Campaigns and Elections
American Style

TRANSFORMING AMERICAN POLITICS
Lawrence C. Dodd, Series Editor

Dramatic changes in political institutions and behavior over the past three decades have underscored the dynamic nature of American politics, confronting political scientists with a new and pressing intellectual agenda. The pioneering work of early postwar scholars, while laying a firm empirical foundation for contemporary scholarship, failed to consider how American politics might change or to recognize the forces that would make fundamental change inevitable. In reassessing the static interpretations fostered by these classic studies, political scientists are now examining the underlying dynamics that generate transformational change.

Transforming American Politics will bring together texts and monographs that address four closely related aspects of change. A first concern is documenting and explaining recent changes in American politics—in institutions, processes, behavior, and policymaking. A second is reinterpreting classic studies and theories to provide a more accurate perspective on postwar politics. The series will look at historical change to identify recurring patterns of political transformation within and across the distinctive eras of American politics. Last and perhaps most importantly, the series presents new theories and interpretations that explain the dynamic processes at work and thus clarify the direction of contemporary politics. All of the books will focus on the central theme of transformation—transformation in both the conduct of American politics and in the way we study and understand its many aspects.

FORTHCOMING TITLES

Congressional Politics: The Evolving Legislative System, Second Edition, Leroy N. Rieselbach

Cold War Politics, John Kenneth White

Young Versus Old: Generational Gaps in Political Participation and Policy Preferences, Susan MacManus

The New American Politics: Reflections on Change and the Clinton Administration, edited by Bryan D. Jones

Congress and the Administrative State, Second Edition, Lawrence C. Dodd and Richard L. Schott

Broken Contract? Changing Relationships Between Citizens and Their Government in the United States, edited by Stephen C. Craig

Campaigns and Elections American Style

edited by
James A. Thurber
and
Candice J. Nelson

American University

Westview Press

BOULDER • SAN FRANCISCO • OXFORD

Transforming American Politics

Copyright © 1995 by Westview Press, Inc.

Published in 1995 in the United States of America by Westview Press, Inc., 5500 Central Avenue, Boulder, Colorado 80301-2877, and in the United Kingdom by Westview Press, 12 Hid's Copse Road, Cumnor Hill, Oxford OX2 9JJ

Library of Congress Cataloging-in-Publication Data
Campaigns and elections American style / edited by James A. Thurber and Candice J. Nelson.
    p.   cm.
Includes bibliographical references and index.
ISBN 0-8133-1966-8. — ISBN 0-8133-1967-6 (pbk.)
1. Electioneering—United States.   2. Politics, Practical—United States.   I. Thurber, James A., 1943–   .   II. Nelson, Candice J., 1949–   .
JK2281.C353   1995
324.6'3'0973—dc20
                                                                94-32609
                                                                CIP

Printed and bound in the United States of America

The paper used in this publication meets the requirements of the American National Standard for Permanence of Paper for Printed Library Materials Z39.48-1984.

10   9   8   7   6   5

To Claudia and Dick

Contents

Tables and Figures   xi
Acknowledgments   xiii
Introduction   xv

1   THE TRANSFORMATION OF AMERICAN CAMPAIGNS   1
    James A. Thurber

2   THE PRINCIPLES OF PLANNING   14
    William R. Sweeney

3   WHO WILL VOTE FOR YOU AND WHY:
    DESIGNING STRATEGY AND THEME   30
    Joel Bradshaw

4   CONTEMPORARY STRATEGY AND AGENDA SETTING   47
    Denise Baer

5   STRATEGY AND TACTICS FOR CAMPAIGN
    FUNDRAISING   62
    David Himes

6   COMPETITION, CONTRIBUTIONS, AND MONEY
    IN 1992   78
    Frank J. Sorauf

7   PAID MEDIA ADVERTISING   84
    Jay Bryant

8   WINNING THROUGH ADVERTISING:
    IT'S ALL IN THE CONTEXT   101
    Steven Ansolabehere and Shanto Iyengar

9   THE BEST CAMPAIGN WINS:
    LOCAL PRESS COVERAGE OF
    NONPRESIDENTIAL RACES   112
    Anita Dunn

10 REPORTING CAMPAIGNS: REFORMING THE PRESS   126
    John R. Petrocik

11 ORGANIZING THE FIELD   138
    Will Robinson

12 FIELD WORK, POLITICAL PARTIES, AND
    VOLUNTEERISM   152
    Paul S. Herrnson

13 POLITICAL POLLING: FROM THE BEGINNING
    TO THE CENTER   161
    William R. Hamilton

14 THE PROMISING ADOLESCENCE OF
    CAMPAIGN SURVEYS   181
    Raymond E. Wolfinger

15 THE ETHICS OF POLITICAL CAMPAIGNS   192
    Wilma Goldstein

16 CAMPAIGN ETHICS AND POLITICAL TRUST   200
    Linda L. Fowler

17 STRATEGIC PERSPECTIVES ON THE 1992 CAMPAIGN   213
    Samuel Popkin

18 DO CAMPAIGNS MATTER?   224
    Marni Ezra and Candice J. Nelson

References   233
About the Book and Contributors   241
Index   245

Tables and Figures

TABLES

3.1   Vote scenario and percent-of-effort calculation for
         candidate Smith   35

FIGURES

2.1   Examples of the use of a lotus diagram in campaign
         planning   18
2.2   Secondary audiences   21

3.1   Three types of voters   31
3.2   Targeted voters   32
3.3   Our voters: supporters and targeted undecideds   32
3.4   Campaign strategy and targeted voters   33

10.1   Party voting in congressional elections, 1952–1992   129
10.2   Candidate issue agendas in presidential campaigns,
         1952–1988   134

Acknowledgments

The rich experience of the Campaign Management Institute (CMI) for both students and professors was the genesis of this book. The Campaign Management Institute was started by campaign professionals and academics in 1981 and is offered twice a year at the Center for Congressional and Presidential Studies. It consists of two intense weeks of hands-on experience organizing actual campaigns and elections, which then receive professional evaluation and guidance from pollsters, media specialists, campaign managers, and academics. We thank the hundreds of students and dozens of campaign professionals who have attended and spoken at CMI. The campaign professionals who have written for this book are all regular lecturers for CMI. Special thanks to these authors for sharing invaluable practical knowledge about the strategy and tactics of campaigns and elections in America. They also have been wonderful mentors to CMI students and alumni who are working in the campaign management field.

Our thanks go to individuals at Westview Press for their enthusiasm about this book. We especially thank Jennifer Knerr, our editor at Westview, for her original interest and support of our idea of combining the knowledge of campaign professionals and academics in a single volume. She had a direct responsibility for making sure this book makes a contribution both in the professional campaign world and in academia. We also thank Professor Larry Dodd, the Westview series editor, for his review and helpful comments on our manuscript. We must also thank project editor, Mary Jo Lawrence, and copy editor, Ida May B. Norton, for her timely and careful editing.

Special thanks go to Tim Evanson, Sharon Drumm, Stephanie Slocum, Tina Fink, and Heather Walters for helping with the conference on campaigns and elections. We also thank Sharon and Stephanie for editing the papers for the conference that were the first drafts of the chapters for this book. Sharon Drumm, our outstanding Assistant Director of the Campaign Management Institute, has always been selfless in her dedication to CMI, and her efforts had a direct impact on this volume. Finally we thank Marni Ezra for her continuous help with editing and seeing this project through to completion.

The funds for this project were provided by the Center for Congressional and Presidential Studies of the School of Public Affairs (SPA) at The American University in Washington, D.C. We owe a special debt to the SPA Dean Cornelius M. Kerwin for his unfailing support of the CCPS and the Campaign Management Institute. This book would not have been written without his backing.

James A. Thurber
Candice J. Nelson

Introduction

THE 1992 AND 1994 ELECTIONS
AND THE CONTINUING TRANSFORMATION OF
AMERICAN CAMPAIGNS

The 1992 and 1994 elections introduced new candidates and issues and brought about a revolution in American politics; however, the principles and process of campaign management described in this book contributed mightily to this turn of events. The basic thesis of this book is that election campaigns influence voter behavior. Professional campaign management strategies and techniques certainly made a difference in the 1992 and 1994 elections.

In 1992 the Democrats recaptured the White House with President Bill Clinton's victory of 43 percent of the popular vote in a three-way race with President George Bush and Ross Perot.[1] For the first time since the Carter Administration (1977–1981) the same party controlled both the White House and Congress. In the 1992 U.S. House of Representatives races, 368 incumbents sought reelection and 325 were successful, bringing 110 new members to the House and a net loss of ten members for the Democrats. The House bank scandal and redistricting led to high levels of retirements and some defeats, especially in party primaries.

The 1994 midterm election campaign brought an overwhelming victory for the Republican Party and revolutionary changes in the policy agenda and structure of Congress. It was the biggest midterm loss for an incumbent president since 1946 when fifty-five Democratic seats were lost in the Truman administration midterm elections. As a result of the 1994 election, divided party government returned to Washington: Eighty-seven freshmen entered the House and eleven new members came to the Senate. In the 104th Congress, one-fourth of the Senate will have less than three years' experience. In the House, almost half the membership will have served less than three years. Since 1990, well over half of the House of Representatives are new members.

The results of the 1994 midterm election were devastating for the Democratic Party at all levels. With the Democrats losing fifty-two seats in the House and eight Senate seats (plus one additional Democratic seat was lost when Senator Shelby changed party affiliation), it was the first time in forty years that the Republican Party gained control of both the House and Senate. No incumbent Republican House member lost. Republicans gained a net of seventeen in the fifty-two open seat House contests and lost only four Republican-controlled House open seats to the Democrats. Thirty-five House incumbent Democrats lost, including House Speaker Thomas Foley (the first Speaker defeated for reelection since 1860); Chairman of the Judiciary Committee Jack Brooks; indicted former chair of the House Ways and Means Committee Dan Rostenkowski; Intelligence Chairman Dan Glickman; and Appropriations subcommittee chair Neal Smith. And for the first time in sixty years that the Republicans have parity with the Democrats at the national, state, and local levels of government with the Democrats' loss of ten governorships, six state senates and nine state houses.

The 1994 election was the most negative, most expensive, most anti-Democratic Party incumbent, anti-Washington, anti-incumbent presidential campaign in modern times. The campaign was "nationalized" with a clear theme and message from Newt Gingrich's "Contract with America" (Gingrich will be Speaker of the House for the 104th Congress). The late Tip O'Neill, former Speaker of the House of Representatives, once said that "all politics is local." In the 1994 elections the Republican party disproved that statement. In the fall of 1994 more than 300 Republican congressional candidates met on the steps of the U.S. Capitol in Washington to sign the "Contract with America." Together these Republicans pledged that, if elected, they would support changes in congressional procedures and bring to a House vote a series of proposals long supported by many in the Republican party. These proposals included a balanced budget amendment, a line-item veto, and term limits for members of Congress. By collectively signing such an agreement, the Republican candidates were pledging to run on a set of national issues, not just issues of importance to a particular congressional district. It is difficult to know if the Republican party was successful at nationalizing the elections; enough Republican candidates were elected to gain control of the House and Senate, but exit polls showed that most voters had not heard of the Contract with America. However, the election proved that all politics are not local, that "pork barreling" can be a liability. The electorate voted for change and they got it.

The 1994 vote also revealed a continuation of southern incremental realignment that seems to be turning into a permanent realignment of southern white males from the Democratic Party to the Republican Party. The 1992 Perot supporters voted more Republican than Democratic in 1994 (68 percent in 1994 as compared to 51 percent in 1992). Independents also voted more Republican (57 percent in 1994 to 46 percent in 1992). Men voted more Republican (57 percent in 1994 to 48 percent in

1992). Whites voted more Republican (58 percent in 1994 to 50 percent in 1992). Ninety percent of those who said they identified with the religious far right voted Republican.[2]

The 1992 presidential election called into question any claims of Republican realignment or a durable change in the distribution of party support by voters, but the 1994 midterm election confirmed the incremental realignment (or "secular realignment") especially of conservative southern Democratic white males moving permanently to the Republican Party. President Clinton's narrow popular vote victory of 43 percent in 1992 raised questions about Democratic dominance; and the 1994 Republican sweep in the House, Senate, gubernatorial races, and state legislative assemblies left no doubt that Clinton's narrow victory did not mean the Reagan Democrats had come back home permanently. The three-way race in the 1992 presidential election was a dealigning election; old voting patterns broke down without being replaced by new ones. Nearly twenty million voters (almost 20 percent) rejected both major parties and voted for Ross Perot. This weakening party loyalty led to the overwhelming Republican victory in the 1994 election with significant numbers of independents and Perot voters voting for Republican candidates at the national, state, and local levels of government. The 1994 midterm election revealed a continuing change in the regional base of Republican Party support in the South. The 104th Congress has a majority of Republican senators and representatives from the South.

The 1992 and 1994 election campaigns both used all of the campaign management strategies and techniques discussed in this book. All of the campaign professionals and several academics who have written chapters for this book worked in the 1992 and 1994 campaigns. Every election both builds on previous campaign experience and brings innovations and new tools to the campaign arena.

What was different about the 1992 and 1994 election campaigns? The 1992 campaign moved away from simplistic and emotional appeals to the voters and included extensive discussion of the issues through the debates and campaign themes and strategies. The media covered the issues more thoroughly. The campaign turned more on issues and less on personalities. Clinton, Bush, and Perot avoided blatantly negative and deceptive advertisements such as the infamous "Willie Horton" advertisement of 1988. The quality of the campaigns was well received by the voters with 77 percent of the voters saying they were satisfied with the campaign and had learned enough about the candidates and issues to make an informed choice.[3]

Each election cycle brings new opportunities for innovations in campaign strategies and techniques; the 1992 and 1994 election cycles were no exception. During the 1992 presidential election changes occurred in the way both earned and paid media influenced the campaign, in the way field organizations were used, and in the assumptions about when the general election began. In 1994 paid media again used a new technique to influence voter decisions; the Republican party tried to nationalize the congressional elections; and preliminary Federal Election Commission data suggest record spending in the congressional elections, as well as changes in campaign funding for some candidates. The 1994 election campaign turned back to more blatantly negative attack advertisements and it was successfully nationalized by the Contract with America. Bringing home the pork and the "all politics is local" attitude became a liability to many House incumbents. Voters' distrust of government and politicians continued in the 1992 and 1994 elections as indicated by the growth of the term limits movement and high levels of cynicism expressed in the polls.

In elections prior to 1992, candidates at all levels had to compete for coverage by broadcast and print media, and consequently relied on paid media to get their campaign messages out to potential voters. In 1992, at least for the presidential candidates, earned media became much easier to obtain. Both George Bush and Bill Clinton, and, at the times he was a candidate, Ross Perot, were regular guests on the network talk shows. Bill Clinton received both acclaim and criticism for playing the saxophone on the Arsenio Hall show, and tried to deliver his campaign message to young people by appearing on MTV. Even the format of the presidential debates changed. In past presidential elections candidates had been questioned by panels of journalists; in 1992 one of three presidential debates occurred in front of an audience of "undecided" potential voters, who were invited to ask questions of Bush, Clinton, and Perot.

Because earned media became more important in 1992, the format of paid media changed. In both 1984 and 1988 candidates Reagan and Bush produced paid media that ran nationwide—Reagan's "morning in America" ad, Bush's "Boston Harbor" ad, and "Dukakis in a tank" advertisements. In 1992 Clinton tailored his media to specific states; earned media supplanted paid media nationwide.

In 1992 Perot disabused the notion that Americans will only tolerate paid media in 30- or 60-second television spots. He paid for a series of 30-minute "infomercials" using charts and graphs to illustrate his vision of the problems with the U.S. economy. An estimated nine million Americans repeatedly turned on their television sets to view Perot's paid advertisements.

The 1992 campaign also brought innovations in the use of campaign field operations. Prior to 1992 field operations were used primarily for voter contact: to identify a candidate's supporters and potential supporters and to get those supporters to the polls on election day. In 1992 the

Clinton campaign used its field operation not only for voter contact but also for message delivery. The field operation was told what the candidate would be talking about each day. This enabled the field staff, in their contacts with voters, to reinforce locally what Clinton was saying nationally. As a result, the Clinton campaign message was delivered not just by the candidate, but also by thousands of field staff around the country.

Prior to 1992 the tradition was that the general election campaign began the day after Labor Day. Candidates typically used the time between the summer national party conventions and Labor Day to plan general election campaign strategy, or, in some cases, to take a break from campaigning altogether. In 1992 the Clinton campaign began the day after the Democratic Party convention closed. Bill Clinton, Al Gore, and their wives left the convention in New York and immediately began a campaign bus trip through the midwest. The Clintons and Gores were very well received in the communities they visited, and consequently received very favorable earned media. While the Bush campaign was still preparing for the Republican Party convention, the Clinton campaign was already under way.

The 1994 congressional elections also brought changes in the campaign landscape. Paid media saw the introduction of a technique called "morphing," in which one candidate's face was electronically transformed into another candidate's face. This was most successfully done by Republican candidates attacking their Democratic opponents; Democratic congressional candidates all over the country were "morphed" into President Clinton.

Finally, 1994 saw record spending in the congressional elections. Although final Federal Election Commission figures weren't available as of this writing, reports through mid-October 1994 indicated spending increased 18 percent over 1992. Moreover, preliminary figures seemed to indicate that in 1994 Republican challengers and open seat candidates in the House of Representatives had unusual financial success in 1994. Republican challengers to Democratic incumbents are typically the lowest funded candidates, generally being outspent at least four to one by their Democratic opponents. Preliminary evidence suggests that 1994 saw a particularly strong group of Republican challengers and open seat candidates who were better funded than was previously typical. Preliminary figures also indicate that 1994 median spending by Republican challengers almost doubled 1992 spending, and median spending by Republican open seat candidates increased 60 percent over 1992.

The 1992 and 1994 campaign themes, strategies, and messages helped to bring about a major change in American politics. Campaigns do make a difference for governance as can clearly be seen in the shift of the policy agendas of the 1992 and 1994 elections. Campaign professionals continued to play a central role in the campaign processes of 1992 and 1994. The lessons learned and shared by the unique combination of campaign professionals and academics in this volume are essential to understand the major transformation of American campaigns and elections.

NOTES

1. For two works on the 1992 election see Paul R. Abramson, John H. Aldrich, and David W. Rohde, *Change and Continuity in the 1992 Elections* (Washington, D.C.: CQ Press, 1994), and Michael Nelson (ed.), *The Election of 1992* (Washington, D.C.: CQ Press, 1993).

2. Tim Curran, "House Pickups at 52 After GOP Blowout," *Roll Call,* November 10, 1994, p. 10, using Voter New Service exit polls.

3. William Schneider, "When Issues, Not Personalities, Rule," *National Journal,* December 5, 1992, p. 2814.

1

The Transformation
of American Campaigns

JAMES A. THURBER

This book is a marriage of knowledge from academics and campaign professionals on the topic of campaign management and elections. These two worlds rarely overlap, and when they do, the basis of knowledge and evidence is often quite different. Academics use scientific methods for making systematic observations about campaigns and elections, whereas professionals rely on direct experience for their generalizations.

Academics are careful to make statements about voters and elections that are based on large data sets and systematic testing of hypotheses. Academics attempt to explain individual and collective political behavior and try to answer questions about who votes and why. When political scientists write about campaigns and the process of getting elected, their approach is based upon scholarly analyses rather than experience.

Campaign professionals also focus on who votes and why but solely in the development of a winning strategy to attract those voters that support a candidate. When they write about campaigns, it is often in the form of how-to-win manuals (Napolitan, 1972). Professionals are hired activists; they develop strategies and tactics to influence voters and election results (Sabato, 1981). Simply put, they are focused on one thing: how to win (Runkel, 1989). Political scientists try to understand voters, candidates, elections, and the consequences of electoral battles for governing and the direction of public policy.[1] Campaign professionals base their knowledge on their experience and collective wisdom from previous campaigns.[2] They know what works because they have experienced winning or losing elections. They have wisdom derived from their tangible campaign seasoning.

Campaign professionals often assert that the academic literature on campaigns and elections is either obvious or wrong. However, most campaign professionals also say they do not have time to read the latest political science research findings. Academics often argue that campaign professionals are just promoting the latest folk wisdom about campaign tactics and that they do not know whether it works or not until it is too late. Academics study campaigns and elections but rarely talk with campaign professionals or know the latest developments in campaign strategies, tactics, and tools. Campaign professionals are objects of research for political scientists, but academics rarely enter into the world of political campaigns. There is often distrust and even fear and loathing between campaign professionals and academics. Political science research is criticized as too academic, not applicable to the real world of election campaigns. The practical how-to-do-it knowledge of professionals is considered interesting by political scientists but not scientific—not based on the systematic collection of data and tests of hypotheses that are part of a broader theory. Add commentary about campaigns from political pundits, journalists, and retired political leaders to those of academics and campaign professionals, and it is difficult to know what is truth, what is myth, what is marketing, and what is simply political "spin."[3]

When a well-published academic works as a professional on a campaign, as Professor Samuel Popkin did for the Bill Clinton organization in 1992, the involvement is remarkable because of its rarity (see Chapter 17 for Popkin's discussion of the Clinton campaign). The worlds of academics and professionals rarely mix, but when they do we all gain from their new insights, as is shown in this book. Whether explaining or managing campaigns, whether treating campaign management as a science or an art, academics, professionals, and pundits all agree that there has been a dramatic transformation in American election campaigns in the last thirty years.

Campaign professionals and political scientists confront each other's perspectives in this book. The result is that they capture the major changes in the organization, operation, and impact of campaign strategies and tactics at the local, state, and national levels that have had such a significant impact on American elections in the last three decades. Essays by campaign professionals and political scientists are paired to cover the major elements of a campaign from two viewpoints. Our authors do not always agree. The perspectives of the professional and the academic on the same campaign topic are often quite different. The disagreements reveal distinct bodies of knowledge. The dialogue between the two views offers a new understanding of election campaigns.

DEFINING ELECTION CAMPAIGNS

Webster reminds us that "campaign" comes from military vocabulary: "a connected series of military operations forming a distinct phase of a war" or "a connected series of operations designed to bring about a particular result." Winning an election is like winning a war to those who establish "war rooms" and manage campaigns. William Safire defined campaign as "the term applied to virtually all phases of an effort to win any kind of election, but most particularly the phase involving open, active electioneering" (Safire, 1978).

Campaigns are competitions over ideas. Candidates and campaign organizations are attempting to capture government through the democratic process and to advance policies. Campaigns are battles to define public problems and to develop public policy solutions to those problems. Election campaigns are combat over ideas and ways to persuade groups of voters to support those ideas.

For candidates and professionals, campaigns are zero-sum games or even minus-sum games: There are always winners and losers, and there are always more campaigners disappointed by the election outcome than pleased by it. Campaigns are objects of analysis for academics. For scholars, election campaigns do not represent a personal gamble, a deeply felt ambition, or a commitment to the objective of winning (Maisel, 1986). Campaigns are not political causes to academics but rather a focus of intellectual interest. Academics are interested in why people vote; professionals are interested in how to get them to vote, especially for a particular candidate. Academics study who contributes money to campaigns and why; professionals are interested in how to get people to give funds to their candidates. These perspectives seem to be worlds apart, but in order to understand campaigns they must be brought together. This book joins these two worlds and shows how one needs both perspectives to understand how to manage election campaigns and how to understand and explain them.

Managers of election campaigns, be they presidential or down-ballot (local and state races), evaluate the web of political circumstances surrounding their campaigns, develop strategies and plans within that political environment, pursue a strategic theme and message for a candidate, establish an organization, solicit and use campaign money, buy advertising and attempt to use free (news) media, schedule candidates, organize and use a field organization, use opposition research, and conduct survey research and focus group analysis among a variety of other activities. These basic elements of all campaigns have changed dramatically in the last three decades because of the decline of political party organization, increasing nonvoting, the growth in the power of interest groups, the power of the media (especially television), and the professionalization of campaigns. What has not changed is that successful campaigns, just as in the 1960s, need to develop an explicit strategy, theme, and message.

CAMPAIGN STRATEGY AND PLANNING

Campaigns are dynamic. They do not happen in a vacuum, and they are not predetermined by economic and political circumstances. The web of economic and political conditions influences a campaign and candidates, and campaigns have an impact on those circumstances. For example, the 1992 presidential and congressional campaigns were managed in an environment that could not be immediately changed. The constraints and opportunities of the voter's perception of the performance of the U.S. economy, the demise of the Soviet Union, the challenges of the European Community and Japan for world markets, disinterest in Desert Storm, the political framework set by having three presidential candidates on the ballot, and normal party balance could not be ignored by candidates in 1992. Taking these objective facts into account, Clinton focused his strategy on the economy and pushed a new issue on the public policy agenda: health care reform. Clinton could not ignore the economy; as his campaign headquarters sign reminded people, "It's the Economy, Stupid." He was able to link a new problem to an objective condition (the rest of the sign said, "and don't forget health care"). President George Bush did not focus on the economy or health care reform. It behooves candidates and their campaign managers to evaluate environmental conditions early and develop campaign strategies and plans that take advantage of them but revise the plans when events call for it.

Campaign strategy, planning, and tactics must take objective economic and political facts into account. Some think that a campaign plan must be adhered to with "almost military discipline and precision."[4] Campaign strategy simply charts the path to win the election and recognizes that campaigns are dynamic and in constant change, reacting to events and opponents. Campaigns are also frequently underfunded, disorganized, and understaffed, and their personnel lack enough information to make rational decisions. However, to start with a strategy and plan, it is essential to develop a campaign theme and message, making the best use of campaign resources, reducing liabilities, and establishing a set of objectives whose achievement will maximize the probability of winning an election or attaining a plurality—50 percent plus one of the total votes cast. The campaign plan to achieve this is a program of specific activities designed to accomplish the set of objectives and, of course, eventually to win the election within a given political and economic environment. This sounds simple, but the key elements of a campaign strategy and plan are complex. Campaign strategies and plans must take into account a vast number of factors, such as the candidate, the constituency, the level of office being sought, the nature of the electoral system, the party organization (or lack of it), the financial and political resources available, and the nature of the voters.

Campaign strategy and tactics were the sole realm of political parties in the early 1960s. Today they are the domain of the campaign professionals: campaign managers, campaign finance specialists, survey researchers, get-out-the-vote specialists, grassroots experts, media buyers, television producers, schedulers, and many others (Sabato, 1981). Campaigns have evolved in the last thirty years into complex organizations featuring distinct divisions of labor and elaborate teams of professionals often outside of party organizations. However, recent studies of the impact of political party organization and funds from the parties on campaigning may reveal a new trend toward local parties playing important roles in campaigns.[5]

Successful campaigns must develop a message that is focused on groups of voters that will help the candidate win. All campaigns have similar functions: They must analyze the political environment of the campaign, decide what tactics or tools will be used to implement the campaign strategy, and establish the campaign budget (the allocation of money, time, and personnel to each element of the campaign plan). Campaign tactics are the specific activities designed to achieve the strategic objective: victory in the election. Campaign tactics, managing the message to target groups of voters, are at the operational level of the campaign.

The critical elements of a campaign strategy and plan have not changed significantly over the last thirty years, but the methods for achieving strategic goals have changed dramatically. William R. Sweeney, a founder of the Campaign Management Institute and a campaign professional with more than twenty years experience in the field, describes how to develop a successful campaign plan in Chapter 2. He argues that "a campaign without a plan is a journey without a map."

In Chapter 3 Joel Bradshaw of the Campaign Design Group adds to Sweeney's discussion of campaign planning with a discussion of campaign strategy and theme. Bradshaw describes campaign strategy as simply how a candidate will win. Campaign strategy answers the questions of who will vote for the candidate and why. Bradshaw's principles of sound campaign strategy are the same whether the candidate is running for a seat on a school board or for the presidency of the United States. He presents four dimensions of campaign strategy: (1) dividing the electorate into three groups in any given contest (supporters, opponents, and the vast majority of voters who are generally uninterested in the candidate and the campaign); (2) using political research to determine the voters that fall into each of the three groups, (3) targeting campaign resources to get the votes necessary to win the election; and (4) identifying how to win the necessary numbers of voters by directing campaign resources (money, time, effort, message) to those key voters. Resource allocation is defined by campaign strategy, the necessary steps to attract the critical voters needed to win. Sweeney and Bradshaw argue that a campaign begins and ends with the campaign plan and strategy. The campaign begins with a written plan of the strategy, and it ends with the achievement of that plan: winning the election.

Campaigns are run within a framework of political parties, voters with party loyalties, and interest groups (collections of individuals with similar political attitudes and behavior). These factors must be taken into account when developing a campaign strategy and plan. Professor Denise Baer, a student of political parties and elections, describes the importance of party identification and party organization in campaigns in Chapter 4. Her partisan food chain of political agenda setting describes the partisan environment of a campaign.

CAMPAIGN FINANCE

Money is the mother's milk of politics, as the late speaker of the California Assembly, Jesse Unruh, said in a lecture to the department of political science at Indiana University in September 1968. Campaigns need money to be successful, and they are increasingly expensive. The average U.S. House incumbent spent almost $595,000 in 1992, 41 percent more than the average incumbent in 1990. The average incumbent candidate for the U.S. Senate spent $3.8 million in 1992 (Ornstein, Mann and Malbin, 1994). How money is raised and how it is spent have changed significantly in the last thirty years, a shift that tells an important story about the transformation of American campaigns. David Himes (Chapter 5), a campaign finance professional, and Professor Frank Sorauf (Chapter 6), a political scientist who studies campaign finance, describe the money chase from the professional and academic perspectives. Himes describes how to organize and accomplish a successful campaign finance effort, focusing on the nuts and bolts of attracting money into a campaign. How does a campaign successfully get its second most important resource, financial backing (first is the candidate)? Incumbents often collect large amounts of money in the belief that it helps to deter the opposition (Squire, 1991). Early money for presidential candidates helps with the matching provisions of public financing. Early money in any campaign shows strength and helps to bring in even more money. Success breeds success. Candidates need to receive money from the right sources to get matching funds, from the right places to meet state limits, and at the right time— as early as possible. The method of getting campaign money and the amount of money collected and used in a campaign can raise ethical questions that may become an issue in a campaign.

Skill in using the money collected is central to a campaign strategy. Money can be allocated for staff, advertising, television time, survey research, almost everything that is essential to a successful campaign. Sorauf responds to Himes's advice about campaign finance with a discussion about competition, contributions, and campaign money in 1992. Sorauf argues that fund-raising is bilateral in nature, and that both contributors and candidates pursue political goals and formulate strategies.

CAMPAIGN ADVERTISING AND THE MEDIA

Paid advertising is a cardinal element in a modern election campaign. Most Americans rely heavily on the news media to keep informed, especially about candidates and issues in a campaign. Candidates who have enough money to buy significant amounts of advertising and who attract positive free media (news coverage) benefit by becoming better known. They are better able to frame issues and influence voters to support them than are candidates without advertising and news coverage.

In Chapter 7, campaign media specialist Jay Bryant describes the use of paid media advertising in political campaigns. In his history of the use of paid media in campaigns, he makes a distinction between commercial products and candidates, arguing that political and product advertising have little in common. He describes five basic functions of political communication: name identification, candidate image, issue development and exploitation, attack, and defense. Bryant gives examples and advice on the application of several communications principles for political campaigns.

Political scientists Steven Ansolabehere and Shanto Iyengar elaborate on Bryant's general overview of campaign advertising and draw on empirical political science research that demonstrates how campaign advertisements, television news, and voters' prior beliefs jointly influence voter choice. In Chapter 8 they develop and test several hypotheses concerning the nature of the interaction among voter beliefs, advertising, and television news.

In Chapter 9 campaign media specialist Anita Dunn draws on her experience with local media and argues for reform in the volume and content of media coverage of down-ballot elections. There is a substantial decline in press coverage from prominent to down-ballot offices, resulting in almost no press coverage of challengers for less prestigious, entry-level offices. Dunn calls for greater coverage and improved content of coverage of these low-visibility races.

Professor John R. Petrocik, a political scientist who studies elections and campaigns, responds to Dunn's call for reform in Chapter 10. He reminds readers there is little evidence that limited coverage of down-ballot races has had a major effect on election outcomes. Extensive coverage of these races would simply reinforce the partisan proclivities of the voters, since the press would be repeating largely partisan appeals by candidates. It is also unclear how the press would "promote a public dialogue." Is it a reporter's or editor's task to tell a candidate what topics and issues must be dealt with during the campaign? Petrocik argues that we should be cautious about demanding reforms from the media.

FIELD ORGANIZATION AND GRASSROOTS CAMPAIGNING

Often the success of an election campaign relies on the ability of the staff; thousands of volunteers and party activists have to get out the vote during the critical last few hours that the polls are open. Although these field organizations do not capture the attention of the public or the press, their functions—voter registration, targeting, distribution of literature, and get-out-the-vote drives—are integral elements of campaigns and elections. There is no substitute for a well-organized and focused field operation. If a campaign has a strong field operation working phone banks and the streets to identify supporters, to reinforce the candidate's message, to persuade voters to support a candidate, and to get out the vote (GOTV) of those supporting a candidate, this staff will help determine the success of the campaign strategy. Field operations need to be linked to the campaign strategy and plan. These operations were formerly performed primarily by the party organization. The party organization is still the most important building block for a campaign, but in modern campaigns, a field operations specialist is often hired to assist with a campaign.

Will Robinson is an expert in field operations and an instructor in American University's Campaign Management Institute. Robinson describes the purpose and activities of a successful field organization in political campaigns in Chapter 11. He emphasizes that voter contact is at the heart of the field operation. The structure, duties, and size of a campaign field operation depend upon the strategy and plan of the overall campaign. Robinson shows how some successful campaigns have no field operation. Other campaigns that have a field operation still cannot overcome the odds against a particular candidate. Robinson argues that the more local the political office and the smaller the campaign, the more likely a field operation is needed and will make a difference.

Professor Paul S. Herrnson, a scholar of political parties, reveals in Chapter 12 how field work, political parties, and volunteerism have an impact on modern campaigns. The major focus of Herrnson's chapter is on three aspects of campaign field work: voter identification and targeting, campaign communications, and voter mobilization. He discusses how these activities are performed and what impact they have on a campaign. Herrnson concludes with a discussion about the transformation of field work and its implications for political party organizations and volunteerism in election campaigns.

CAMPAIGN SURVEY RESEARCH

Survey research and focus group analysis are also essential tools in modern election campaigns. The need to analyze political attitudes and opinions in the electorate has become a central, often driving element in campaigns. Survey research, focus group analysis, and tracking polls are used primarily to find the most persuasive messages for a candidate and to identify the key target groups for the campaign. Public opinion polls are usually undertaken at the beginning of a campaign to assess the public's reaction to salient political issues and to find out how voters perceive the candidates in a race. Opinion surveys also help the campaign organization make strategic decisions about how to allocate scarce resources and to direct campaign tactics to achieve the goals of the campaign. Surveys are often used to test the effectiveness of television advertising. Focus groups are used to evaluate voters' reaction to a candidate's image, the message and theme of a campaign, the effectiveness of political advertising, negative attacks on a candidate, counterattacks, and a variety of other communications going on in a campaign. Another innovation in political surveys is the tracking poll. These are public opinion polls based on daily monitoring of voter attitudes with samples sufficiently large for analysts to determine immediate public reaction to campaign messages, events, and the candidate. Tracking polls have become essential tools for timely evaluation in implementing the campaign's strategic plan and reacting to the dynamic events of a campaign.

In order to understand the importance of political polling, it helps to trace the history of survey research in politics. William R. Hamilton, a well-known survey research specialist with almost thirty years in the field, is our guide to polling's important history in campaigns. Hamilton describes the transformation of the art and science of modern political polling during the last thirty years. In Chapter 13 he argues that polling has become the major influence in strategic decisionmaking in modern U.S. political campaigns. Polling has not always been at the center of American campaigns, but the importance of analyzing voters' opinions has grown as the power of political party organizations has weakened and the power of television and specialized groups has grown. The need for direct feedback from the electorate is insatiable during a campaign, and political polling is the primary tool to satisfy that demand. Since pollsters are at the heart of the communications system in a campaign (or should be), they have gained enormous influence over a campaign's strategy and plan. Pollsters influence television advertising, media buying, campaign scheduling, campaign theme and message, and ultimately the election campaign endgame.

Voting scholar and survey research expert Professor Raymond E. Wolfinger of the University of California at Berkeley discusses the evolution and impact of survey research on election campaigns in Chapter 14. He describes the growth of nonacademic survey research by newspapers, television stations, broadcasting networks, and political campaigns. Much of this growth has stemmed from changes in the technology and methods of survey research, such as focus groups, people meters, telephone surveys, improved sampling, and exit polls. Wolfinger compares the application of contemporary survey research methods to election campaigns twenty years ago. He evaluates differences between academic and nonacademic surveys. He argues that academics lag behind political pollsters in use of data collection techniques. For example, people meters and advertising testing are not employed in academic research. Academics use survey research to test hypotheses and explore assumptions about political attitudes and behavior. Campaigns use surveys to help implement winning strategies and predict voting behavior. Wolfinger reveals the differences between campaign and academic survey research through analysis of the growth of the independent voter and the academic explanation of the outcome of elections using fundamental analysis (i.e., the notions that party identification will determine most of the votes in an election and that the main dynamic factor is the economy unless there is war or significant scandal).

ETHICS AND CAMPAIGNS

Political scandal comes too often in contemporary campaigns. Candidates and campaign staff may act in a perceived or actual unethical way that causes great damage to a campaign (e.g., dirty tricks, Watergate, questionable campaign finance and spending). Sometimes this comes from going negative, (misuse of campaign funds, unethical campaign solicitation, or perceived character flaws of a candidate, for example). Campaign professional Ed Rollins learned that his remark about using "walking-around money" to "buy" African American ministers in New Jersey to suppress traditionally Democratic voter turnout for Governor James Florio in 1993 was ethically unacceptable. The statement was offensive to the ministers and to black voters. It was considered unethical and even illegal by Democratic Party activists (and by many Republicans) in New Jersey. Whether true or not, the implication of improper behavior by Rollins caused him immeasurable harm in the campaign management profession. After twenty-five years, and at the top of his profession, he was seriously hurt by that one statement. The law and norms of ethical behavior in campaigns and elections have changed dramatically since the days of George Washington Plunkett of Tammany Hall when "he saw his opportunities and took advantage of them." Watergate and the campaign finance activities of Richard Nixon's Committee to Reelect the President changed campaign ethics fundamentally, but every campaign must be alert to setting a high standard of proper behavior or all the plans and strategies of a campaign will be for naught.

Ethics in political campaigns is discussed by Wilma Goldstein in Chapter 15. Her observations are those of a campaign professional who has been concerned about increased public cynicism regarding campaigns, campaign professionals, and candidates for public office. Professor Linda L. Fowler from Syracuse University discusses ethics in campaigns and the political trust in Chapter 16.

CONCLUSION

A marriage of academic and professional viewpoints occurred when Samuel Popkin, political scientist from the University of California at San Diego, worked for the 1992 Clinton campaign. Professor Popkin helps to conclude this book in Chapter 17 with his insights on the 1992 campaign from inside the Clinton campaign organization. As an academic he describes what political scientists can contribute to a campaign but points out that they can be wrong. The economy was the issue of the 1992 campaign, but traditional economic models of voting were spectacularly wrong in predicting the outcome of the election. The standard economic models of presidential elections predicted that President George Bush would win comfortably with 57 percent of the vote, but he received only 38 percent. Ross Perot's candidacy and the voters got in the way of the political science models. A *Washington Post* national exit poll immediately after the 1992 presidential election found the economy to be the single most important issue of the campaign. Almost half the voters surveyed cited jobs and the economy as their central concerns. Among voters who felt that their economic prospects were worsening, Clinton won by a 5-to-1 margin. Voters concerned with foreign policy were very few but supported Bush by an overwhelming 9-to-1 margin (Edsall and Dionne, 1992).

Popkin reminds us that candidates and campaign professionals can be strikingly wrong also: "The road to Washington is littered with the geniuses of campaigns past." Bush's strategy of raising Clinton's negatives (the character issue) rather than raising his own positives worked between Nixon and McGovern in 1972 and against Michael Dukakis in 1988, but it failed miserably in 1992. The Clinton campaign's war room learned how to negate the attacks and kept the focus on the economy, a factor of great concern to the American public even though unemployment and inflation were not high in mid-1992. Professor Popkin reminds us that proposed policies and campaign plans do indeed make a difference in an election. Popkin argues that the American public perceived Clinton as a new kind of moderate Democrat willing to address economic performance, the budget, debt, health care improvements, and welfare reform with something more than traditional Democratic tax-and-spend solutions. The Clinton-Gore ticket revealed a new posture of moderation on racial issues and ideology and a new economic plan to help the United States pull out of a continuing recession. The electorate was not interested in the traditional Republican cries against taxes, regulation, and affirmative action. Family values and Clinton's character issues, two fallback themes of the Bush campaign, did not sway a significant number of voters.

Marni Ezra and Candice J. Nelson conclude the book with a historical perspective of what is known about campaigns from the viewpoints of professionals and academics. They answer the question of whether campaigns make a difference or not. They describe what political scientists know about campaigns and what the professionals know. The rivalry and collaboration between political scientists with their scientific knowledge and professionals with their revealed truth from campaign experience are themes that complete the analysis.

Few changes have transformed American elections more in the past three decades than the professionalization of campaign management. What began in the 1960s as the waning of political parties evolved into the increased importance of campaign professionals, which has become a major industry involving hundreds of millions of dollars being raised and spent in each election cycle. Campaign professionals are a staple of contemporary elections. This book describes and evaluates this crucial development, the professionalization and transformation of American political campaigns.

NOTES

1. For examples of scholarly works on campaigns, see Edie N. Goldenberg and Michael W. Traugott, *Campaigning for Congress* (Washington, D.C.: Congressional Quarterly Press, 1984); Stephen Hess, *The Presidential Campaign* (Washington, D.C.: Brookings Institution, 1978); and John H. Kessel, *Presidential Campaign Politics* (Chicago: Dorsey, 1988).

2. For scholarly case studies of specific campaigns, see Sidney Blumenthal, *Pledging Allegiance: The Last Campaign of the Cold War* (New York: HarperCollins,

1990); Marjorie Randon Hershey, *Running for Office: The Political Education of Campaigners* (Chatham, N.J.: Chatham House, 1984); and L. Sandy Maisel, *From Obscurity to Oblivion: Running in the Congressional Primary* (Knoxville: University of Tennessee Press, 1986).

3. For a case of "political spin" by a campaign professional after an election, consider Ed Rollins's comments about the importance of "walking-around money" in depressing voter turnout among African Americans in the 1993 New Jersey gubernatorial race. See articles in the *Washington Post* and *New York Times*, November, 1993.

4. Paul Allen Beck and Frank J. Sorauf, *Party Politics in America* (New York: HarperCollins, 1992), pp. 315–316, argue that a rigid plan is the conventional wisdom of most campaign professionals. As will be shown in this book, that is not the modern approach to campaign strategy and planning.

5. See Paul S. Herrnson, *Party Campaigning in the 1980s* (Cambridge, Mass.: Harvard University Press, 1988); and John P. Frendreis, James L. Gobson, and Laura L. Vertz, "The Electoral Relevance of Local Party Organizations," *American Political Science Review* 84 (1990): 225–235.

2

The Principles of Planning

WILLIAM R. SWEENEY

"Would you tell me, please, which way I ought to go from here?" "That depends a good deal on where you want to get to," said the cat. "I don't much care where," said Alice. "Then it doesn't matter which way you go," said the cat.

Lewis Carroll

A campaign without a plan is a journey without a map. Although Saint Brendan did find North America without a map, Neil Armstrong could never have reached the moon by simply pointing the rocket. The average, competitive congressional campaign in the 1990s has a life cycle longer than one year and easily approaches $1 million in expenditures. Thus, the financial, technological, and competitive realities necessitate the routine implementation of a planning process for politics.

A political campaign is fundamentally a communications exercise about choices between the aspirants for public office and the audience of voters (Brenner, 1992). Sometimes it is a two-way dialogue between the political figures and the voters. More often than not, the campaign is a monologue that hopes to provide the information voters need in order to make a political decision. The victorious political campaign can be a semirational effort to communicate a message to the voting-age population based on an understanding of the aspirations of the population and the comparative agenda for the future of the two opposing candidates. However, a winning political campaign can also be a disorganized, haphazard mess that produced victory more because of political circumstance and luck than of any professional application of communications or organizational technique. The mythology of political lore and of American political tradition suggest the absence of a rigorous planning effort, but the reality of modern politics, particularly for significant positions—city council, mayor, state legislature, or constitutional offices—should mandate a serious planning effort.

In order to plan a campaign, the first hurdle is often attitude. People

14

have not usually invested in the planning process of politics and thus do not wish to bother with committing to time, energy, and confrontation early in the process. Since a political campaign, unlike a business or other institution, is usually considered to be a temporary creation, there is regular resistance to efforts beyond the perceived immediacy of campaign tasks. Planning involves investment in a process to produce a consensus and a work product created principally by volunteers at the beginning of a campaign, at the expense of other organizational tasks. Moreover, a plan often involves choices on direction or objectives that are often beyond the vision of the people involved in the beginning of the process. The most important rationale for the necessity to plan is simply to minimize the chance of losing, in both the nomination process and the general election campaigns (Luntz, 1991).

THE RESOURCE EQUATION

Campaigns are very simple. All have the same basic elements with adjustments for size and resources. Although some fine tuning is required in accordance with the local political culture and the market's mechanisms for voter communication, the reality is that all campaign managers are dealing with a similar recipe of fundamental resources. One must first acknowledge that there is a structure to gain some sense of the elements to a campaign. There is no definitive listing of the categories of resources, but there are plenty of anecdotes. Gary Hart often compared the design of a campaign to the construction plan of a Gothic cathedral, financed in large part by the donors of the complicated stained-glass windows. Speaker Thomas P. O'Neill, Jr., described four elements to a campaign: "the candidate, the issues, the people (organization) and, of course, the money." The chairman of the Democratic National Committee, Charles T. Manatt, used a formula of "votes, media and money." Other professionals have defined the structure as PMS—people, money, strategy.

THE EXCUSES

If the objective is to have a plan for the campaign, there are some routine excuses that must be overcome by the campaign team or else the process will simply fall apart. Among the usual range of excuses that cripple the planning process are attitudes and techniques to delay or avoid the commitment to a plan. Politics is fairly ephemeral by definition, and planning for political communication can be even more removed from the daily reality of most people, including successful candidates for office. Thus it is helpful to bear in mind certain principles.

First, *every idea of the campaign team needs to be written down or it is lost forever.* Regardless of the planning tool (brainstorming, deployment flow-charting, mind mapping, metaplanning, lotus diagram, or just plain conversation), there has to be a commitment to paper. "If it's not in writing, it doesn't exist." Paper connotes discipline and commitment to the business of political communication. Paper is evidence of the ability to share ideas and involve more minds in the process. Paper also is a permanent record of ideas that may lead to accountability and confrontation. Unfortunately, paper is also work, usually done by volunteers at the beginning of the process. There is no planning process without a commitment to the product, and there is no plan without paper.

Second, *time is the enemy of all political efforts.* Since elections in the United States are set by law and tradition in time, there are a limited number of months, weeks, days, hours, and minutes available to implement all the activities of the campaign. Unlike other marketing efforts, the political campaign must receive all of its favorable consumer decisions on one day of action in a voluntary marketplace. The intensity of time as a dwindling resource separates political efforts from all other public relations or marketing efforts. A political campaign without the immediate sense of the time remaining in the election burned into its consciousness for daily accountability is virtually running blind.

Political planners, therefore, must always have a calendar at hand so as to plot the time involved in every step of an activity. Many campaigns adopt a process known as "election day backward" and count the days remaining until election day so that there is a constant understanding of the time left to communicate with voters and organize for the election. This number is often posted daily in campaign headquarters. Planning involves a constant commitment of the time resource throughout the campaign. The proponents of the competing organizational tasks of the campaign will attempt to save time by eliminating the time to plan. Although such an argument is counter to most managers in business, it is routine to hear claims about being too busy to plan the campaign.

Third, *perceived disparity from region to region is often cited as the reason to keep the process as informal as possible* (meaning no written documents and hence no records or accountability). Campaign managers claim they do not need plans from Maine to Utah to Alaska to Florida because "it's different here." However, voters in every democratic society make decisions about political leadership based on virtually identical sets of information delivered to them through identifiable communication channels. The United States has selected regional and demographic distinctions, but none are sufficient to overcome the homogenizing or nationalizing influences of American citizens' accepted ways of collecting and organizing information for voting (Goldenberg and Traugott, 1984). With the possible exception of Hawaii's unique electoral traditions, the campaign pattern does not vary greatly across the United States in my experience. At the same time, the business of politics is not as uniform as McDonald's hamburgers either.

Fourth, *political planning is always imprecise,* since one has to make assumptions about the future in order to continue toward election day. Because there is an absence of data on many questions, campaign teams have to choose among becoming paralyzed, guessing, or abandoning the planning process. The easiest route is to abandon the planning process because "we don't know the answers." Michael Berman, Democratic campaign professional with the Duberstein Group in Washington, D.C., introduced the WAG (wild-assed guess) as an acceptable tool to keep the planning process alive. A WAG is a reasonable guess about the future. The basis of the WAG may be diverse—history, sociology, political science, management, local folklore, marketing, military sciences, sports— since political planning borrows randomly from many disciplines and has no exclusive ownership of ideas, tactics, technology, issues, or organizational styles. A WAG can also be employed to break the "paralysis of analysis" when there is too much information in one area.

Finally, *situational problems in the planning or execution process can be legitimately addressed by answering "it depends"* rather than by permitting planning to cease. Since no "fact" about the future is immediately available, "it depends" forces the planning team to refine this answer into a question: "It depends on what?" Participants then can start to define the factors affecting the decision challenging the planning team.

THE PLAN

Every campaign team eventually designs or borrows its own methodology to address the planning process. Most prefer delay or task avoidance for as long as possible. As in business, there is no fixed formula for success. Each political professional and campaign has a style or tool that matches the talents and tools available in the kitchen cabinet (a small group of the candidate's closest advisers and friends) of the campaign. Since campaigns should be intuitively responsive to change, no political plan can ever afford to be final. The rationale for a plan and a structure is to have a document to revisit in order to form the basis of new tactics and strategies as events unfold. Management must enforce the regular review of the plan through a series of meetings which are, of course, on the general campaign calendar. It is critical to merge the draft documents with a calendar and the campaign resources budget documents to produce the final planning document. One element of the process or one isolated piece of paper does not constitute a plan. Of course, if it is not in writing, it does not exist.

The "lotus diagram" is a personal favorite planning tool developed by the students of Mount Edgecumbe High School in Sitka, Alaska. My original inspiration for the lotus diagram came from lessons concerning the "Continuous Improvement Process," and the reason for the design was to assist English classes in writing essays and short stories (Crawford-Mason and Dobyns, 1991). Adaptation of this simple "tic-tac-dough" methodology allows the political planning team to bring the elements of the campaign into separate and combined focus.

The lotus diagram produces an initial nine aspects of the campaign plan. Each box in the diagram then becomes a lotus diagram of its own, with campaign brainstorming generating eight aspects of that particular part of the campaign. In the example given in Figure 2.1, the candidate, one aspect of the intitial campaign plan, becomes central to a second lotus diagram, and eight topics related to the candidate make up the second diagram. Similarly, the campaign team, one box in the initial diagram, becomes a second lotus diagram, with the respective components of the team filling in the boxes.

The diagram allows the campaign planning staff to focus on the issues surrounding each particular element rather than be overwhelmed by the spectrum of tasks associated with each step of the campaign. The linear thought process usually produces exhausting lists of to-do items that never get addressed. The lotus diagram makes all tasks more equal. Once the initial brainstorming process has been completed so as to draw out all possible ideas from the campaign planning team, the lotus diagram can offer one structure for the campaign plan.

Candidate	Team	Environment
Donors/Audience	Plan	Time
Resources	Opponents	Coalitions

Personal	Spouse	Family
Style	**Candidate**	Geography
Philosophy	Lists	Opposition

Candidate	Finance Chair	Finance Director
Campaign Staff	**Team**	Coalitions
Friends	Events Committee	Finance Committee

Figure 2.1   Examples of the Use of a Lotus Diagram in Campaign Planning

THE CANDIDATE

In this cynical era, candidates for public office, better known as "politicians," are usually dismissed as craven or corrupt and are often considered secondary actors to the goals of society. For example, Secretary of State James Baker stated, "A candidate is the lowest form of human life" (Williams, 1992). I believe that the overwhelming majority of people attracted to public service are committed to "the energetic clashing of conflicting ideas" in order to "play a part in helping the country along" (O'Neill, 1987, p. 337).

Although anyone in the political profession is free to agree or disagree with either set of attitudes, people involved with the campaign process should recognize that the ambitions of their candidate constitute the fundamental rationale for the existence of the campaign. The campaign is, in fact, an undertaking aimed at affecting public will, but it does not exist without the candidate's personal determination to seek party nomination and public office. Conversely, the absence of ambition can undermine the campaign.[1]

The challenges of the campaign to the candidate are varied. For example, the Republican National Committee's 1989 campaign organization manual itemized these roles for the candidate: "Central Figure, Chief Cheerleader, Chief Spokesman, Chief Fund-Raiser, Chairman of the Board, Chief Campaigner, Trusting Boss, Family Support, Good Guy, Initiator, Innovator and Leader." For purposes of this discussion, the central issue is leadership. Leaders not followers, are elected to political office. As the leader, the candidate must display the personal characteristics necessary to inspire the campaign—volunteers, staff, contributors, coalitions, allies—and the community of voters. The campaign process is often the first time the candidate can show the impact of his or her personality in the public marketplace (Womack, Jones, and Roos, 1988). There is a value to the enthusiasm and emotional commitment that political competition brings out in people (Guber, 1988). Conversely, if the candidate or the candidate's hard core of supporters is disappointed in performance, it is difficult to persuade complete strangers to elect the candidate to a position of public trust (McCabe, 1988).

As the product of the campaign, the campaign plan must virtually dissect the candidate so as to organize campaign activities to mirror human strengths and minimize human frailties. Personal characteristics—such as whether the candidate can be a morning person; can communicate in person better to small groups or large groups; can talk in sound bites to a microphone or a camera; can remember faces and names; or can be charged with unfortunate racial or sexist attitudes—are critical to the campaign's success. Some issues, such as the personal morals and habits of the candidate or the family, are beyond the ability of even the best campaign to affect, but the campaign team should be the first to know its candidate's faults (Cramer, 1992). The timing, inflection and subtleties of human relationships of the candidate's interactions with people are the business of the campaign (White, 1973).

The life choice of a partner is undeniably a message to the community about the values of the candidate. The success or failure of the family and individual family members is another set of messages. Parents, spouses, and children are potential assets to the campaign as surrogates for appearances, as volunteers, and as additional voices, arms, legs, and brains to add to the "people power" of the effort (O'Brien, 1975). Unfortunately, there are also numerous examples of the family becoming a hindrance to the campaign's success. In addition to understanding candidates and their families as people in this process, it is also critical for the campaign to review the candidate's and the family's personal histories and public record of accomplishments in order to be certain of all the details and assured of their fundamental veracity. Failure of the team to undertake a research effort on its candidate can be a fatal mistake in the personality-driven politics of the 1990s.

THE AUDIENCE

What is the primary purpose of the campaign? There is often a confusion within campaigns with respect to this question. Is the objective to elect the candidate to office? to win the competition? to exceed expectations? A campaign should acknowledge that the electoral success of the candidate is its primary objective. The candidate is the leader of the effort, and the candidate probably receives more quality information about the fate of the campaign than any other individual. All campaign efforts eventually become known to the candidate, and as such the candidate becomes a constant audience because he or she is, after all, the boss.

The primary audience of a campaign should be the voters, particularly the campaign's committed voters and then those people who are not yet committed to the candidate. Choosing the vehicles for communication to those possible voters and then delivering that message should be the road map to victory for a political campaign. The research needed in order to identify the audience of all possible voters for the candidate is a combination of demographics, psychographics, and public opinion research. It reflects an understanding of the constituency based on voter registration lists, precinct evaluation based on voting histories, geography of the constituency, and then the media markets of the television, radio, and print media (including mail) that provide information to possible voters.

There are competing secondary audiences of the campaign (Figure 2.2). Political campaigns, like all organizations, have the magnetic quality of pulling energy into themselves at the expense of the mission. The initial secondary audience therefore consists of participants in the campaign who, to date, do not equal the 50 percent plus one vote necessary for victory in the election. The campaign structure itself becomes an internal audience of its own workers and volunteers with a parallel external audience of campaign consultants (pollsters, media, fund-raisers), campaign contributors, and the political party structure of amateurs and professionals. The demand for information to satisfy this internal audience can shift a campaign away from its primary focus.

The next category of audiences includes the people just outside the circle of allies and friends; these are persuadable organizations and contributors. Some are friendly—civic organizations, associations, and opinion leaders not yet endorsing the candidate, or people who are still considering a financial contribution. They are interested, positive, and open to making a commitment. The sum of the aforementioned committed supporters and these identifiable persuadable voters should result in sufficient numbers for victory. The interactions among the candidate, the

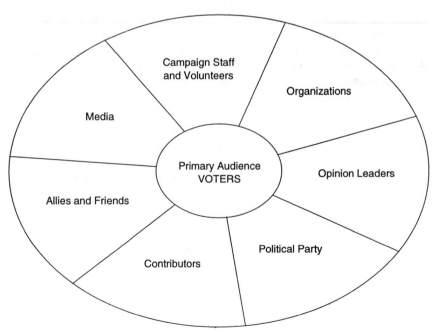

Figure 2.2   Secondary Audiences

campaign, and this audience may be sufficient to elect the candidate to public office (MacDougall, 1977). However, the quest for organizational support can also become an end in itself. In 1984 John Glenn correctly complained that the Democratic message to the constituency of the whole (Honomichl, 1980)—the voters—was being lost in the quest to secure endorsements from anyone with a letterhead and a mailing list (Germond and Witcover, 1985).

Another secondary audience is composed of the transmitters of information. A portion of this audience is the opinion leadership of the community. The media are a more distinct portion and are defined as neutral if not hostile. Although a campaign has no choice but to engage in a dialogue with the media to gain access to the listening, reading, and watching audiences, the relationship of the candidate and the campaign with reporters, journalists, producers, and commentators can consume all the energy of the campaign. The campaign must constantly resist the allure of individual publicity or community approval for campaign workers at the expense of the candidate. If the campaign loses respect for its own candidate, the opinion leaders and media will be the first to broadcast such internal discouragement.

There is no precise response to the dilemmas posed by the quest to define audience for a campaign. There is a rainbow of secondary audiences: the campaign itself, the political party, the media, the coalition of endorsing organizations, the contributors, and the opinion leaders of the community. Each of these fulfills a portion of the election process. From a planning perspective, the campaign should anticipate the competing audiences and structure itself to accommodate the needs of the audiences without losing its vision of the primary goal. When the campaign wanders toward secondary audiences of less value to the candidate's election, campaign disintegration in this time-sensitive competition is under way. If the campaign has a definition of secondary audiences and a structure prepared to respond to those audiences, it is able to maintain focus on the central objective. If a campaign can timely identify what it needs to satisfy the demands of the secondary audiences, it can address them as a resource rather than as a management issue. The answer to many of these internal audience conflicts becomes "it depends."

THE ENVIRONMENT

Although it usually feels as if the campaign worker is in a hostile cocoon during the campaign, the fact is that a political campaign should be an interactive dialogue with its surrounding cultures—political, economic, and social. The political culture usually does not make the daily list of concerns, interests, or activities of most voters, but the mundane political process is fundamental to the development of the political campaign. Political planners should first look at the ballot—the instrument by which the voters will elect or defeat the candidate for public office supported by the planners' campaign:

- Who is on the ballot?
- Is it a presidential or a gubernatorial year?
- Is a U.S. senator running for election or reelection?
- Are mayoral or other local offices on the ballot?
- Are there initiatives, constitutional amendments, or referendums on controversial issues or on local tax increases or bond measures?

In other words, the planning team wants to know what other choices are going to be made by the voters who will be making a decision on its candidate during their review of the ballot.

Once the terms of the campaign have been established by a review of the ballot, assessment of the political situation is in order:

- Which races are competitive?
- Which campaigns will attract resources?
- Will the party be united?
- Will the voters be satisfied or conflicted over their choices?
- How will voter reactions to the ballot help or hurt this campaign?

A second environmental concern that must be addressed in a campaign by the planning team is the economy:

- Where is consumer confidence?
- What is the unemployment rate?
- Are local or national businesses hiring or firing?
- How many new homes are under construction, and what are current real estate sales?
- Do the numbers translate into national optimism but local pessimism?
- Is there an opportunity for the most important political issue—the status of the economy—to be a reason to vote for or against the candidate?

The central issue of the 1992 campaign was posted in Bill Clinton's Little Rock headquarters: "It's the Economy, Stupid!" The economy is often voters' foremost concern. National polls consistently reveal that pocketbook issues (state of the economy, unemployment, interest rates, inflation) are the most important ones confronting the voters (Germond and Witcover, 1985).

The third element is the society surrounding the campaign—the social

environment. Most campaigns rely on the tools of public opinion research (polls, focus groups, feeling thermometers) to measure the mood
of the voters. However, there are more data to assimilate and to articu-
late before delivering a message to voters. Statisticians review demographics. Media analysts review Nielsen ratings or other measures of audience for television, radio, and print literature. *Hotline* (a political
newsletter) monitors opening routines of late-night talk shows for insights. Whether the task is forecasting, trend watching, or reading *Rolling
Stone*, the political campaign has to be in touch with the voters. In short,
there is a world surrounding a political campaign that usually has more
meaning to voters' understanding of the candidates than the political
messages of the campaign have (Center for National Policy, 1991).

THE RESOURCES AND BUDGET

A political campaign is often the most difficult enterprise in the United
States to finance for a number of reasons. Costs of campaigns are always
rising because of communications, technology, and an electorate that demands information and service. Federal, state, and local election laws are
complex and constantly changing. There is a constant suspicion of the
motivation behind the contributions made to campaigns; therefore media
attention to political dollars is usually negative. No tax deduction is
available for a political contribution as there is for other charitable gifts.
Finally, the solicitations are often extraordinarily amateurish because of a
failure to understand and anticipate the financial requirements of the
campaign by the candidate and the campaign staff. The checkbook is often the only document involved in many campaigns' financial planning.
Expenses are met through contributions from the candidate and assorted
activities termed "fund-raising," which then become particularly important as either the checking account diminishes or a major expense of the
campaign, usually communications costs, becomes imminent.

From a planning perspective, resources are brought to the campaign
through people or money. The people are either volunteers of their time
and energy or donors of some tangible resource, such as money, but there
are also in-kind donations. The process usually begins with an estimation
of the amount of money needed to win, based on a review of the current
costs of communications, the tools needed for campaign activities (headquarters, telephones, office machines, staff, postage, materials), and candidate expenses, principally for travel (Popcorn, 1992). Once those anticipated expenses are organized onto a sheet of paper, many campaigns
mistakenly believe they have a finance plan and a campaign budget.

Since political campaigns are funded through voluntary contributions,
logic would suggest that it is necessary to consider where the resources

are coming from and how they will be solicited before one can devise a plan for when and what the resources will be expended. However, time limitations and human nature do not allow a campaign such luxury. It is imperative for a campaign to think of resources and budget simultaneously and in relationship to each other. Four components of the finance plan help to structure this relationship.

The finance plan should begin with the resource of people rather than dollars. Most gifts to political campaigns are the result of personal solicitations by the candidate and the candidate's allies. Since most political activity is voluntary and limited to a few hours, the people resource in finance is critical because it takes time to solicit people through any process—mail, phone, in person, special events, candidate meetings. Thus, the first calculation for the planning team is the size of the sales force of campaign allies who will solicit people on behalf of the campaign. This resource is often structured into a finance council or events committee that becomes a separate campaign activity. Once this people component is known, the next factor to consider is the amount of money necessary to win the campaign. This figure is usually the result of both the itemization of expenses, some assumptions of financial success, and more than a few WAGs.

The third component is the calendar. The answers to the first question—when is the money needed by the campaign?—for all the expenses itemized earlier should be placed on the calendar. The process of soliciting and receiving money usually takes some time—a day, a week, a month, or longer. Thus, a campaign will get a sense as to when the people resource has to go into action in order to have the necessary money at the critical times. In practice, this calendar exercise produces a set of monthly targets in the beginning of the campaign that quickly become a set of daily or weekly finance targets in the closing weeks of the campaign. The real mistake to avoid is allowing individual special events or program successes to interfere with a monthly objective set by the resource budget process.

The fourth component of the finance plan becomes expansion and renewal of the people resource. Most volunteers have a limited set of associates who will contribute to a political campaign. Once that list is exhausted, the value of the finance volunteer is also exhausted for a time, but the campaign's financial demands remain and often accelerate. Therefore, recruiting more people and organizations into the finance process must become a planning objective. Finally, these data are reviewed periodically in order to determine how to remedy any financial shortfalls and whether there are sufficient campaign allies and activities to meet the targets according to the campaign's schedule of expenditures.

The companion to this planning process is the budget. From a planning perspective, one should first budget to win the campaign regardless of the political and financial reality tests that will be imposed shortly. How much does it cost in dollars to carry the message to the voters in order to encourage them to vote for the candidate of this campaign? Once the campaign planners understand the cost of the Cadillac approach, they can begin to address the reality of the situation. The merger of the budget-to-win proposal with the finance plan will demonstrate the necessity of scaling back some campaign activities, and the initial victims usually are paid campaign staff or political consultants. Such confrontation and compromise among the programs of the campaign produce the first real campaign budget.

THE STRUCTURE AND ORGANIZATION

The modern political campaign should not be designed or maintained with any concept of patronage. The era of political jobs for people unqualified, unable, or unwilling to work is no longer a fiscal option for most campaigns. More important, such an attitude has no place in the competitive team setting that is the political campaign of the 1990s. All organizations must first define their inner workings to themselves in order to be successful in any contest, and political campaigns are no different from any other effort organized to win a competition. However, there is enormous resistance to the concept of structure in a campaign as well as to the necessary bureaucratic trappings, such as titles and job descriptions.

Yet it is imperative that the planning process address the internal organization of the campaign at the beginning. The initial task is to define roles through written job descriptions for the candidate, the candidate's family, the campaign's significant volunteers (principally fund-raisers and senior advisers), and the paid staff or full-time volunteers. Since most campaigns start with a few volunteers and friends and paid staff, this challenge is often avoided until the absence of an organization, personality conflicts, or overlapping duties cause real damage to the campaign effort.[2] The rationale behind this investment in how people conduct their business is to create some divisions of labor within the campaign and to establish internal accountability.

The job descriptions usually focus on the campaign chair, the campaign manager, the finance chair, the finance director, the treasurer, the volunteer chair (or director or coordinator), the scheduler, the communications director (press secretary and media person), the office manager or headquarters chair, and the spectrum of assignments under field operations. All campaigns should have an attorney, and most larger campaigns have an accountant involved as well. There is also an assortment of committees that need some definition and role within the campaign. Most candidates have a network of advisers who become the kitchen cabinet and experienced managers try to identify those advisers as early as possible. Most campaigns also have a political committee of community and party leaders and need to organize a finance committee. Additionally, campaigns often form committees based upon geography (city, town, county committees); identities (e.g., Ukrainians, Koreans, veterans, Catholics); and special projects such as a voter registration drive. The party committees' handbooks are extraordinarily useful to campaigns attempting to define their internal structure. There are models of organization charts and job descriptions for virtually every task. The real structural challenge is to take the time to adopt an infrastructure and gain consensus as to that structure.

THE MESSAGE

Political plans should focus on the information provided to the voters by the campaign. Because of the limits of time, the lack of financial resources, and the physical size of most electoral constituencies, most voters will not have a personal visit with the candidate, the candidate's family, or even a representative of the campaign. It is hoped that the voters' information needs will be met by the assortment of materials transmitted to them by the media, the campaign, its opposition, and a spectrum of informal channels.

Planning for message starts with the candidate. Personal values or belief systems and personal history are vital bits of information people use to make decisions about other people. In the United States in the 1990s, public policy questions often collide with the candidate's personal beliefs on sexuality, personal freedoms, or religion. A campaign sensitive to its environment and its candidate will allow the candidate the time to prepare an answer rather than be surprised or confronted with personal moral dilemmas in a public setting. Message also involves the history of the candidate and the opposition. There does not appear to be any moment of a public figure's life that is allowed to remain private, and a campaign must research itself as well as its opposition does in order to prepare for the attack-counterattack of the current style of personal political comparisons.

Issues should matter in political campaigns because the disposition of issues constitutes the job of most elected officials, and a candidate and his or her campaign must invest resources in understanding and developing issue positions in partnership with its coalition of supporters and possible voters. Issues also need some framework unique to the candidate. Liberal, conservative, Republican, or Democratic may be a sufficient label, but many candidates avoid easy typologies or pigeonholing in this complex era, particularly when personal and social issues overlay the public policy questions.[3] Issues should be transformed into an agenda by the candidate and the campaign in order to answer the question posed by most voters: "What are you going to do with the office?" Bill Clinton consistently answered this question within the framework of his "agenda for change" in 1992; many would argue that George Bush never put "the vision thing" into the 1992 race.

Delivery of message is often as critical as substance. Since the audience is voluntary in politics—voters have to listen and then have to act—the campaign has to plan the delivery of its message by a series of stages in communications. The candidate must earn recognition and credibility in order to be deemed able to fill the voters' job definition of the office and to be considered knowledgeable on the issues. The candidate thus either must pay (advertisement delivered by private media) to communicate the message to the voters or must devise a mechanism (press conference, forum, event, letter to the editor) that places the message before the voters at the time of decision. Like every other element of the campaign, this process involves time and should be mapped onto a calendar. Finally, one cannot forget that the setting of a political campaign is competitive. There is an opponent who is trying with equal commitment to deliver a message about the team's candidate and the candidate's agenda for the future (Maddox and Lilie, 1984).

CONCLUSION

A political campaign's components can be organized so as to present a message to voters about the candidate as a leader. Such a commitment of time, energy, and thought to the process results in a plan (if it is in writing) or an endless series of conversations. The value of a written plan to a campaign is the presence of an organizational vision in a chaotic process that has earned the support of the majority of participants in the enterprise. The plan is always subject to revision and debate, but it should become an internal compass.

NOTES

1. See Christine M. Black and Thomas Oliphant, *All By Myself: The Unmaking of a Presidential Campaign* (Chester, Conn.: Globe Pequot Press, 1989), p. 6: "Beware of candidates who spend most of their time deciding whether to run, instead of why and how . . . beware of buttoned up candidates who instinctively distrust rhetoric, television, and other politicians; beware of candidates who seek to dominate the detail in their campaigns, a species that ironically includes the

chronically indecisive and insecure; and beware of the candidates who stress means over ends, trees over forests, detailed content over thematic style."

2. See Winter Park Group, "Proposed Gary Hart 1988 Business Plan," Winter Park, Colo., August 1986, pp. II-1: "In 1984, there was de facto anarchy at the top. The result was erratic coordination between the ground and the plane and between the local and state organizations at critical stages of the campaign."

3. See Institute for Strategic Management, (1984) "Campaign Groundwork: Strategy, Planning and Management," Washington, D.C.

3

Who Will Vote for You and Why: Designing Strategy and Theme

JOEL BRADSHAW

Modern political campaigns are becoming increasingly complex. Spending tens of thousands or even hundreds of thousands of dollars is more and more common, even for small local offices or state legislative seats. Increased expenditures generally provide greater communication to and with the voters and the use of more technology, sophisticated targeting, polling, direct mail, broadcast media (including cable television), and campaign professionals. However, whether this increased level of spending, technology, and sophistication actually produce a successful candidacy depends on how well the campaign deals with the fundamentals of strategy, theme, image, and issues. Many campaigns never come to grips with the need to determine a basic strategy or theme, and they pay the price at the ballot box.

Many, if not most, modern political campaign personnel lack a clear sense of what the campaign is trying to accomplish. They know they are trying to win, but they never come to a resolution as to how they are going to win. In short, they fail to define a strategy. Instead, most campaigns, even ones for high office, begin with a group of the candidate's friends, joined perhaps by some people who have worked on campaigns in the past, discussing the campaign. Drawing on their experience and their observations of other campaigns, they begin by making a series of lists. These lists include the following: tasks to do (get a headquarters, announce the candidacy); people to call (past candidates, party leaders); items to buy (buttons, bumper stickers); and materials to write or print (brochures, position papers). Most of these initial meetings raise no money, and participants spend little time addressing the financial aspects of a campaign.

Under the best of circumstances in this scenario, the campaign personnel begin with a list of activities to be completed, and proceed down the path of doing these activities until some external event interrupts. The campaign personnel react to the event and either return to activities on the original list or generate a new list based on the new circumstances. The campaign inevitably becomes a series of unplanned reactions to unanticipated events. The ultimate outcome is thus dependent on external circumstances, the opponent's campaign, the ability to react, and luck. Such campaigns are usually in chaos and often in crisis. They frequently change their message and tactics, and they always seem to be a day late and a dollar short. This kind of campaign lacks definition and focus. It has no strategy.

A campaign strategy is simply a definition of how you will win. It answers the following questions: Who will vote for you, and why will they do it? The principles of a sound strategy are the same whether the candidate is running for a seat on the school board or for the presidency of the United States. Of course, the techniques used to construct the strategy will vary based on the resources available to the campaign (particularly for research), but a sound strategy for a campaign is needed in order to have a clear sense of how to find and persuade the voters needed to win.

A campaign strategy is based on four very simple notions. First, the electorate can be divided into three groups in any given political contest: your supporters, your opponent's supporters, and the vast majority of voters who are generally uninterested in you and your campaign, uninformed about the race, and undecided on the vote that they will cast in the far-off future (see Figure 3.1). Second, by using political research, it is possible to determine the voters in various locations that fall into each of the three groups. Third, it is neither possible nor necessary to get the votes of all people, everywhere, to win the election. Rather, research and knowledge must be used to make a rational selection of a subset of the undecided voters sufficient to create a victory when they are added to the initial supporters (see Figure 3.2). Once this selection is made, the two sets of voters—our supporters and the targeted undecideds—become "our voters" (see Figure 3.3). There must be enough voters in this category to win, and the strategic focus of the campaign should remain on these voters at all times.

The fourth and final notion of campaign strategy is that once we have identified how to win, we can act to create the victory we have envisioned in that strategy. Once we have defined our voters (supporters plus

OURS	UNDECIDED	THEIRS

Figure 3.1   Three Types of Voters

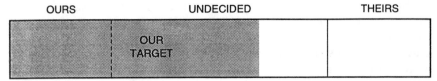

Figure 3.2   Targeted Voters

the targeted undecideds), we direct campaign resources—money, time, effort, and most of all, message—to those voters, and we direct *no effort anywhere else or at anyone else* (see Figure 3.4). Thus, resource allocation is defined by strategy, and that is the secret of running a strategically focused political campaign and conducting it to assert and retain control of the public debate. At this point, we have defined the first part of the key question of who will vote for you, and we know that we will speak only to those voters.

DECIDING A STRATEGY: WHERE?

There are three steps to deciding a strategy: understanding the political behavior of the jurisdiction in which the campaign will be conducted (the *where* of campaign strategy), understanding the nature of politics in that area from the voters' point of view (the *who* of your strategy), and understanding the contrast presented to the voters by the candidates (the *why* of your strategy).

The first step in deciding a strategy is to understand the political behavior of the jurisdiction in which you are running. The best tool available to predict voter behavior is to look at past behavior. By evaluating comparable elections in the past, we can learn with relative precision how many votes will be cast in the election for the office for which our

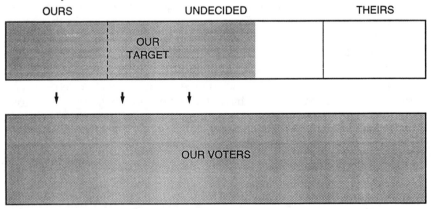

Figure 3.3   Our Voters: Supporters and Targeted Undecideds

Figure 3.4   Campaign Strategy and Targeted Voters

candidate is running. Once we know this, we determine the number of votes needed in order to win. In addition, by breaking down the jurisdiction into its component parts (counties in the state, wards in the city, towns or counties in a congressional district), we are able to learn the geographic distribution of the vote. This is the first important strategic fact, because as we have already determined, the allocation of resources must follow the strategy.

For example, in a statewide election in Colorado, the most basic fact to know is that roughly 85 percent of the votes cast come from only ten of the state's sixty-three counties. Clearly, the election will be decided in those ten counties. The victor will win a substantial portion of the vote in those ten counties overall but must win a majority in only some of the counties. Which counties a candidate must win becomes the core part of the campaign's strategy. The anticipated performance and the margins of victory or defeat in each of the sixty-three counties, but particularly the ten largest, should be reflected in a vote scenario. The scenario, which contains vote goals for each county, is thus the first step in assembling a strategy.

In order to determine how many votes we need to win, we first must decipher how many votes will be cast on election day. To do this we need two facts: the number of registered voters and the percent of voters who historically turn out in races at this level in this jurisdiction, both by geographic unit. It is important to use historical data that are as analogous to your race as possible, such as a race at the same ballot level in the appropriate year (presidential or nonpresidential). The key principle of race selection for use in vote targeting is *comparability*.

Once we know how many votes will be cast in this race and how they are distributed geographically, we need to know how many our candidate is likely to get. In partisan general election campaigns, the results of comparable past elections provide a series of important facts that will help us to identify our candidate's voting bloc. First, we determine the average performance for candidates of each party—that is, the percent of the vote that each party's candidate typically receives in an average year with an average campaign and an average candidate. Second, we find the baseline party vote for each party's candidate, or the vote that historically goes to the weakest of the party's candidates. Third, we compute the number of persuadable voters, those voters who are "up for grabs." The persuadable voters historically split their votes between the parties on one ballot or switch between the parties from year to year.

When this analysis is completed, we know the following things about the election:

1. How many votes will be cast
2. How many votes are needed to win
3. How many votes we can expect (performance)
4. How many voters are persuadable
5. How many votes we will receive if we do not get any persuadable voters (baseline party vote)

In order to build a meaningful strategy, we should undertake this analysis for each of the geographically subordinate parts of the jurisdiction. Using this knowledge, we can immediately determine the nature of the jurisdiction and some things about our campaign. For example, in a district with an average Republican performance of 55 percent, a Republican baseline party vote of 46 percent, and a persuadability factor of 14 percent, a Republican candidate is in a stronger position than would be the case in a district where the Republican performance is 47 percent, the baseline is 41 percent, and the persuadability is 18 percent. Victory in the first district relies much more on reinforcing the traditional Republican voters than victory in the second district. In that second district, a Republican would need to win a substantial number of votes from non-Republican voters. The campaign in the district with lower performance is likely to be more centrist and less ideological, and therefore the campaign strategy will be more message-oriented and less reliant on organization than the race in the first district, where mobilization will be a more integral aspect of the campaign strategy.

It is also necessary to consider the geographic distribution of our candidate's political strength throughout the district. In every competitive political jurisdiction, there are relative pockets of strength and weakness, and in the development of the geographic component, we need to take this into account. In general, the campaign should seek to maximize both voter performance and turnout in pockets of strength, maximize persuasion in some but not necessarily all of the areas of midrange performance and high persuadability, and hold losses to acceptable levels in areas of the opponent's strength. The result of this approach is the creation of a winning vote scenario containing vote goals for each of the subdivisions of the jurisdiction.

From left to right the columns in Table 3.1 show: the 1992 voter regis-

Table 3.1 Vote Scenario and Percent-of-Effort Calculation for Candidate Smith

	1992 Registered Voters	1992 Estimated Turnout	1992 Estimated Votes	1992 Persuadability (percent)	1992 Democratic Performance (percent)	1990 Smith Vote (percent)	1992 Expected Smith (percent)	1992 Expected Smith Votes	1992 Persuadables Required (percent)	1992 Percent of Effort Index (percent)
Lealman	2,643	59.6	1,575	19.6	56.1	57.0	56.5	890	58.0	5.0
Pinellas Park	27,002	63.5	17,158	20.5	50.5	57.0	51.0	8,751	53.1	48.0
St. Petersburg	1,300	67.5	877	21.8	50.2	–	51.0	447	54.0	2.0
Kenneth City	5,562	68.3	3,798	20.7	49.8	55.0	54.0	2,051	70.2	11.0
Largo	15,253	63.5	9,689	20.8	50.1	–	52.0	5,038	59.3	28.0
Clearwater	1,582	53.0	839	16.0	59.2	–	58.0	487	51.5	3.0
Dunedin	1,831	58.7	1,074	18.7	51.7	–	51.5	553	50.7	3.0
Total	55,173	63.5	35,010	20.4	50.8	56.0	52.0	18,217	56.9	100.0

tration total; the 1992 estimated turnout; the number of votes expected to be cast in 1992; the percentage of those votes deemed persuadable; the average Democratic performance percentage; the percentage Smith received in the part of the district Smith had in 1990; Smith's 1992 vote goal expressed as a percentage; the 1992 vote goal expressed as number of votes; the percentage of the persuadable votes required to reach the vote goal; and the percent-of-effort index, or PEI. The PEI is a guide for the allocation of campaign resources across the geographic or demographic subgroups of the district. In a geographic scenario, it is simply a measure of the relative share of the winning vote total allocated to each community, and it is the way to allocate the candidate's campaign time consistent with the campaign strategy.

This particular district is a swing district (Democratic performance of 50.8 percent), meaning it has a relatively high (20.4 percent) level of persuadable voters. This scenario was created for a one-term incumbent who represented 63.8 percent of the district (the rest is part of another district because of redistricting). In the scenario, 35,010 votes would be cast, and we would need 18,217 to achieve our 52 percent goal. This would be a very modest 1.2 percent improvement in the Democratic performance of 50.8 percent. We would need 56.9 percent of the persuadable vote, also relatively modest. In some districts, those with strong party performance for the opposition, over 75 percent of the persuadables would be required to achieve a winning scenario. As shown in the scenario, the most dramatic increase over average Democratic performance would be in Kenneth City (from 49.8 percent to 54 percent); it would require persuasion of 70 percent of the persuadables. This lofty goal was chosen in part because in the 1990 election, this candidate did win 55 percent of the vote in Kenneth City. According to our calculations, the battleground communities in this race would be Kenneth City, from the old district, and Largo, the largest portion of the new district, because the vote scenario would require the largest increase over Democratic performance in these two communities.

In addition to the historical voting behavior, the strength of the candidate and of the opponent in each place must be factored into the vote scenario. The voting behavior study provides the lay of the land based on previous voter behavior. Polling, on the other hand, helps in setting the targets above and below the historical averages. In some campaigns, like primaries or nonpartisan elections, voting behavior studies based on the two political parties are of no help in building a vote scenario or strategy. In cases like these, strategies are instead built by ascertaining the expected vote and its geographic distribution in order to know where to concentrate resources, and then creating a vote scenario based on the results of polling.

DECIDING A STRATEGY: WHO?

Now that we know where to focus our efforts, we next need to decide which types of voters are going to be in the "our voters" box. At this juncture in the process, it is necessary to conduct survey research. Whereas historical voting behavior tells us how voters have behaved in the past by geographic unit, polling informs us about voters' contemporary attitudes by both geographic and demographic classifications. The latter factors include political party, age, gender, level of income, level of education, political ideology, race and ethnic background, religion, marital status, and union membership. A poll indicates who likes your candidate now, who never will like your candidate, and what issues are of interest to the persuadable voters. A poll also measures the mood of the voters, thus helping the campaign to define the political environment in which the campaign will be conducted. To do this, most pollsters frame a question on whether respondents think the direction of things in the country, state, or district are on the right or wrong track.

In 1992, the number of people answering "wrong track" reached record proportions before the elections. In California, Pennsylvania, and Washington, between 70 and 85 percent of poll respondents indicated that they felt the country was on the wrong track. It was clear that voters were in a surly mood, and in many states, voters were angry. Their anger was focused on incumbents. Many voters simply said they were voting against all incumbents. However, this sense that things were going wrong and needed fixing was not uniform across states or demographic groups. Within Florida, for example, voters in some legislative districts were much more upbeat than voters in the state as a whole. Voters with higher incomes were less pessimistic about the direction of the country and the direction of their state. Women were more pessimistic than men. When a candidate is putting together a strategy, these details are the key. In this climate, an incumbent would be more likely to target men with higher incomes than women with lower incomes.

This was the mood in 1992, but in any election, there are many subtexts and subgroups. The key to successful strategy is not to try to appeal to everyone on his or her particular flash point but instead to select the types of voters you can most easily persuade based on the contrasts presented by the candidates.

DECIDING A STRATEGY: WHY?

Ultimately, the voters will make a choice between two or sometimes among three or more candidates. Most contested elections are decided at the end of the campaign. For voters who are making decisions late in the campaign, the choice rarely, if ever, comes down to an evaluation of a candidate's position on any one issue or any combination of issues. Rather, the selection is made more on the traits and characteristics of the candidates, and issues serve as a backdrop. It is a comparative choice, as the candidates are contrasted with each other. In order to fill in the final part of the strategy, therefore, it is necessary to evaluate the candidates. We need to see how they fit the district or state, how they fit the mood of the electorate, and how they stack up against each other. There are three types of positioning to consider. Presented in the rough order of their importance to voters who are deciding at the end of the campaign, they are the following: incumbency, party ideology, and style or image of the candidate.

Incumbency is the key factor. If there is an incumbent in the race, he or she is the issue in the campaign. The choice will come down to a referendum on the incumbent's performance in office. If voters are surly, as they were in 1992, the incumbent is at a disadvantage because there is a predisposition to change. If the campaign is decided on change, it is difficult for incumbents to win. If, on the other hand, the race is about experience, it is the challenger who is positioned poorly. Challengers cannot prevail unless they can convince the voters to replace the incumbent. The challenger says of the incumbent, as Bill Clinton did, "He has done a bad job. He should be fired." The incumbent says, "I have done a good job and we need my experience," which works only if it fits the voters' perception. The other typical response of the incumbent is, "Wait. You can't trust him. He is inexperienced." Other claims might be "he is deceitful" or "he lacks values." President Bush at one time or another tried all of these and more. Ultimately, the presidential campaign was decided on the voters' perception of the incumbent's performance.

Incumbency is just as important a factor in low-visibility races. In 1992, in Orlando, Florida, a young woman who had never run for office and had not voted in Orlando before September 1992 defeated a twelve-year Republican veteran in a district with a 44 percent Democratic performance. He started campaigning earlier, spent more money, attacked her nonparticipation as a voter, attacked her for running a dirty campaign, and tied her to the very unpopular Democratic governor. She convinced over 80 percent of the persuadable voters to vote for her. For the voters, the race was about the incumbent, and they decided that he should be fired.

If there is no incumbent in the race, a strategy must be constructed to make one of the candidates more acceptable than the other. One choice available is to run as the incumbent: to assert having more experience, better qualifications, and more accomplishments and, in extreme versions, to claim the seat and act as if it is yours. Walter Mondale adopted this strategy in his 1984 primary quest for the Democratic nomination.

He diminished his opponents' experience, dressed formally, and had a large entourage in order to make him look presidential. Mondale relied on his support among Democratic political institutions and ran a very institutional campaign. He was the pseudoincumbent, and ultimately he prevailed for the nomination.

The other option is to run as the challenger and make your opponent appear to be the incumbent. This worked well in several places in 1992; one of the most notable cases was the U.S. Senate race in Washington State. State Senator Patty Murray, the "mom in tennis shoes," was the ultimate outsider. Her general election opponent was Republican incumbent Senator Rod Chandler. Chandler tried to run against the Democratic majority in Congress and take the change message for himself. When that failed, he attacked Murray's inexperience and suggested that electing her would be too risky, a classic incumbent contrast with a challenger. Chandler's approach fed into Murray's message of being a different voice, an outsider. Since Murray was running in an open seat as the challenger, in a state with high voter dissatisfaction, she won by ten points. The contrast between challenger (outsider) and incumbent (insider) favored her because it matched the voters' mood.

If the incumbent-challenger contrast is not available for some reason, campaigns in an open seat often move to the next level of candidate positioning: party ideology. After incumbency, the next most important factor to voters is party or, to some, ideology. For people undecided in October, party labels are something to focus on easily and quickly. To most voters, the terms Republican and Democrat mean something. Ideology, in this context, means more than right or left, liberal or conservative. It also means views on specific issues that individual voters feel strongly about. It is the shorthand language that voters, who are not paying much specific attention, use and understand.

In some places, it is sufficient to be a Republican or Democratic nominee to win; the partisan performance is so strong that nothing overrides it. Localities like this generally have few contested general elections. An example is Middlesex County, New Jersey, where only 10 percent of the voters are likely to split their ticket or switch between parties. There is a strong tradition of Democratic voting, and although Republicans sometimes win, it takes a very good Republican year or an extraordinarily weak Democratic candidate. Democratic candidates link themselves in such a place to the Democratic tradition and the accomplishments of previous Democrats. That message usually prevails. In primaries in particular, candidates can get the persuadable votes they need by identifying with a particular ideological faction—liberal for Democrats, conservative for Republicans—or with a powerful group such as organized labor in Michigan or the Mormon Church in Utah.

Some candidates attempt reverse ideological positioning. In the 1988 Florida U.S. Senate campaign, Connie Mack ended his television advertisements with the phrase "Hey, Buddy [McKay, his opponent], you're a liberal." In 1988, with Bush pounding on Dukakis and setting an ideological tone for the presidential campaign, it was too much for McKay. Mack barely won, with only 50.5 percent of the vote, but this tactic worked because it fit into the context in which voters were deciding. It moved just enough people for Mack to win.

In general, party, political ideology, and issues are important as determinants of voter preference to issue activists, partisans, and others engaged in the political process on an ongoing basis. These people are not very likely to be deciding the outcomes of close elections by making up their minds at the end of October; they traditionally decide early in the race. The undecided voters remaining (after some have decided on incumbency and others on party, ideology, or issues) vote based on the contrasting traits and characteristics of the candidates. This is the image of the candidates that voters form based on what they see and hear during the campaign.

The concept of image is often misunderstood in political campaigns in two ways. First, consultants and managers do not create an image for a candidate out of whole cloth. This does not work for two reasons: The voters are hard to fool, and the opponent will enumerate to the voters all the ways your candidate is trying to be something he or she is not. What really happens in strategic campaigns is that our research and knowledge tell us which of our candidate's traits match best with the qualities the voters are seeking. Here again it is a comparative choice for the voters: one candidate against the other. Thus the selection of an image is a two-step process: Understand the district and the voter, and then maximize the contrast between the candidates in a way that places your candidate closer to what the voters seek.

The other misunderstanding about the concept of image in campaigns is that people think it refers to hairstyle, makeup, and clothing. Paul Tsongas made much fun of the advice he got from his handlers. "They told me to buy a blue suit and a red tie. I hope you like it." What Tsongas said resonated with the voters who were paying attention to the presidential primary campaigns. They believed that this is literally what his handlers did, but in fact they were using that dialogue to reinforce Tsongas's existing image as a nonpolitician. They knew this image would sell because they knew the voters were in a surly mood and were tired of politics as usual.

A candidate's image is made up of many things: age, appearance, gender, speaking style, body language, accomplishments. Image is the person that the candidate is perceived to be by the voters and, in high-visibility races, by the press. One of the first exercises any campaign should conduct is to gather a group of the candidate's close friends and supporters to do an assessment of strengths and weaknesses on all of the candidates. This process never fails to produce a basic list of traits and characteristics of the candidates. In well-funded statewide campaigns, focus groups are often the next step. This gives the campaign the benefit of a structured discussion among voters of their basic concerns, their mood, and their perceptions of the candidates. Focus groups provide qualitative information and generate ideas to test in subsequent baseline polling. In smaller local campaigns, one has to do the best one can with the available information. A broad group of supporters and activists can serve as a mini–focus group and help campaign planners to make the best judgments they can about the mood and concerns of the voters.

Once we have an assessment of the district, an awareness of the mood of the voters and their concerns, and an understanding of the image of the candidates, the strategy can be completed. At this point, we should know which types of voters are going to vote for us and what our vote goals are across the jurisdiction. When we match up our strengths with the mood and concerns of the voters and contrast them with the opponent's weaknesses, we have the answer to the second half of the strategic question of why they will vote for you. Our strategy is now complete.

Or is it? In many campaigns, the first question asked after the campaign decides on a strategy is how and when it will be changed. In order to answer the question, it is important to understand the context in which it is asked. The essence of a strategy is that it defines choices the campaign has made about what it will and will not do, and where it will and will not do them, within the context of available resources. Much of the value of strategic closure is that you know what you are *not* going to do. This understandably makes candidates and their advisers very uncomfortable. People in politics are conditioned to try to keep their options open and, frankly, to try to keep to a minimum the number of people unhappy with the candidate. This approach is in opposition to a strategic concept that limits the focus of the campaign to only those voters and topics necessary for victory. Therefore, the desire to change is often a reflection of the desire to open up more options or to reanalyze decisions already made.

So when should we change? Since having a strategy has no value unless it is executed, the answer is not very often. The only instance is when you have clear, unrefutable evidence that what you are doing is not working, *because the fundamental circumstances in which the race is being conducted have changed.* Examples of this kind of basic alteration in the political landscape are the Los Angeles riots in spring 1992 and Hurricane Andrew in Florida that fall. If the presidential election had occurred in early

1991, the collapse of the Soviet Union would have meant the same sort of fundamental change in the landscape. When an event such as this occurs, the appropriate response is not to change the strategy but to do additional research (polling) in order to assess the impact of the changed environment. Then evaluate the strategy in light of the new information.

Changes in the relative standing of the candidates, the narrowing of the race, or the opposition spurting ahead generally should not signal a change in strategy. It takes time for things to work, and if your research was sound and your judgment good, your strategy should be valid. If you change too soon, you will never give anything a chance to work, and you will have a campaign of unplanned reactions to unanticipated events. Here again, the appropriate response is to do more research. Look before you leap.

THEME

Once a strategy is determined, the campaign must be won. In order to get potential voters to go to the polls and vote for your candidate, you have to communicate with them. The information your campaign provides is only part of the information the voters will receive. They will also be receiving information about your candidate and his or her opponent from the other campaign and the press. Furthermore, the voters have a lot more important things on their minds than political campaigns. Most of the people we are trying to reach with our message do not think about this at all until late in October. They do not read all the news magazines, the *Wall Street Journal,* and two local dailies. They are not waiting impatiently to receive your position paper in the mail. They do not watch CNN and C-Span. They watch *Wheel of Fortune,* and they think about politics and campaigns less than five minutes a week. So if you want them to get the point you are trying to make about your candidate, you have to help them.

A campaign must have a theme to communicate to voters. In the campaign context, "theme" is not a word that should ever have an "s" on the end; there is only one theme. You can get one point through to voters who think about this five minutes a week or less. There may be examples of the theme and many different specifics you use to illustrate it, but all those examples must add up to one point: *A campaign theme is the rationale for your candidate's election and your opponent's defeat.* It is the single, central idea that the campaign communicates to voters to sum up the candidate's connection with the voters and their concerns and the contrast between your candidate and the opponent. It answers the question, Why should your candidate be elected—to this office at this time? Further, a one-sentence summary of the theme should always be the candidate's response to the question, Why are you running? It either states or implies why your opponent should not be elected—to this office at this time—and it is specific to the circumstances of time and place. However, it is general with regard to the candidate.

A good campaign theme has six characteristics. It must be clear, concise, compelling, connected, contrasting, and credible. It helps also if it can be communicated in an easily understandable and memorable way.

Clear means easy to communicate and understand. Many politicians have difficulty meeting this criterion.

Concise means short and to the point. A campaign theme that is not disqualified under "clear" is often disqualified under "concise."

Compelling means conveying a sense of emotional urgency. Voters require a strong reason to choose you over the other person, and in politics emotional motivation prevails over rational motives every time.

Connected means relevant to voter perceptions of the circumstances in which the race is being run. The better connected the theme is to voters, the more compelling it will be to them.

Contrasting means establishing clear differences between the candidates, and it is part of making the theme compelling. Often voters will choose the candidate they dislike the least.

Credible means believable. When voters compare what you say to what they see, the two had better be consistent.

When it is time to develop the theme, start with the strategy. We know who we need to persuade, and our research tells us what traits voters want in the candidate they choose. Typically, voters want someone who cares about people like them, works hard, is honest and effective, will make a difference, gets things done, or has experience. Next, focus on the contrasts between or among the candidates in order to find the differences to highlight for the voters. Then select the traits and characteristics that you want to highlight in your candidate to connect well with the voters and simultaneously to make the contrast clear.

An example of how this approach worked occurred in the 1992 elections. Voters wanted change in many places. They were angry and frustrated. Women candidates did particularly well in congressional campaigns in part because voters generally did not perceive women to be part of the problem in Congress. Voters saw them instead as something new and different. In short, many women were *compelling* as candidates because they were able to connect better with the mood of the voters.

Barbara Boxer, the eventual winner in the six-year Senate seat in California, was engaged in a three-way primary with Lieutenant Governor Leo McCarthy and incumbent Los Angeles Congressman Mel Levine. The issue differences were minimal. Levine was much better funded, and McCarthy much better known, having run for statewide office three times in the previous six years. Boxer was seen by those who knew her as a fighter with a vibrant and feisty style. Her two opponents in the primary were both more deliberative and rational in their presentation to voters, not as good a match with the voters' mood as was Boxer.

Boxer campaigned for a year telling the story of how she and seven other women members of Congress went to the Senate to demand that Anita Hill's allegations against Clarence Thomas be heard. She related how they were told, "We don't let strangers in here." She then asked, "If seven women members of Congress with more than eighty years of experience among them are strangers in the United States Senate, what about you?" By telling this story over and over, she established herself as the outsider in the race and, by implication, made the other two the insiders. She connected with the voters' sense that the Senate needed to be changed and shaken up. The way she told the story elicited an emotional response that helped to establish the urgency Boxer needed in order to move voters to her candidacy against her better-known and better-funded opponents.

Clearly, gender was a big part of the contrast. Women were a key target group, but men also responded to the shake-up theme. Boxer's ability to express a rationale for her candidacy in terms that connected emotionally with the voters propelled her to a stunning upset victory. It is important to note that in this case, the winning theme relied more on contrasting styles than on issue differences.

Repeating the Theme

The key to achieving your strategy is the repetitive communication of your campaign theme. If you stick to it and say it often enough, you will define the criteria for the voters that they should use to make their choice. In other words, you communicate your theme by stressing the same message to voters over and over. In that 1992 primary, Boxer said: "Vote for the one who you think will shake up the Senate." That was a test Boxer—and only Boxer—could credibly pass.

If the theme is the case you build for voters for your candidate's election, the issues and the way you deal with them are the evidence you use to build the case. If the case you want to build is that you are a fighter who will shake up the status quo in the Senate, you can talk about the Hill-Thomas hearings and the march to the Senate. You can talk about standing toe-to-toe with Jesse Helms to protect a woman's right to choose. You can talk about forcing the Pentagon to have competitive bidding on defense contracts so that taxpayers do not pay $7,000 for coffeepots. Or you can talk about the need to make U.S. allies pay their fair share of defense costs, which would free up funds to be spent to help the nation by creating jobs and improving education and health care.

Boxer used all of these issues to make the point that she wanted to shake up the Senate. They were examples of how she would make things different. She wasn't saying, "Vote for me because I am pro-choice" (so were both her opponents). She was saying, "Vote for me because I think we need to shake things up and I am the best person of these three to do that, and here are some examples that demonstrate that." This theme was extremely compelling because it was so well connected to what the voters were thinking and feeling. It worked so well that Boxer was able to sustain the disclosure of 143 overdrafts at the House bank less than two months before the election, and her consistent advocacy of her message prevailed.

In the final stages of a competitive campaign, voters will be receiving messages from two campaigns. If both campaigns are thematically focused and have relatively equal resources devoted to communicating their themes, the one that prevails is generally the one that is the better connected to the voters, provides the sharper contrast with the opponent, and offers a compelling reason to vote for the candidate.

A look at the comparison between the closing days of the 1992 presidential campaign with the 1984 presidential campaign will help make this point. In 1992, Clinton was running on change and hope, saying that the country was on the wrong track, that we must change, and that we can change. The Bush campaign was raising doubts about Clinton, saying that he could not be trusted, that he lacked integrity, and that he would bring back the days of tax and spend. The Bush campaign was also saying that the economy would turn around and that he had earned the voter's trust. In 1984, Reagan was saying that things were good, that he had fixed the economy, and that it was good to be an American. Reagan said that the United States had the respect of the world and that it was morning in America. On the other hand, Mondale was saying that it was midnight in America, that things were getting worse, and that we needed to change. The key difference between these two elections is not that Jim Baker did a better job as Reagan's campaign manager in 1984 than he did as Bush's campaign manager in 1992 or that Reagan's media specialist, Roger Ailes, did not do Bush's media. The difference is that Bush's theme was not connected to what the voters really cared about and Clinton's was. Clinton's theme was connected, consistently expressed, and compelling. Reagan's 1984 message was connected and compelling, and Mondale's was not. *If you want to move and motivate voters, start where they are, not where you are.*

CONCLUSION

A campaign begins and ends with the strategy. The campaign begins with the establishment of a strategy, and it should end with the achievement of the strategy. If you are able to establish a winning strategy, with a precisely defined set of persuadable voters to move to your candidate, you are able to define *clearly* a *concise* rationale for your candidate's election that offers the voters timely, *compelling*, and *credible* reasons for your candidate's election and sharply *contrasts* your candidate with the opponent. If you do this, your campaign will have focus. If you are focused on what you want the voters to think about your candidate and the opponent, and you are rigorously disciplined and consistent about what and how you communicate to voters, you can define the debate and make your opponent react to your definition. If the campaign is decided by your voters on your turf, consistent with your definition of the debate, you will win.

4

Contemporary Strategy and Agenda Setting

DENISE BAER

Political campaigns are increasingly coming under attack by journalists and the public as too negative and even dishonest and underhanded. Ironically, political science scholarship has traditionally treated campaigns as less important in the outcome of elections than economic and political factors. Elections are explained primarily as the result of preexisting voter loyalties to the two major parties. The popular view of campaigns is that elections are determined through the cynical manipulation of independent polling consultants and "spin doctors." What is the truth? Are candidates marketed like soap with campaigns based on themes irrelevant to important policy concerns of the American public? Are elections determined simply by party identification of voters and the state of the economy?

Campaigns are a complex mechanism through which alternative readings of the pulse of the public are tested and compared. Incumbents and challengers must visit voters where they live to defend and justify their record and make promises. The process is one that may offend the aesthetics of some.

Understanding the theory and practice of campaign strategy is essential to understanding how they work and, yes, enhance democracy. Candidates must persuade citizens in their homes, in their union halls, and at their chamber of commerce meetings why they should be elected. The mobilization of this support is based on how well each individual campaign structures its strategy, frames its message, and communicates with voters. In the contemporary party system, the quality of the strategy is increasingly crucial, as argued by William R. Sweeney (in Chapter 2) and Joel Bradshaw (in Chapter 3).

Ironically, political science has paid scant attention to campaign strategy. After World War I, the "hypodermic model" was in sway—propaganda could be injected into consumers and its effects would be complete and immediate. Like the manic-depressive whose mood swings from one extreme to another, political science has alternated from treating campaigns as propaganda with vast power to alter voter preferences, to deeming them irrelevant, to again viewing campaigns and campaign strategies as quite potent and effective in determining elections.

WHY POLITICAL SCIENCE IGNORED
CAMPAIGNS 1940s–1960s

Voting behavior is considered the most scientific subfield of American politics. However, until recently, there has been little direct research on campaigns (Asher, 1983). One reason may be that theories of campaigns were actually theories of something else: rational-choice models derived from economics; psychological theories derived from psychology; or consumer marketing, developed after World War II, derived from business administration.

The first voting studies of the 1940s (Lazarsfeld et al., 1944; Berelson et al., 1954) approached voting behavior as a variant of consumer marketing (Natchez, 1985). There followed the individualistic social-psychological model of *The American Voter* (Campbell et al., 1960 and 1964) and political scientists found little evidence for campaign effects. With most voters having a strong identification with one of the two major parties, mass communications and voting behavior research conducted in the decade after World War II found that the major effect of campaigns was to reinforce already existing attitudes rather than to create new ones. When over 80 percent of voters were tied to a party, as was true in the 1950s, the potential for campaign effects was indeed small.

Campaigns were further constrained by the social nature of campaign communications. Voters were ill-informed and paid little direct attention to either campaigns or the media. Instead, voter knowledge was garnered indirectly in conversations in nonpolitical groups with attentive opinion leaders. This two-step flow of communication informed voters by giving them information consistent with preexisting group affiliations (Berelson et al., 1954).

Similarly, econometric and rational-choice models also came to the conclusion that campaigns were irrelevant to the outcome of elections. Rational-choice theories (e.g., Downs, 1960; Page and Brody, 1976) downplayed the role of campaigns because rational incentives encouraged candidates to be ambiguous about their issue positions. Candidates would seek to maximize votes. Partisans would have no other place to go, and the largest numbers of votes would cluster at the moderate consensual center point, at least if the political preferences of Americans were normally distributed. This left the ideologically passionate voters with little choice; they had no alternative party to turn to. Econometric models predicted the outcome of elections based on the functioning of the economy (see Samuel Popkin, Chapter 17) but also minimized the importance of the campaign.

Neither the rational-choice model nor the econometric model posited a mechanism through which campaigns were minimized, and their complementary theoretical support for the weakness of campaign communications reinforced the lack of attention scholars paid to campaigns. The model of campaigns produced by these researchers was the *militarist campaign* (Jensen, 1969). The militarist style stresses contact with partisans and mobilization of voters already committed. It is based on the model of the "political army" of the party machine: Campaign strategy, not persuasion, is the strategy of turnout. Campaigns have minimal consequences, and winning campaigns are those that most effectively mobilize the already committed partisans.

MASS MEDIA CAMPAIGNS 1970s–1980s

By the early 1970s, scholars increasingly viewed campaigns as extremely influential in persuading voters and identified the *mercantilist campaign* (Jensen, 1969). The mercantilist style is based on public relations and the liberal use of media techniques in appealing to a broad, undifferentiated electorate. Diametrically opposed to the militarist model, it is conducted without regard to party identification and in many instances is directed toward independents.

Dan Nimmo's *The Political Persuaders* (1970) first raised serious questions about the role of "professionally mediated" campaigns. In this early work profiling the new campaign management industry, Nimmo proposed a theory of perceptual effects to explain how campaigns really did have strong effects on election outcomes.[1] In his analysis of the developing field of communications research, Nimmo argued that the mass media and television in particular were used by modern campaigns to change the perceptions of those with low involvement. In contrast to the law of minimal consequences that ignored low-involvement voters, Nimmo articulated a "field theory of campaign effects":

> The less important to a person the subject considered, the more likely is persuasion, or learning without involvement. . . . His relatively low involvement makes him the primary target of professional campaigners. They bombard his weak perceptual defenses. . . . The candidate is presented as the ideal leader in whom we can place faith and trust; his image remains sufficiently ambiguous to permit the . . . voter to "fill in the gaps" by projecting his own private needs. The effects of political campaigns thus result from role-taking in a field of action. (1970, p. 182, pp. 192–193)

By using message repetition and stressing the form and imagery of the message over content, Nimmo concluded that campaigns can have large effects by mobilizing voters who previously showed low or no participation.

Nimmo raised three concerns later echoed by many others (e.g., Burnham, 1985) about the use of television. First, image or appearance may count for more than reality; second, campaigns may no longer be battles between candidates but between titans of the campaign industry "working on behalf of those personalities"; third, there is a concern that those candidates able to buy the best consultants will ultimately be able to buy public office (1970, p. 197). Sidney Blumenthal later argued that "politicians are ephemeral," but consultants have become "permanent" (1982, pp. 17, 23).

This view raises a key question for democracy. Can candidates indeed be sold like commercial products (e.g., soap)? Recent research tells us that these early fears were unfounded. One reason is that the technology is neither so complex nor so expensive that the issue of equal access raised by Nimmo and Blumenthal leads to the "buying of office." Another key reason is that many outside observers of the rise of the professionally mediated campaign have misunderstood the fundamental purpose of campaigns and campaign themes and how the nature of political competition radically separates the structure and practice of campaign communications. Consumer marketing is a poor fit in politics where the nature of competition is radically different from the marketing of consumer products.

THE PURPOSE OF CAMPAIGN STRATEGY AND TACTICS

Campaign themes are usually about changing the future: Each opposing candidate offers a different version of what the future can or should be. Campaign themes come from a candidate and his or her closest adviser's assessment of current trends and problems, from the views of partisan groups and factions, and from the entrepreneurship of the individual candidate.

Voters choose among alternatives presented by the candidates and thereby choose the mandate for change presented by the winner. By successfully persuading a plurality of the voters to their view, winning campaigns can change the future. Mandates can be created in the nomination process within the party or by winning an election. In the general election, one candidate's team is placed into office rather than another, and one party's interest groups are provided greater access than the losing party's coalition. As Howard Phillips, chair of the Conservative Caucus, noted concerning Dan Quayle's selection as George Bush's vice-presidential running mate in 1988, "It gives us a place at the table, a focal point for our concerns. It's the first personnel decision, and personnel is policy" (Stokes, 1988).

A campaign strategy is a long-term "action-based frame of reference" (Wirthlin, Breglio, and Beal, 1981) that (under ideal circumstances) is designed to bring the campaign theme to life in the persona of the candidate. The best strategic campaign plan is organically linked to the campaign theme and message(s). Those outside of the campaign are rarely privy to the campaign's strategy, but its theme is well known because it is the public face of the campaign. A well-formulated strategy is the campaign plan that structures how the campaign is to act and react to the opposing candidate and campaign's initiatives. The tactics of a campaign are a series of individual actions that create news and implement the strategy.

Tactics are devices (campaign appearances, dress, style of contact, dramaturgy) used to reinforce and reiterate the campaign theme. Tactics that go beyond the experience of the opposing campaign team or the ability of the candidate to compete equally (personal knowledge, speaking skill) enhance the campaign's ability to maintain momentum and control of the agenda. But the diffusion of campaign technology and tactics is nearly immediate. As Gary Mauser (1989, p. 45) put it, "the genie is out of the bottle," and what one campaign does is added to the repertoire of future campaigns.

Although the tactics of a campaign may change in response to external events or actions of the opposing candidate(s), ideally the overall strategy should be one that animates the campaign from start to finish. It is important to maintain momentum. To the extent possible, tactics should be aimed at going outside of the experience of the opposing campaign. This increases the ability of the campaign with the more diverse array of tactics to catch the opposing campaign off guard and unable to respond.

The 1992 campaign theme for Bill Clinton was "change"—by itself a simplistic concept. This campaign theme was communicated in part by Clinton's strategic use of a grassroots-campaign speaking style and the famous bus tour after the convention. Specific support groups were given specialized messages about what this change meant to them (the "narrowcast" message); others were given a general message ("broadcast" message). For example, the narrowcast message to blacks, a key Democratic support group, was to assure them that change meant an attack on racism and a concern for the policies they cared about (urban areas). The tactics varied but included campaigning in black churches, receiving the endorsements of major black leaders, and visiting Los Angeles after the riot following the verdict acquitting the officers accused of beating Rodney King. The general broadcast message to voters was that Clinton was not an extremist or a captive of Democratic interests. This was communicated by the tactics of attacking the concept of quotas, of publicly criticizing Jesse Jackson shortly before the Democratic convention, and of presenting a tough stand on crime by refusing to grant clemency to Rickie Lee Rector, a brain-damaged Arkansas convict who was to be executed. "Change" worked for Clinton because it separated him from his opponents in both the primary and the general election campaign.

Regardless of the race, the basic principle of a good campaign strategy is to polarize sharply the campaign's theme and message into two sides—yours and your opponents. A wide variety of potential issues may be used in any campaign, but it is important to be able to personalize the message. For example, the Democratic and Republican parties and their candidates usually take opposing positions on the issue of abortion. Yet abortion has been successfully used as a general election issue only in those few campaigns in which the opposing candidate can be personally linked to the "wrong side" of the issue. The point is not that the pro-choice or the pro-life positions are wrong per se (usually viewed by the average voter as a position of conscience), but whether the opposing candidate can be defined as an extremist (antifamily or antifemale). The opposing candidate must be made personally responsible for an unpopular view or policy. The 1989 Virginia governor's race between Doug Wilder and Marshall Coleman is presented as a model for how abortion could be successfully used by a Democrat to come from behind and defeat a Republican. The issue worked in Virginia because the Wilder campaign was able to use Coleman's own words against him by repeating his statement that he wished abortion policy was like it was in his childhood—all abortions were illegal, even in cases of rape and incest. By the same token, candidates may insulate themselves against a possible attack by stressing their personal compassion for those on the opposing side.

The purpose of campaign strategy is to use tactics to convince voters that it is important that you represent them. To be given the grant of power to speak for people requires that they trust you. This is not a generic or diffuse trust in character but rather a political trust that you, the candidate, have the same priorities they have. Campaign tactics and themes may seem simplistic to those who prefer position papers and well-reasoned and referenced analysis, but their purpose is to invite trust, not to appeal to the intellect. Trust takes a long time to build, and it can be destroyed in an instant by a breach such as Gerald Ford's attempt to eat a tamale in Texas with the shuck still on or George Bush's ignorance of the price of a container of milk.

THE THEORY OF POLITICAL CONFLICT AND STRATEGY

Political scientists argue that there are two factors that have a significant impact on the outcome of elections: turnout and voter preferences. One way to assess these variables is through targeting: Make an assessment of average aggregate turnout and expected levels of support district by district, and compute how much the campaign needs to gain to win the magic 50 percent plus one vote on election day. This approach can misrepresent the strategic nature of political conflict. Candidates and parties have finite resources to devote to campaigns. Thus, the activities of the campaign focus on existing groups and networks of politically active individuals. Candidates also seek to magnify the effect of their campaign communications by strategically focusing "their efforts to coincide with salient issues, minimal distractions, imminent decisions, and close political contests" (Rosenstone and Hansen, 1993, p. 162).

As E. E. Schattschneider made clear more than thirty years ago, a central facet of campaigns is the scope of conflict (Schattschneider, 1942). As more participants are brought into a conflict, the nature of the game changes, and therefore the salience of issues and issue preferences change. Thus, as turnout increases, preferences are altered. This is the "socialization of conflict" through which groups not specifically affected by an issue become involved. This process changes the nature of the conflict and materially changes how the conflict is defined (Thurber, 1991, pp. 302–348). As preferences are altered, turnout is affected. Campaign strategy not only is affected by but also structures the scope of conflict. "In view of the highly strategic character of politics we ought not to be surprised that the instruments of strategy are likely to be important in inverse proportion to the amount of public attention given to them" (Schattschneider, 1960, p. 6). Framing the issues one way as opposed to another can limit the scope of the conflict—which Schattschneider termed the "privatization of conflict" (Schattschneider, 1960, p. 7). Conflict is contagious and unstable. It not only draws in new participants who participate in redefining the conflict but also mobilizes opposing groups who countermobilize their partisans (Duverger, 1954).

Modern campaign techniques, designed to increase the efficiency with which campaign resources are used, employ targeting. This targeting focuses on likely voters. This can be measured demographically either by focusing voter mobilization efforts on localities with a high voter turnout or by using a voter identification program in which voters who regularly vote are sent targeted information. The new campaign technology ignores communities with a history or pattern of nonvoting. Earlier mass mobilization techniques, such as rallies and door-to-door campaigning, were addressed to all citizens. Although targeting is necessary because of limited resources, it can undermine the recruitment and socialization of new voters. The important point is that parties and their candidates do not always act to increase turnout. It must be strategically in their interest. It is strategic when it is a close election to increase turnout among voters with a low turnout expectation.

The expansion of the scope of conflict in a campaign dramatically changes the role of strategy (Berry, 1993; Thurber, 1991). The 1991 Louisiana governor's race between Edwin Edwards and David Duke resulted in a record turnout despite what many commentators decried as an excessively negative campaign. But, as Samuel Popkin pointed out, "people will turn out in record numbers to choose between an unabashed rogue and a former Klansman as well as Nazi sympathizer when the campaign is big enough to keep people mobilized" (1992, p. 167).

A campaign with an expanded scope of conflict requires leadership and well-honed strategy. Leadership can be shortsighted, and some campaigns can be badly structured. Bad campaigns deserve to lose. One key issue is not the quality of a candidate's ideas but how well they are conveyed to voters. "Campaigns that matter" are not mechanistic (Popkin, 1991; 1992). The 1993 New Jersey governor's race provides a good example of this maxim. Much commentary and speculation focused on the admission (later repudiated) by Ed Rollins, the campaign manager for Republican Christine Todd Whitman, that the campaign paid black leaders to dampen black turnout. Whitman won in an extremely close race against incumbent Democrat Jim Florio. Although most commentators focused on the activities of the Whitman campaign, the real lesson is that this strategy would never have worked or even been credible (as a scenario—true or not) if the Florio campaign had worked to mobilize black support. The black share of the vote decreased from 12 percent in 1989 (when Florio was first elected) to 8 percent in 1993. Florio received 75 percent of the black vote, a rather anemic level of support for a Democrat. If Florio had mobilized blacks to turn out at their 1989 level, even with the low 75 percent share he received overall, he would have won the election. If the first principle of campaign strategy is to shore up support among likely supporters, the Florio campaign failed—and deserved to lose.

WHY CAMPAIGNS ARE IMPORTANT

Gary Mauser argued that marketing principles are extremely important in "strategic positioning" (Mauser, 1989). Consultants do not simply map the preferences of the electorate but actually test which campaign message will move likely supporters and likely voters. Testing strategies does not result in a remaking of the candidate but rather allows a campaign to select which strategies are the most effective. The role of the consultant is to provide some objective criteria to resolve differences of opinion among staffers, not to provide a candidate makeover.

Candidates seek to frame issues (Popkin, 1991; Riker, 1986). Voters use a clinical form of reasoning in which information is processed by putting it together in a narrative. Campaigns can help form this narrative in a way positive to the candidate by providing context. This affects how topics are defined for voters—what points of view and what attitudes are brought to bear on an issue: "What we incorporate into a picture or narrative depends on the point of view or frame we use" (Popkin, 1991, p. 81).

Issue framing and manipulation of public opinion have severe limitations. Partisan groups also seek to frame issues and define the political agenda. This means that issue framing is useful only when there is no opposing group or when opinion is so mixed on an issue that ambiguity is a desirable strategy. An example is how the Reagan campaign dealt with the gender gap in 1984 (Mueller, 1988). The gender gap is defined as an average difference between political responses of men and women, not as an indigenous or concrete group. It is thus a contrived category available only to pollsters. Lake and Heidepriem (1988) concluded that "women and men do not have separate policy agendas, but often think about the same issues in different ways." They argued that by using early polling and paying "special attention to the shape and content of your message, the identity of your messenger, and your means of communication," any candidate—Republican or Democrat—can target women voters successfully (1988, p. 37). In 1984, funded by the American Medical Association's political action committee, Reagan pollster Richard Wirthlin subdivided women into sixty-four categories based upon age, marital status, and employment (Witt, 1985). Wirthlin's profiles were later collapsed into eight groups based upon Reagan's strengths and weaknesses and were used to target women through direct mail, media, and personal appearances (Peterson, 1985). Reagan was thus able to minimize his loss of support among women.

The validation and reinforcement of inchoate attitudes during a campaign does not pander to existing attitudes but involves a leadership role for competitive campaigns in forming opinion. The quality of campaigns is critical to democracy and differs substantially from the marketing of products like soap or cereal.

CANDIDATE-CENTERED CAMPAIGN STRATEGIES

The contemporary paradox is that the more candidates structure campaigns that are individually focused, the more party is strengthened. Candidate-centered campaigns are not forged in a vacuum. In the marketplace of campaigns, the self-interest of candidates acts as the invisible hand that regulates the supply of and demand for genuine alternatives and effective constituent representation. Alternately, as V. O. Key put it, the collective is responsible even if individual voters (or candidates or campaign activists) are not. The driving mechanism is that dissatisfied losing candidates always have an incentive to "unseat the governing status quo" (Carmines and Stimson, 1989, p. 7). Governing parties do not. Candidate-centered campaigns provide an enhanced opportunity for the "natural selection of issues" through the vehicle of generating "new issue conflict" in campaigns.

Strategic candidates, those who run if they believe they have a reasonable chance of winning, are interested in their own success, not simply in pushing their policy preferences to voters. Party control of recruitment is weak. There is no longer a party boss who can tell a candidate to run or not to run. Parties now operate according to a consensus model under which competitive candidates must determine their support among the rank and file. David Rohde in his study of the postreform U.S. House of Representatives concluded that partisanship has increased among House members precisely because party primary constituencies across the nation are more homogeneous and exert similar pressures on their party's candidates in separate election campaigns (Rohde, 1991).

Party organizations have fewer direct ties to the voters. Instead, parties are often mediated through the candidates it recruits, the activists it can mobilize and train, and the campaigns its candidates run.[2] There is no unemployment market for unnecessary volunteers. On the contrary, the Democratic and Republican Parties work hard to expand the available pool of volunteers. Parties do so by offering campaign training. In my own research, an overwhelming majority of party leaders have taken campaign training courses.[3] Although it is true that fewer Americans are contacted by the less labor-intensive contemporary campaigns than was the case in the 1960s when about one in four Americans was contacted (Rosenstone and Hansen, 1993), volunteers still remain in short supply, and campaigns compete for their valuable services during campaign season.

Those who say that candidates are unimportant in a strong party system are ignoring the issue of factional conflict, a predominant feature of contemporary parties (Baer, 1993). Party nominations are a battle for control of the party. Winning factions gain temporary control of the party. If they win the general election, they have a chance to do more—gain temporary control of government. But a winning faction that loses the general election also loses control of the party. Even though campaign managers usually meet candidates after they have declared, each individual campaign strategy will be fundamentally affected by the past associations of each individual candidate and by the citizen activists they attract to their campaign.

placed into homes through voter contact. Third, the advent of new types of media (e.g., cable) and the market segmentation of contemporary radio stations allow very specific targeting. In contrast to the position of David Broder who pioneered the use of "truth boxes" in 1990 to compare candidate ads with the "facts," research has shown that information about issues comes largely from campaign commercials—the paid media. The mass media primarily provide credibility for the campaign theme through the focus of studies and corollary stories built around the theme.

The general election provides an opportunity for candidates to find out how well their campaign has done in persuading voters. Even though the two parties disagree on major issues, there is some evidence that the campaign closer to the center wins (Baer and Bositis, 1988). There may be wedges and magnets, but there are no silver bullets that will permanently win the day. Campaigns require going out into the country and facing the citizens.

CONCLUSION

Campaign strategy, tactics, and agenda setting have changed in the post-reform party system. Candidates must form a strategy that has an overall theme (broadcast message) and maintains momentum but that also effectively targets specialized groups (narrowcast message). Campaigns must effectively separate themselves from their opponents and personalize their message. Unlike in the strategy used in consumer marketing, where advertisers attempt to make their products resemble others in the market, politicians must distinguish themselves from their competitors and give voters a reason to choose them over their opponents. Clinton, by using a theme of change as well as specialized messages, effectively won over voters in 1992. He convincingly separated himself from his opponents and showed that elections and campaigns are important.

NOTES

1. In his later work, Nimmo (Nimmo and Savage, 1976) argued for an interpretation of campaign communications based on "candidate image" rather than on the party identification of the law of minimal consequences.

2. Some views of party organization (e.g., Joseph Schlesinger's ambition theory) have fused the campaign organization with the party (Cotter et al., 1984, p. 4). Nothing in this section should be construed as endorsing this view.

3. These data are from the 1988 study by Baer, Bositis, and Jackson (1991).

5

Strategy and Tactics for Campaign Fund-Raising

DAVID HIMES

In his discussion of campaign planning in Chapter 2, William R. Sweeney describes various ways to look at the resources of a campaign. Some strategists describe campaign resources as "the candidate, the issues, the people, and the money." Others describe resources as "votes, media, and money." Still others define resources as "people, time, and money." Yet however the resources of a campaign are described, money is always a critical resource. It is difficult, if not impossible, to conduct a successful campaign without money. Consequently, campaign fund-raising is an extremely important part of any political campaign, irrespective of the office sought.

There are five truths that apply to campaign fund-raising:

1. No campaign ever lost because the candidate spent too much time raising money.
2. Many campaigns have lost because they failed to raise enough money to implement a winning campaign plan.
3. No one can raise money more effectively than the candidate.
4. Do not rely on political action committees (PACs), direct mail, telemarketing, or special events with important personalities to raise money. Rely on personal solicitation.
5. Everyone loves to sit around and talk politics. But the real measure of your commitment to winning an election is the willingness to personally ask another person for a contribution.

If the candidate is uncommitted to raising funds personally for the campaign, the campaign is doomed right from the start. There are no shortcuts to raising money or winning elections.

THE FINANCE PLAN

Raising money for a political campaign does not happen by accident. People are not walking the streets with extra money, just waiting for someone to pass by so they can contribute money to the campaign. Once, while I was deputy director of finance for the National Republican Congressional Committee, the executive director's assistant came into my office with a bewildered question. In her job, she saw the regular finance reports, which showed millions of dollars being raised. "Every time I walk by your office, all you are doing is talking on the telephone," she said. "How do you raise the money?" One of the most important things we do is plan. Planning is the guide to all successful efforts. Fund-raising is no different. Successful campaigns must have a finance or *fund-raising plan.*

The first step in preparing a finance plan is to determine the revenue budget or projection. How much money can you raise? That is almost always the first question a candidate asks or is asked when considering an election campaign. It is the wrong question. The right question is, How much money do you need to raise? This is why a written, detailed campaign plan (discussed in Chapter 2) and budget must be completed prior to beginning work on the finance plan. Once you know how much you need for the campaign plan, you can address the sources of money and techniques of successfully soliciting it.

SOURCES OF MONEY IN A CAMPAIGN

There are five principal sources of campaign funds: the candidate and his or her family, individuals in the district, individuals outside the district, PACs, and political party committees (the Democratic and Republican National Committees, the senatorial campaign committees—the National Republican Senate Committee and the Democratic Senatorial Campaign Committee—and the congressional committees—the National Republican Campaign Committee and the Democratic Congressional Campaign Committee). In a very real sense, these five groups constitute five distinct audiences or markets. Each market must be analyzed to determine the best message and best medium for that message, in order to motivate successfully the people in each market to make contributions to a campaign.

The Candidate and Family

No one, other than the candidate, can really say how much money he or she will give to the campaign. Some candidates are like most Americans—they can make a contribution but not very much. Some candidates may be able to contribute $100, some $500, some even $1,000. Other candidates can write checks for their entire campaign. John Heinz did it when he first ran for the U.S. Senate. Others have done it too. But when Pete du Pont ran successfully for governor of Delaware, a central theme of his campaign was that he was not using his own money to finance his political aspirations. In 1988, Linda Bean-Jones, an heir to the L. L. Bean family fortune, spent more than $500,000 trying to win the Republican primary for a U.S. House of Representatives election. Only $5,000 came from contributors—the balance from her own pocket. She lost to a campaign financed with less than $65,000.

Personal wealth does not guarantee success in the election business. Nor does it guarantee failure. It is simply another source of money that must be managed and used properly. If the candidate has family wealth, the candidate must determine how much can be used in the campaign. Because of the U.S. Supreme Court's ruling in *Buckley v. Valeo*, a candidate personally may use an unlimited amount of personal finances. Since the Federal Election Campaign Act does not require a spouse's funds to be maintained separately, a candidate's spouse may actually give an unlimited amount as well—but it must be reported in the name of the candidate. Other members of a candidate's family—mother, father, brothers, sisters, cousins, children, in-laws—are each subject to the same limits as any individual: $1,000 per candidate per federal election ($2,000 total).

Individual Contributors
Within the District

Contributors inside and outside the district should be distinguished because there is a significant political difference between them. If a campaign gets a gift from a voter in the district, the candidate can feel confident that he or she also has at least one vote. In one survey, done by the U.S. Chamber of Commerce, one contribution translated into ten votes because that contributor was likely to become a very active and vocal opinion leader on behalf of the campaign. If a campaign gets a gift from an individual who lives outside the district, all it gets is a gift—still useful—but getting votes as well as money is a valuable bonus from a well-planned and well-executed fund-raising campaign.

In the end, individuals within the district are probably going to be the single largest source of money for a campaign. In my view, that is the way it should be. The people who vote you into office should be the people who give you most of the money to pay for the campaign. The more true this is, the greater the chances of winning the election.

Individual Contributors
Outside the District

When I first got involved in soliciting political contributions, I often took the lists of wealthy contributors to my desk and perused them. I was curious to know which celebrities gave to the Republicans and which ones gave to the Democrats. What was most surprising was how many gave to both, and this was especially true of businesspeople, the giants of industry.

That is one of the problems with outsiders. They may have other motives for giving to a campaign. If a campaign plans to raise a significant amount of cash from outsiders, it will probably have to focus on the very wealthy or the very political. If it focuses on the wealthy, there is some possibility it can go to a major city outside the district and, if the candidate has some connection, raise a substantial sum at a reception or special event. Recent political history is filled with stories of candidates traveling to New York or San Francisco or Chicago or Dallas for a reception with major donors.

Political Action Committees

PACs are an important channel for political contributions. I use the term "channel" deliberately. PACs represent larger numbers of people who have pooled their financial resources—and sometimes other resources as well—to promote their own political points of view.

It is easier for incumbents to raise money from PACs than it is for challengers and open-seat candidates. Incumbents know that and have a good idea of how much they can raise from PACs. Nonincumbents need to plan to work very hard to get PAC money, but they should plan on getting none. That way if they do get some they will be thrilled, but the failure to get as much as they would like will not cost them the campaign.

PACs often give to candidates or incumbents with whom they agree on some specific set of issues. PACs will usually ask for some evidence that a candidate can or is likely to win. PACs will give more to incumbents than to challengers because they are a more sound investment. A challenger may think his or her campaign will be the exception to this rule and they may be correct, but the odds are against it. Most challenger campaigns simply do not receive much money from PACs, (though Democratic challengers have had some success in getting contributions from labor PACs).

In reviewing a list of PACs to solicit for contributions, the campaign personnel should look for one or more of the following connections:

1. A business PAC that represents a major plant located in the district state.
2. An association PAC that represents a major industry in the district state.
3. Any PAC that has someone known to the campaign as an influential member or even as the primary contact person.
4. A professional PAC that represents the candidate's profession—or simply one that the candidate may be politically in tune with.
5. An ideological PAC that shares the candidate's political viewpoint either in general or on a specific issue.
6. PACs that would like to see the candidate's opponent defeated.
7. PACs such as BIPAC, AMPAC, and others that may have a large national-level PAC as well as similar state or local PACs. However, an endorsement from the state or local PAC usually is necessary before you can get a contribution from the national PAC.

PACs will want information about a candidate and a campaign including committee name and address, the treasurer's name, district profile, voting history, primary date, opposition research, special interest group ratings, key personnel, budget, and endorsements. The campaign must give it to them. These items cover the kind of information most PACs will find helpful and informative, but every PAC proposal will not be the same. Different PACs have different reasons for existence; proposals should reflect those differences.

After the PAC proposal is prepared, there are two things not to do. Challengers do not raise money from PACs by holding a reception somewhere in Washington, D.C., unless the candidate already has good contacts. PACs do not make contributions in response to direct-mail solicitations. The best way to solicit contributions is similar to how money is raised from your major individual contributors. This means personal solicitation and perhaps some events. The most common PAC-oriented event is the Washington, D.C., reception. Nearly every incumbent has such a reception, and occasionally so does a Republican running in an open seat or against a Democrat. But the incumbents do much better at raising PAC money.

Political Party Committees

In many ways, the party committees are like PACs. The difference is in how much money they have and how much money they can give away. Before any party money is included in a finance plan, all of the appropriate party committees should be contacted and asked for their criteria for making contributions to a campaign and for participating in coordinated expenditures. Typically, the primary factors considered in these decisions are potential for winning, quality of the campaign, the campaign plan, extent of local party support, and extent of other local support. Most campaigns overestimate the support the party committees can give them. A campaign should find out first if the party committees have funds available to give the campaign and what the state or federal limits are on contributions from each of these committees to the campaign.

The foregoing criteria should determine how confidently a campaign can expect to get any money at all. Once again, incumbents almost always get some funds if they need the money. Others get part of what is left. Party committees do not automatically give to every campaign. They give to campaigns that have a campaign plan with a budget and district support and that are realistically winnable. In addition, the Republican and Democratic National Committees (RNC and DNC) can legally make coordinated expenditures for campaign committees. Often, these are consulting services. Other times, the RNC and DNC will actually pay bills for a campaign. In the case of candidates for the House of Representatives, the congressional campaign committees are often designated as the agent of the RNC or DNC for the purpose of making coordinated expenditures for specific campaigns.

FUND-RAISING STRATEGY

There are three goals behind a fund-raising strategy:

• *To raise all the money needed to finance the political plan, in a timely and cost-effective manner.* The emphasis here is on timely and cost-effective. A campaign has to raise the money before it can be spent. And it has to raise more than it spends to get the gifts. This is just common sense—but too many finance directors and candidates forget these basic points.

• *To ask more people to give to a campaign than have ever been asked before.* There is an axiom in fund-raising that has never been successfully violated by any person, campaign, organization, or institution—regardless of its cause or constituency: Activity results in contributions; the absence of activity results in the absence of contributions. Thus, a campaign simply must do something to raise money. It does not just come floating into the campaign. The best fund-raising efforts include the most variety of activities directed to the widest possible market. In its simplest form, a fund-raising strategy outlines which fund-raising tactics will be used to reach each of the markets. In fact—without any doubt—a campaign may clearly use every tactic to reach every market, but that strategy is not the most productive. Certain tactics historically are more effective in certain markets.

• *To ask every donor repeatedly to give again until all donors reach their legal or financial limit.* Just because someone gives to a campaign once, do not fail to ask that donor to give again. Alumni associations are notorious in their unwillingness to ask a graduate to give more than once each year. That is because universities use their alumni associations or "annual fund" campaigns to get people into the habit of giving. They go for the large contributions in their capital campaigns. Political campaigns do not have that luxury. They must ask again and again. The campaign should use every tactic that fits with a market. If a donor gives for the first time by buying a ticket to a dinner, send him or her every fund-raising letter mailed. If someone responds to a direct mail piece, invite the person to a private reception in someone's home. For example, in 1987, the National Republican Congressional Committee mailed an invitation to its entire donor list—everyone who had given $15 or more in the last two years or so. The invitation was to a dinner that cost $1,500 per person. The committee sold well over one hundred tickets—$150,000—and raised an additional $500,000 from people who could not buy a ticket but sent a contribution anyway. Colgate-Palmolive does not rely just on television advertising to sell its toothpaste. Campaigns should not rely on any one fund-raising tactic to finance the election campaign.

RAISING SEED MONEY

Seed money is the initial funds needed to get the campaign going. It is the first $20,000–$30,000 a campaign needs to have a benchmark survey taken, get a campaign plan written, and perhaps hire a manager—to pay the first few expenditures of the campaign. Seed money can be raised using virtually any technique discussed in this chapter. PACs are less likely to provide seed money to a candidate challenging an incumbent, but they are more likely to help in an open race. There are three primary ways to get seed money.

• The *direct-mail approach* is usually viable for seed money only if a campaign already has a contributors list. A campaign should consider using direct mail only if it has donors to a previous campaign (if not this candidate, perhaps, donors to the last party candidate to run for this seat).

• In *individual solicitation*, the candidate, the finance chairman, or both can approach potential major donors. This can be done either on a one-to-one basis or in small intimate groups. The campaign should concentrate specifically on people who can give $500 to $1,000.

• If *the candidate* is financially capable of providing the seed money, that should be considered. However, it is important to be sensitive to the possible political ramifications of the candidate making such a large initial contribution. If this option is chosen, I strongly recommend the candidate make a loan to the campaign committee.

Of these three approaches to raising seed money for a campaign, the wisest and, usually, a very successful approach is individual solicitation by the candidate among a small intimate group of personal acquaintances. It is often easiest to expect the candidate to put up the seed money for the campaign, especially if the candidate is financially able to do that, but it is often a politically unwise approach.

However, raising seed money does not replace the need for a solid finance plan. It's somewhat like the five dollars your father used to give you to put a little gas in the tank. It's enough to get around for a while, but you can't take any long trips on it.

TACTICS FOR SOLICITING CONTRIBUTIONS

The tactics available to solicit contributions fall into just two categories: *personal* and *direct response.* Personal solicitation tactics include any approach that essentially involves organizing individuals to solicit gifts on a one-to-one basis. Direct-response tactics involve the use of advertising media, such as mail, telephone, radio, television, or print ads, to solicit a large number of people simultaneously.

The challenge of putting together an effective finance plan requires the proper matching of these tactics to the available markets. With some markets, such as individuals inside the district, a campaign can use virtually every technique available. With others, such as the party committees, the only way to solicit contributions is by the candidate making personal calls and visits to the proper party officials.

Personal Solicitation Tactics

There are three tactics that fall into this category: personal solicitation by the candidate, finance committees, and special events. The theme of these tactics is people. This is personal selling.

The candidate. There is no way around it. The most effective fund-raiser for a campaign is the candidate who is on the ticket. Unfortunately, many challengers and even more incumbents spend much of their time trying to avoid this role. Admittedly, another serious problem arises when the candidate is actually a poor salesperson for himself or herself. If the candidate does it well, he or she can be the complete finance committee. In some instances, the candidate's spouse may be a better fund-raiser than the candidate. If this is the case, it may be easier for the spouse to focus on fund-raising while the candidate is out on the road campaigning. If not, building an effective organization of people to raise funds in the candidate's name on a personal basis may become the key to the campaign's financial success.

The campaign finance committee. The campaign finance committee deals with personal solicitation by the individuals organized into two major groups: the major gift ($500 to $1000 per election) committee and the general gifts committee. Some people may use different labels for these groups, but the concepts are there. The candidate and other knowledgeable people should create a list, by name, of anyone they know who is financially capable of making a $500 or $1,000 contribution (major gift) to the campaign. The candidate should ask virtually everyone he or she thinks can give $500 or more. This guideline never works in reality but should be tried anyway. If it works, the campaign will raise more than it expects. Anyone the candidate will not ask should be asked by members of the *major gifts committee.* There is one absolute prerequisite to being a member of the major gifts committee: They must make a major gift.

The *general gifts committee* is organized to solicit contributions of less than $100. The idea behind this effort is to identify as many target groups as possible and recruit a volunteer to solicit contributions from that group. A *target group* (or peer group) is an identifiable group of people who have a common characteristic, such as a social interest, profession or occupation. Some examples are nurses at hospitals, bank tellers, farmworkers, bus drivers, retail clerks, construction workers, garden club members, secretaries, teachers, chamber of commerce members, and civic club members. Another type of target group is the issue-oriented group such as the local chapter of the National Rifle Association, right-to-life (antiabortion) groups, right-to-work groups, environmental groups, education groups, or veterans organizations such as the Veterans of Foreign Wars or American Legion.

Special events. Special events can take many forms. A campaign's first decision is what type of special events it will have. Special events include a wide range of activities. Dinners, VIP receptions, private receptions and public receptions, are just a few of the events a campaign should plan. The two most common and successful for political campaigns are the dinner and the reception. Special events often have the dual function of raising funds and of providing positive publicity for the candidate. As with the finance committee, success usually depends on a good organization.

For *dinners and VIP receptions,* it is important to think in terms of gross income and net income when setting a price for tickets. Gross income is the total amount raised. Net income is what is left after all expenses are paid. Dinner tickets should be priced between $100 and $250 per plate. There is not a district in this country where $100 tickets cannot be sold.

The objective of a dinner is to raise money, not to have thousands of people—although having thousands of people is fine, if they have each paid $100 for a ticket.

If a major national figure will be featured at a dinner, it may be a little easier to sell tickets. But the mere presence of a VIP there does not guarantee success. In 1978 in Texas, two Republican candidates had dinners with VIP speakers. The cities were of comparable size. One candidate's dinner featured then Governor Ronald Reagan; the other featured John Connally. The Connally dinner netted $80,000 for one candidate; the Reagan dinner netted $12,000 for the other. The difference was not Reagan or Connally. The difference was organizing people to sell tickets.

Special guest speakers and other VIPs can certainly add some level of attractiveness to a major event. However, even an event featuring the president of the United States must be sold a ticket or table at a time. Additionally, with a guest speaker or VIP usually comes a lot of additional logistical problems and expense. It may be worth the cost and the trouble—often it is—but campaign planners should recognize all the advantages and disadvantages of inviting a major VIP.

If there is a VIP reception preceding the dinner, tickets should be priced from $250 to $500 per person (depending on the VIP), noticeably higher than dinners without receptions. This reception should be appropriately private, so those attending feel a specific sense of intimacy with the candidate and any VIP guest. The campaign should consider making attendance at this reception by invitation only. It is not uncommon to raise as much money at a VIP reception as at the dinner itself. *A successful special event depends on how well the campaign organizes to sell tickets—not on which VIP is in attendance.*

- The first step in planning a major dinner is to appoint a *dinner chair.* The finance chair should recruit this person, but in many cases the finance chairman is the dinner chairman. The major responsibilities of the dinner chairman typically include (1) overall responsibility for the dinner's success, (2) recruitment of cochairs whose main goal is to sell a specific number of tables at the dinner, and (3) recruitment of ticket salespersons who will each sell ten tickets. The main focus is on recruiting people and selling tickets. A campaign wants a chair who will get on the phone and call people. If the prospective chair hesitates when told about this role, the campaign should look elsewhere for another prospect.
- An alternative approach to helping the ticket-selling process is to organize a *host committee* to sponsor an event. A host committee is a group of supporters who buy tickets, allow their names to be put on the invitation, and agree to sell tickets. Typically, the candidate or finance director contacts potential hosts by telephone or letter. The hosts should

reflect a wide range of the business sectors represented in the district. The host committee is a method of adding prestige and recognition to the task of selling tickets to an event.

Having prominent figures in the local community, especially current or past elected officials, builds some credibility for the event and shows community support of the candidate. But this is important only if the candidate is unknown or lacks credibility. The single most important responsibility of the hosts is to sell tickets. The hosts should take an active role in getting people to attend the event and make follow-up calls to their friends, neighbors, and coworkers encouraging them to attend. When the event actually takes place, it is important to make sure the hosts are recognized by the candidate or program chair. The candidate should make a special effort to talk to and thank each one.

Receptions can be one of the most productive—and easiest—methods of raising funds for a candidate. Here is why:

1. Several receptions can be easily scheduled and coordinated per week, even in the fall months.
2. Receptions do not require much of the candidate's time.
3. Receptions serve the dual purpose of raising money and building support.
4. Receptions can be geared to different target groups.
5. Receptions are inexpensive. Supporters who host them can cover the cost as an expenditure over and above their individual $1,000 limit. They can spend up to $1,000 ($2,000 for a couple) per election. If they spend more than this $1,000 limit, the excess applies against their contribution limit.

The campaign should select the target groups it wants to raise money from via receptions. Then, the campaign should decide how many receptions it wants to hold for each group. Hosts for the receptions should be identified as early as possible. Receptions should be scheduled as the hosts are recruited.

There are three types of fund-raising receptions that may and probably should be included in the finance plan. The first is a VIP reception, previously discussed, which is most commonly associated with a major dinner event. The second type of reception is a private reception. It is private because it usually involves inviting the host's personal circle of friends. The response to private receptions is usually pretty good because the campaign is relying on the personal relationship between the host and the people being invited. People respond best to requests from their friends and others whose opinions they trust and respect. Receptions in private homes can raise from $2,500 to $5,000.

The third type of reception is a public reception, which is open to any individual who purchases a ticket. Generally, this type of event is promoted to a fairly broad audience. Both public and private receptions have a place in a fund-raising campaign. Each event should have a goal for how much money the campaign needs to raise, and that goal should relate to a specific project in the campaign.

Breakfasts are another special event often successful in campaigns. Breakfasts are about the same as dinners. However, they are especially good where a candidate has strong business support and can bring in a strong free-enterprise speaker. Eggs are still inexpensive, so net income on a $50 breakfast will be higher than on a $50 dinner.

The essence of politics is people, and special events get people together to discuss politics. This is why special fund-raising events are so effective in campaigns. These events also help a campaign manage its cash flow more effectively because the campaign can easily schedule the timing of each event. After a few events the campaign will quickly get a feel for estimating the number of tickets it will sell to each event and also the cost per ticket. A campaign should be able to keep its expenses to no more than 30 percent of the gross income from events. If expenses are higher, the campaign is not charging enough for the tickets or it is wasting money.

Direct-Response Solicitation Tactics

A campaign can use every advertising medium to solicit contributions but probably should not follow that course. There are two direct-response media that have a long history of being successfully used for political fund-raising: direct mail and the telephone (often called telemarketing).

Direct mail. Direct mail is a powerful medium and very popular for political fund-raising. But it ranks behind personal solicitation as the most effective fund-raising medium. Although direct mail can be an effective way to raise money, it is comparatively expensive. It takes time to build up a donor mailing list to a point that direct mail can be effective for fund-raising. Incumbents usually use direct mail more successfully for fund-raising than challengers. However, for political purposes, direct mail remains a potent medium for any candidate. The basic principle about direct mail is that the letters should be as personal as possible. It would be best to have the candidate write a letter by hand to every name on the list. Every step away from that weakens the letter a little.

Since most candidates will not handwrite letters, the letters should look as if a secretary prepared them. This principle of personalization and appearance should be applied to all letters. But there is more to direct-mail fund-raising than how it looks or how it is produced. There is an old debate in the direct marketing industry about which is more important, the text of the letter or the mailing list.

• Evaluating and selecting mailing lists are key tasks. Mailing lists are essential to the direct-mail process. Obviously, if the campaign does not have a list of names and addresses, it cannot mail a letter to anyone. There are basically six types of lists the campaign can use. Here they are, from best to worst:

1. *House lists* are lists the staff maintains. These should include lists of current or previous contributors, people who have written to the candidate, and volunteers. The campaign should keep a record of how much they gave, what volunteer work they did, or what they wrote about.

2. *Outside lists* are lists of contributors to various causes other than the campaign and who are ideologically in line with the candidate.

3. *Compiled lists* are usually lists created by combining several other lists. Compiled lists include lists of doctors, lawyers, businesspeople, mothers, fathers, accountants, truck drivers, and similar categories.

4. *Commercial or direct-response lists* are available through list brokers, who have a wide range of lists available. They include lists of magazine subscribers, people who buy products through the mail, and many other lists. The most common problem in renting these lists is minimum orders. Almost every list available for rental carries a minimum order of 5,000 names. Only the very largest lists will have that many names in a single congressional district, so the campaign must pay for names it does not get. This problem disappears for most statewide campaigns, but at the congressional level, these lists become almost prohibitively expensive.

5. *Universal lists* are usually not profitable for direct-mail fund-raising by political candidates. However, there are list brokers who can provide a campaign with lists of every name and address in a specific area. Accuracy is sometimes a problem because 20 percent of the people in the United States move each year.

6. *Voter lists* are another tool for a campaign. The Republican Party has compiled the most complete list of registered voters in the country. The only registered voter list that might be better is the one a candidate's own voter registration office maintains. If the state registers voters by party, the campaign should get a copy of the local voter registration list.

• List brokers can be found in any major city. Their main business is selling and renting mailing lists. Normally, they receive a 20 percent commission from the list owner every time they rent a list. For most campaigns, a list broker cannot help much, primarily because the campaign will want lists of names just in the district. Generally, lists that must be confined to a small geographic area are not large enough to be handled profitably by a broker. A campaign can probably get many good lists itself simply by asking someone for the list. For example, to get a list of lawyers, the campaign can ask a lawyer who supports the candidate to get a list of members of the local bar association.

• Building a good prospect list is one of the most difficult tasks facing a campaign in order to make direct mail work. The campaign should get all the existing lists it can, but it also should begin building its own prospect list. I have some suggestions on how to build up this prospect list:

1. If the campaign has a voter identification phone bank, it should put the most favorable voters on the prospect list as soon as they are identified.
2. As the candidate goes around speaking to various groups, attempt to get the names and addresses of all the people who hear the candidate's speech.
3. At every other opportunity, the campaign should find any excuse to get a name and address of a voter and then add that name to the prospect list.

• Response rates are an important consideration in direct mail. Mailings to a candidate's previous contributors can be made as often as every thirty to forty-five days. A campaign can expect from 5 to 10 percent of previous contributors to give again each time the campaign writes a letter to them—they will give, on the average, $30–$50 each. Early mailings to prospective contributors (prospects) for "donor acquisition" are crucial, especially in the long-range perspective. A campaign simply wants to recover its costs when mailing to prospects. New contributors, of course, will get additional appeals, and that is when a campaign begins to show a "profit" in its direct-mail program.

Telemarketing. Fund-raising by telephone has come into vogue during the last few years. Unfortunately, it has been abused as often as it has been used effectively. Most of the negative press coverage on telemarketing has been about rip-off artists who sell nonexistent products and services or who raise money using appeals that come close to being fraudulent. Another telemarketing technique that has received negative press coverage is automated or computer-controlled telemarketing. This technique uses a computer and recordings to deliver and record messages with people.

Political fund-raising campaigns have not generally been guilty of using fraudulent telemarketing appeals, but some have tried to use automated messaging systems—especially for get-out-the-vote efforts. In 1989, 900 numbers became generally available. Their effectiveness for fund-raising in general and political fund-raising in particular has not yet been demonstrated. Whether they will ever be accepted is simply unknown. There are certainly a number of people trying to use them.

There are five strategic objectives a campaign may select from when planning telemarketing efforts. Each of the five has its place in the finance plan—except the last, which is mentioned only so I can point out that it never works:

1. *Reactivation:* Calling donors who have not given in the last year in an effort to reactivate them as current donors. Getting previous donors to reactivate is more cost-effective than trying to find new donors.
2. *Renewal:* Calling donors who gave last year in an effort to get them to give again. People who give two or more years in succession are more loyal and dependable donors than those who give only once every couple of years.
3. *Second gift:* Calling donors who have given once in the current year in an effort to get them to give a second gift this year. Donors who give twice or more in a single year respond at a much greater rate than those who give only once a year. It is advantageous to have a large number of multiple-time donors.
4. *Follow-up:* Calling donors after they have received a fund-raising letter to make a special appeal for responding to that letter.
5. *Prospecting:* Prospecting by telephone can work if a campaign has good lists to work with. It is also a fairly expensive proposition. Perhaps the most troublesome problem for prospecting via telemarketing is the amount of time it requires to identify a large number of donors; the process is very time-consuming.

Telephone calls, especially to contributors, can be an effective way to raise funds. Response rates and average contribution amounts are usually higher. Telemarketing is especially effective because, in part, it bridges the gap between impersonal (media) and personal contact.

CONCLUSION

There are three main resources campaigns can utilize: people, time, and money. Campaigns can capitalize on these resources in a variety of ways. Through the candidate, individuals both inside and outside the district,

PACs, and party committees, the campaign can raise the money needed to make the race competitive. Although some modes of fund-raising may be more beneficial than others, and certain methods of conducting fund-raisers will make them more effective, each type of fund-raising discussed serves a valuable purpose to the campaign: Collectively, they provide it with the money it needs to sustain itself. The more successful the campaign is at maximizing its resources, the higher the chance becomes that the candidate will prevail.

6

Competition, Contributions, and Money in 1992

FRANK J. SORAUF

Not only is there a substantial amount of applied wisdom about how to raise money but also ample data exist detailing who gives and receives campaign contributions. To understand the two-sided exchange, however, it is necessary to know more about why, how, and under what conditions contributions are made and received. In order to address these questions, I examine the 1992 congressional elections. Within them I analyze data chiefly from the campaigns for the House of Representatives, for all of the usual reasons: the relative size of the constituencies and the election of all members of the chamber at the same time.

It is important first to discuss what I think is a fundamental truth about the raising of campaign money: its bilateral nature. The view of the fund-raising transaction among practitioners and academics is often a candidate- and a campaign-centered view. The view of the process among the media and reformers, on the other hand, tends to be contributor-centered. That is where the bad news and big stories are, and that is where they find their devil theories. The intellectual task is to merge the two points of view into a broader picture of the process by which we fund the campaigns for most public offices in the United States. The process is bilateral in that both contributors and candidates pursue political goals, both formulate strategies to achieve those goals through campaign funding, and each group has considerable leverage on the other in arranging the exchange.

COMPETITION IN 1992

The 1992 campaigns demonstrated once again what should be a truism to both practitioners and academics alike: Campaign receipts and spending will rise as the level of electoral competition rises. The most important fact about the House elections of 1992 was their heightened competitiveness. After four cycles of generally low levels of competition and a high incumbent return rate—a rate reaching 98 percent in 1986 and 1988—the 1992 campaigns gave every sign of offering candidates and campaign contributors an opportunity of breaking the low rates of turnover. The signs of heightened competition were there early enough to offer new candidates and any contributor reason to think that they had more favorable electoral opportunities than they had had at any time since 1982.

The 1992 rise in competitiveness had several sources. Above all, the elections were the first after the reapportionments following the 1990 census—reapportionments that shifted nineteen congressional districts to new states and drastically recast the boundaries of many others.[1] Furthermore, 1991 and 1992 were years of popular rebellion against politicians and public officials, an antipolitical animus for which the rise of Ross Perot and the success of term limitations served as only the most obvious markers. For these and other reasons, such as advanced age and campaigns for other offices, 65 House incumbents chose not to run again; they represented both parties. The number of House open seats, those classic centers of competitiveness, rose from 26 in 1986 and 28 in 1990 to 86 in 1992, the largest number since 1912. And large numbers of incumbents who did seek reelection seemed, at least early in the campaign, to be very vulnerable.

In the end the incumbents did much better than even they could have hoped. If one counts defeats in both the primaries and the general elections, 88 percent of the incumbents seeking reelection won it. Moveover, they continued to maintain safe electoral margins. The percentage of incumbent winners with 60 percent or more of the vote dropped only from 75 in 1990 to 67 in 1992. Nonetheless, the House that convened in January 1993 had 110 new members, the largest number since the 118 in 1948. Altogether, it was a combination of circumstances that brought the turnover; some of them were unpredictable, but one was not: reapportionment. The campaigns of 1992 added another bit of evidence that the aftermath of the decennial census may well be the most important limit to the electoral power of congressional incumbents. It is certainly the most predictable.

With expected competition at a high-water mark, the campaigns of 1992 raised and spent far greater sums than the campaigns of 1988 and 1990. In March 1993 the Federal Election Commission (FEC) reported that spending in the House and Senate campaigns totaled $678 million, an increase of 52 percent over 1990.[2] The money raised increased only by 40 percent to a total of $659 million, the difference largely the result both of debt and of incumbents spending large sums from their cash reserves. House campaigns raised $396 million, an increase of 39 percent over 1990, and they spent $407 million, a 53 percent increase. In 1990 a total of

1,370 candidates for the House filed reports with the FEC, but in 1992 the number rose to 2,049.

Incumbents may have been on the defensive in 1992, but they raised campaign money with unimpaired vitality and success. Perhaps, indeed, the fear and apprehension of the year stimulated them to greater effort and more fervent pleas for help in their time of trouble. Then, too, the incumbents had their reserves, their cash on hand. Of the total cash on hand available to House candidates, 93 percent of it was in the hands of incumbents. Thus, although challengers did in fact increase their receipts and spending, they collectively made only modest inroads into the incumbents' funding advantage. In 1990 the average House incumbent in the general election spent 3.7 times more than the average House challenger. In 1992 the ratio dropped a little to 3.2 to 1.[3] In short, the sums of money soared in 1992, but their distribution was only slightly altered. The rising tide lifted all boats—or at least all kinds of boats.

Contributors in 1992 donated pretty much as they did in the less competitive campaigns of previous cycles. In the 1989–1990 cycle, PACs gave 80 percent of all of their money for House candidates to incumbents and 10 percent each to challengers and open-seat candidates.[4] PACs in 1992 gave incumbents 75 percent of all the money they gave to House candidates and only 9 percent to challengers; the remaining 16 percent went to the swollen ranks of open-seat candidates. Thus there was some shift in PAC allocations over 1990 but not enough to cover the shift in numbers of incumbents and open-seat candidates. In other words, PACs actually gave a larger share of their money to House incumbents if one controls for numbers.

Even if one looks at the most competitive races—recognizing that all challengers are not equally worth funding—one sees little change in challenger funding from the previous presidential year, 1988. In election years *Congressional Quarterly* analyzes those campaigns that it determines to be the most competitive.[5] The analysis offers a barometer of competitiveness at the time contributors are making their decisions rather than after the election results are in hand. In the campaigns judged the most competitive in 1988 and 1992, the incumbent to challenger ratios, both in receipts and spending, were just about the same. For example, in the October 15, 1988, data of the FEC, Democratic incumbents in these closest races enjoyed a spending edge of 2.2 to 1 over their Republican challengers. The same ratio held in 1992.

Senate campaigns in 1992 in many ways resembled House campaigns.[6] Senate candidates increased their total receipts by 40 percent and their total spending by 50 percent over 1990. There was also a sharp increase in total number of Senate candidates filing with the FEC, from 158 in 1988 and 151 in 1990 to 247 in 1992. Senate incumbents did not, however, create a dramatic rise in open seats; there were 7 in 1992, an increase over the 3 in 1990 but very close to the 6 in 1988 and 7 in 1986. Senate challengers in recent years have been much better funded than their counterparts in the House. The incumbent-challenger spending ratio was 1.8 to 1 in 1992, almost the same as the 1.7 to 1 ratio when those seats last were filled in 1986.

Thus, the greatly elevated levels of competitiveness in the 1992 campaigns seem not to have greatly altered their financing. Contributors remained highly averse to risk, and not even the opportunities to elect likeminded candidates could lure most PACs away from a commitment to ensuring eventual legislative access by funding incumbents. Indeed, the enormous incumbent power in the bilateral exchange was alive and relatively unimpaired. Perhaps analysts now have firm evidence of how threatening the risks of a competitive election are for many contributors—of how a system of voluntary funding of campaigns for public office is intrinsically committed to the support of incumbents and of likely winners.

In other words, anyone who had hoped and thought that a greater competitiveness might better feed the starved challengers is certainly disappointed. The evidence of 1992 suggests that such an outcome would happen only in a realigning election, one in which large numbers of challengers seem certain to win. It would require an election in which the fortunes of the incumbent party had turned noncompetitively sour—an election such as in 1932, for example. Competition is risk, and riskaverse contributors will choose only the most conservative and self-protective strategies in confronting it. In 1991 and the early part of 1992, there was perhaps a hint of such a great reversal of fortunes, but it had largely faded by summer's crucial months.

CAMPAIGN FINANCE REFORM

As does everything else about American campaign finance, this analysis leads, finally, to thoughts of reform. Certainly the related problems of the starved challengers and funding of competitive campaigns are major items on my agenda for reform. If it is also on a broader agenda, then what are the options? One, of course, is to try somehow through incentives or changed contribution limits to increase funding through the political parties. There is considerable difficulty with that as an option because of the political difficulty in getting a Democratic Congress to agree to it while Republican Party committees are raising more money than their Democratic counterparts. There is also the option of public funding, and I do not minimize the serious problems surrounding it: public opposition, the funding dilemma, and the problems in administering it. Nor do I ignore the importance of specifying what kind of public funding one is talking about—full or partial, mandated or matching. I want to note only that it seems increasingly clear that public funding offers the clearest solution to the problem of challenger funding. It offers best what challengers need most: early money that comes for reasons other than likely victory. It alone provides risk-tolerating money that permits the kind of building and bootstrapping that are the essence of a challenger's campaign.

CONCLUSION

If we cannot bolster the challengers in their races, then the open-seat races will remain as the main source of competition in congressional campaigns. They have always been, collectively, among the best funded of campaigns for Congress, for they are free both of incumbency's electoral advantages and incumbency's power in the bilateral exchange. Even though the surge of incumbent spending in 1992 topped the average for open-seat candidates, open-seat candidates in the House general election campaigns still averaged expenditures of $423,000. At the least, the funding of open-seat campaigns is sufficient to support the elements of competitiveness in most districts.

The question then becomes one of the number of open-seat campaigns one can expect. Clearly the 86 open-seat races for the House in 1992 provided a far greater core of competitiveness to House elections than the 26 of 1988 or the 28 of 1990. For the future one might imagine the creation of open seats by the adoption of term limits for members of Congress. In the absence of that intervention, one looks to the intervention of 1992: the forces making for reapportionments in the states that disturb incumbents and create open seats either by shifting seats to other states or by creating new and less secure districts within states. Population shifts lead to those outcomes, and so do reapportionment processes in the hands of the courts or reapportionment commissions. So, too, do the mandates for minority-dominant districts and for districts of almost equal population. In short, the overlooked lesson of 1992 may be this: that the decennial reapportionment of House seats may serve in the long run as the greatest enemy of incumbent power.

NOTES

I would like to acknowledge the help of my research assistant, Peter Gronvall, in organizing these observations and the data in them.

1. The mandated creation of districts in which there were substantial majorities of racial or ethnic minorities in 1992 added to the usual disruptions inherent in adjusting for population gains, losses, and migrations.

2. These data and those following come (unless otherwise noted) from the March 4, 1993, FEC press release on the funding of 1992 candidates and the funding of candidates in earlier election cycles; it is titled "1992 Congressional Election Spending Jumps 52 percent to $678 Million."

3. The increased number of House challengers in the 1992 general election undoubtedly inflates the challenger average because of the large number of incumbents defeated in primaries and, consequently, the large number of general elections in which the FEC views both candidates as challengers.

4. The data in this paragraph come from the FEC press release of April 29, 1993, "PAC Activity Rebounds in 1991–92 Election Cycle—Unusual Nature of Contests Seen as Reason."

5. The data on spending through the middle of October 1992 come from the FEC press release of October 30, 1992, "FEC Finds Congressional Campaign Spending up $75 million as 1992 General Election Approaches." The *Congressional Quarterly* evaluations of the close or competitive House races appears in special reports it publishes in mid-October of election years.

6. One must always register a caveat about comparing data on Senate campaigns or elections with those of the previous cycle because the one-third of the seats up for election in a year may be quite different from those at contest two years earlier. The most nearly valid comparison is usually with campaigns and elections of six years earlier.

7

Paid Media Advertising

JAY BRYANT

THE ORIGIN OF POLITICAL SPECIES

Humans are political animals, but at the dawn of human history, their political organization was little different from that of other species. That is, political leadership was given to the physically strong: You got to be the clan chieftain because you could beat up anybody else in the clan, and as soon as someone came along who could beat you up, that person was the chief. Thus it was with walrus, hyena, elk . . . and *Homo sapiens.* To this day, across the tundra, the clash of the mighty antlers of the male elk can be heard in season, as the chief elk faces his grueling reelection campaign once again. Can he hold on against the younger buck? Time will tell, but to the winner will go the spoils—the perks of office in the elk political system. These perks are quite basic: the best pasture and all of the females. Doubtless the perks of prehistoric human office were similarly basic, and some would say that modern human political perks, however complex they seem, are not so far removed at all.

Nonetheless, with the coming of civilization, things changed. Civilization began in Iraq, as we know, which was then called Sumer. It happened roughly 10,000 years ago. The question is, why? Why did this particular group of hunter-gatherers cease their immemorial ways and settle down to a sedentary life? Remarkably, some archaeologists believe that it came about as a result of the invention of beer. They have discovered the ancient Sumerian recipe for beer, and they know the name of the beer goddess (Ninkasi). It all makes sense, really. Imagine that in a world where no one has ever tasted an intoxicating liquor, you invent beer. Doesn't it seem likely that your friends and their friends will pretty soon be beating a path to your tent, and that in time, you will not be able to find enough hops and barley growing wild and will have to plant them? And settle down and tend them? And hire helpers to harvest the crop, operate the brewery, and serve up the brimming clay pots to the waiting customers?

Before you know it, you will have a crowd of drunken Sumerians gathered around the bar. And what will they talk about? Politics, of course. Factions will form at once. "We want free beer," the liberals will cry. "Buy your own damn beer," the conservatives will counter. It really is just a hop, step, and jump to America in the 1990s (the first of the 1992 presidential debates was in fact sponsored by a consortium of beer manufacturers).

After the time of the Sumerians, society gradually became more complex, and systems for selecting political leaders did as well. Personal physical power was replaced by corporate physical power. A Roman political commentator might ask, "How many legions does he have?" in assessing the likelihood of a given candidate becoming the next emperor. People also tried heredity as a system for determining political leadership. In the Middle Ages, being the eldest son of a king did not assure you of being the next king, but you had a leg up on everyone else. It was sort of like winning the early primaries.

DEMOCRACY AND COMMUNICATIONS

When the Americans reinvented the infrequently tried idea of representative democracy, they resolved upon a different method of selecting political leaders. Stripped of its mythology, the democratic system works thus: Political leadership is given to those best able to convince the electorate to give it to them. *In other words, a democracy is a political system that rewards communications power, in precisely the same way the older systems rewarded physical power.* In the early years of the American democratic experiment, this communications power was (like physical power in prehistoric times, or with the elk) personal. A premium was thus placed on oratory, and to win an election, a politician had to be able to deliver a thunderous stump speech. As it had been in Periclean Athens, so it was in Lincoln's America.

Later, the ever increasing complexity of the technology of communications led to a shift to corporate communications power. There was the great age of the newspapers, when the trick was to garner (or avoid) the large type. "The Feast of Balshazaar!" screamed the newspapers in reporting James G. Blaine's famous "boodle banquet" with the robber barons, and the coverage, complete with pictures, may have cost Blaine the presidency. With the invention of radio, technology again changed the requirements for communication skills, and we can hear Franklin D. Roosevelt at his fireside chats, manipulating the communications technology of his time in order to convince people to keep him in political power.

TELEVISION

Today's dominant communications technology is television. Ronald Reagan was called "the great communicator" because of his skill at manipulating the television medium, and he richly deserved the sobriquet. However, television, far more than radio or newspapers, is a corporate medium, and its effective exploitation requires a skilled campaign communications team. In a 1990 conversation, Congressman Newt Gingrich said, a media consultant "is a modern knight" hired by a politician to get and maintain political power and is handsomely rewarded for so doing. They are knights armed with camcorders in lieu of sword and shield.

Paid political advertising was not a major force in the politics of the newspaper and radio eras, but with the coming of television, all of that changed. Today, political communication practices have come to include *advertising* as well as *public relations*, or newsmaking. Indeed, television advertising is by far the largest single component of most campaign budgets at the congressional level and above. Thus, a discussion of the use of paid advertising media (particularly television commercials) in politics is perhaps the most important component in understanding how elections are won in America today. However, in focusing on paid media, we must not lose sight of the fact that all communications are intertwined in a campaign. Both the paid and free (or "earned") media obey the same principles, and a winning communications strategy includes both. Television is a remarkable medium, and many learned volumes have been written about its psychological and sociological ramifications. However, with television, it is often difficult to distinguish clearly the real from the unreal. How do the children of the 1990s understand the past, for example? There they sit in front of their (cable) televisions, waving their remote controls. Click. They see *I Love Lucy*, made in the 1950s. Click. There is *All in the Family*, made in the 1970s. Click. *Happy Days*, made in the 1970s, about the 1950s. They see *The Andy Griffith Show* followed by *Matlock*. Did the sheriff quit and go to law school? And about that little kid in Mayberry? Didn't he grow up to be . . . ? Wait, let's click back to *Happy Days*. We of the baby-boom generation can sort all those things out because we lived through them, but how do our kids figure it out?

Reality is difficult to identify on television. We know that a realistic-looking fistfight can be staged without anyone really hitting anyone else. Yet we knew Rodney King was really getting beat up. Or did we? What did that first jury see that we did not? Or were they just a bunch of bigots? What is real? When we believe that we have found reality, we are riveted by it. The Persian Gulf war was real: real Scuds, real Patriots, real reporters trapped in a real city under real attack. And for weeks, you could go home and see it every night on television—the best miniseries ever.

Reality programming is very popular. From *America's Funniest Home Videos* and *Divorce Court* (low-class reality) to *Sixty Minutes* and *48 Hours* (high-class reality), we give high ratings to programs with real people in them. We like game shows for the same reason. We do not believe the *Wheel of Fortune* is fixed; we believe that real people really win. Is the news real? We are somewhat ambivalent about that. Studies show that we do not quite trust the news media, but the fact is that we usually give them the benefit of the doubt.

It seems odd, but among the most real parts of television are the commercials. You can lust in your heart for Vanna White, but you cannot have Vanna White. She is not real to you in that sense. But you can have Cap'n Crunch for breakfast tomorrow morning, and you know this because there is a commercial. Whatever else you may or may not believe about a commercial, you know that at the core of it all there is a product that you can have, and because commercials exist in a market, they do best when they portray a sense of reality. In a very meaningful way, the recession of the 1990s arrived not because of the pronouncements of a gaggle of economists but because the commercials changed.

McDonald's banished its slogan of the 1980s, "Good times, great taste," because it could not talk about good times in the 1990s. So McDonald's started talking about "value." When hamburger commercials are all about value, you know there is a recession on. In its ads, the Old Milwaukee beer company recognized the recession by revising its 1980s claim that "it doesn't get any better than this." These had been very realistic commercials, with men engaging in manly camaraderie—fishing or rafting or whatever in an idyllic yet very real setting—and enjoying a beer at sunset. Any man in America could put himself in that scene, but with the recession, the company could not say "it doesn't get any better than this," and so it resorted to pure fantasy. In the middle of the idyllic scene, a group of buxom blond women (the "Swedish Bikini Team") would parachute in. No man could seriously identify with that, and the ads were soon dropped.

Successful political commercials, like successful product commercials, must strike the viewer as in some way real. This does not mean they cannot be imaginative or creative or humorous, but there must be a core of reality at their base.

PRODUCTS AND CANDIDATES

Beyond the need to deal in reality, principles of political and product advertising have little in common. Indeed, it is tempting to abandon the word "advertising" altogether when dealing with the topic of paid media in political campaigns. Although political media and product advertising utilize essentially the same technology and the same vehicles, the way in which these are applied is radically different. For that reason, extensive training in product advertising is almost counterproductive when it is applied to political media. Thus it is important to understand some of the major differences between the two disciplines:

1. The normal task in product advertising is to convince the consumer to choose one brand over another when, in fact, there is virtually no difference between the two (two brands of gasoline, for example). The normal task in political media, on the other hand, is to convince the voter to base his or her choice on one or a few of a long list of very real and significant differences between the candidates and to ignore other differences.

2. The voter is, in effect, buying at one time all of the product (candidate) that he or she is going to use for the next four years (or whatever the term is for the office in question). Moreover, all voters are making their purchases on the same day. Imagine trying to market soap or cereal under these conditions. Imagine the difficulty of convincing people to try a wholly new brand name, knowing they would be stuck with the choice for years.

3. When consumers buy a product, they get the product. But a voter does not get his or her candidate elected just by voting. A majority (or plurality in some cases) of all the other voters must select the same candidate. Suppose you could not get that new Grand Prix you like so much unless a majority of all car buyers in your state also selected it. And if, instead, they voted for Honda Accord, you were stuck with a Honda Accord too.

4. A product advertisement is almost never news. A political commercial is very frequently news, and it is likely to be picked apart word for word and image for image by commentators.

5. At the very least, a political commercial is likely to be the subject of a scathing review by the opposition, whose press release on the subject will be printed in the newspaper. When have you ever read a news article in which Tums charges that Rolaids do not in fact consume forty-seven times their weight in excess stomach acid?

6. In politics, market share does not count, and winning is everything. Coke and Pepsi can go on forever as fabulously successful companies by dividing up the cola market, even leaving enough for third-party candidate Royal Crown to make a nice profit. Name any product category you want and you can likely become very rich indeed if you can garner 30 percent of the market, but in politics that market share makes you a landslide loser.

7. Another important difference is the vastly different budgets involved. A product commercial typically costs hundreds of thousands of dollars to produce, whereas political spots are done for a few thousand dollars.

8. Finally, the political advertiser's ability to target the message is greatly hampered by the fact that the demographic categories measured by the rating services (Arbitron and Nielsen, for example) are designed for commercial rather than political use. The key political demographics—partisanship, ideology, and likelihood of voting—are not measured and must thus be inferred. Political time-buying is therefore much more of an art and less of a numbers-driven science than commercial time-buying.

POLITICAL COMMUNICATION

All the foregoing differences and others that could be cited are significant enough to warrant the conclusion that a responsible analysis of political paid media must be based on the rules of political communication and not those of advertising. This chapter is therefore organized with that in mind. There are five functions of political communication.[1] Every bit of communications done by a campaign, from news releases to bumper strips (and including all paid media), is designed to serve one or some combination of these five functions.

Name Identification

The first function is *name identification*. Name identification is critical to a successful political media program in a way that goes far beyond its importance in product advertising. The principal reason for this is best understood by considering the advertising concept called "point of purchase." The point of purchase for a product such as laundry detergent is typically in a grocery store or supermarket. The consumer, perhaps pushing a shopping cart, enters the aisle where the various choices are displayed and makes his or her final selection. However, the point of purchase in politics is in the voting booth. Note one important difference: In the voting booth, the advertising symbols of the candidates are not on display. In the detergent section of a supermarket, the packaging of the various products bears colors, logos, and typefaces that the manufacturers have spent millions of dollars—billions in some cases—promoting. Moreover, this promotion may have gone on for years, even decades. For example, Tide was introduced by Procter and Gamble in the early 1950s. Its basic logo design—orange and yellow circles, bold dark blue letters—has remained largely unchanged ever since. In the voting booth, however, it is actually illegal to display the advertising symbols of the candidates.

Instead, the voter is presented with one clue as to the choice he or she should make: the candidate's name. Moreover, this name is in black and white lettering and in a typeface selected not by the creator of the ad campaign but by a bureaucrat somewhere in the bowels of the board of election commissioners. The point is that unless the candidate's name, by itself, can carry the entire weight of the advertising campaign behind it, that campaign has failed.

Name identification is critical because very few voters will vote for a candidate whose name they do not recognize. Indeed, most people will vote for a candidate they know and do not like if they have never heard of the opponent, and if they do not recognize either name, many voters will simply not vote at all for that office. This is an explanation for the phenomenon of "drop-off," the decline in the number of votes cast between the top and bottom of the ticket. The farther down the ballot you go, the more important name identification becomes relative to the other functions. In a race for the state legislature or for offices such as state treasurer or attorney general, name recognition can be the only function one really needs to focus on in order to win.

At the top of the ticket, especially in presidential campaigns, very few resources are expended on name identification, except perhaps in the early primaries. Every voter in 1992 knew the names Clinton, Bush, and Perot; that is why you never see billboards for presidential candidates. Outdoor advertising, such as billboards, is a paid medium that has a very limited range of effectiveness, but correctly used, outdoor advertising can effectively increase name identification. Thus billboards may be an excellent medium for a candidate for county assessor, but they would be a colossal waste of money for a well-known candidate for governor.

An important early decision in a campaign is to determine the candidate's name. It is a decision, not a given. Should one use the full, formal first name and middle initial (John F. Kennedy, for example) or go for the informal approach, as in Jimmy Carter or Bill Clinton? Many factors will go into this decision, but the critical point is that the decision should be made, not just fallen into, and once made, that decision should be adhered to at all times. However, it is important to research the ballot law in your state. It will be a major mistake if the whole campaign is spent promoting Bunky Smith, only to learn on election day that the ballot says Elwood T. Smith. In general, the more ordinary the candidate's last name, the more important the first name becomes. In analyzing the name for its advertising potential, ask, Where is the memorability in this name? In names of identifiable ethnicity, the last name is almost sure to dominate. For women candidates, on the other hand, it is almost sure to be the first name. In matters such as logo design, therefore, women candidates should generally feature both first and last name in more or less equal-sized type. If a candidate's name is not pronounced the way it is spelled, remember that the important thing is to have it visually recognized. If the voter pronounces the name correctly but does not recognize it visually, he or she may miss it entirely on the ballot. Correct pronunciation is far less important: Everyone who went to the polls in 1980 to vote for "Ree-gan" cast ballots that counted for "Ray-gan."

The foregoing logic makes radio advertising a poor medium for promoting name identification. Outdoor advertising and television are the best paid media for name identification. However, television is so expensive that it would be wasteful to run commercials only for name identification. (Besides, what would such commercials look and sound like?) However, if a candidate lacks name identification, his or her television commercials should all feature a high level of name-identification value, both audio and video. Newspaper advertising can aid in establishing name identification in certain local races, but if major daily papers are involved, it will not generally be cost-effective.

Candidate Image

Candidate image may be defined through the answer to this question: What kind of a person is this candidate? Thus understood, it is clear that "image" is not the pejorative term it is often thought to be. A thoughtful voter will certainly want to consider what kind of a person he or she is about to vote for, and these considerations may indeed outweigh specific issue stands taken by the candidates (see next section). In general, it is clear that voters give more weight to image considerations than they do to issue considerations.

In planning a campaign, one should make an early image decision similar to the name decision discussed previously. That is, the campaign should determine how it wishes people to answer when asked what kind of a person the candidate is. This is called the *image statement* and should normally be approximately a paragraph long. The starting point in developing an image statement is that it must be real. This is not a moral decision; it is a political decision. In today's atmosphere, it is simply not wise to attempt to fool the public as to what kind of a person the candidate is.

Consider a typical voter in the voting booth. She looks at both names on the ballot for a given race. She can identify both names. Her next step is to ask the image question: What kind of a person is this? If she can answer the image question for one candidate but not for the other, the candidate for whom the question can be answered will get the vote, virtually 100 percent of the time. Of course, some broad test of reasonability must be applied. One may have a very clear answer to the image question for Fidel Castro, Jeffrey Dahmer, or Imelda Marcos and not be willing to vote for them, but in any reasonable case with ordinary politicians, it is much more important to have an image than to define narrowly what that image is. Consider the 435 members of Congress. They are a very diverse group. Some are old, some young. Some are snappy dressers, some are slobs. There are men, women, whites, blacks, gays, straights, wimps, bullies, brainy types, and street-smart pols who never read a book without pictures, but they all won. Thus, there is no one winning image. Competent media consultants do not attempt to force their clients into a predetermined mold. Rather, they seek ways to present the real person their client is in a positive light.

This insight also serves to guide a campaign in dealing with its candidate's image problems. The key here is that an image problem should not be solved by pretending to be the opposite but rather by seeking to portray the positive side of the quality itself. The classic example, because it encompasses both the positive and negative cases, is George Bush. George Bush's image problem in 1988 was that he was a wimp. In his 1988 presidential campaign, the problem was very much in the forefront. In fact, it made the cover of *Newsweek*. His handlers attempted to deal with it in a feisty interview with Dan Rather, but this did not result in an end to the wimp problem. Did people who saw this interview say, "Gee, I guess I was wrong; he's not a wimp after all"? Hardly. At best they said, "Gee, George overcame his wimpiness tonight." Later, wiser handlers came up with the correct solution. In his convention acceptance speech, Bush called for a "kinder, gentler society." The phrase became a sort of slogan for the campaign, and the wimp problem evaporated. Kindness and gentleness are the obverse of the coin of wimpiness. They represent the good side of the image quality—a *real* Bush character trait.

In the term that followed, Bush mostly behaved as a kind and gentle wimp, but in the instance of the Gulf war, he showed strength and decisive leadership. Of course, the war was not just a one-night performance, as was the Rather interview. It represented the sustained application of leadership over a period of months. The significant display of strength almost caused the public to forget the existence of Bush's wimpiness. The war was a big enough event to accomplish something no mere campaign gimmick could ever hope for, and Bush's popularity soared. However, even winning a war is not enough to turn a (real) wimp into a decisive leader. In the end, the (real) person again emerged, and because the crest of the wave had been very high, the trough was very low. The highest Bush approval rating, 91 percent, is the highest ever recorded for any president; the lowest, 38 percent, is only a couple of points higher than Nixon's 1974 low.

Bill Clinton's image at the time of the 1992 elections was one of the most complex in modern history. A sizable majority of Americans voted against him (he won with the lowest percentage of any president in this century), and even among those who voted for him, a substantial number had serious doubts as to his character and trustworthiness. In October 1992, Bush had a slight advantage over Clinton on the issue of trust and attempted to steer the campaign in that direction, but his advantage was not decisive, in large measure because his own trustworthiness had been seriously undermined by the breaking of his "read my lips . . . no new taxes" pledge. Both candidates ran "trust" commercials. The Bush commercial was a "Clinton versus Clinton" approach, designed to high-light contradictions in the Clinton record. Visually, it featured shots of Clinton with his face obscured by a gray blob. Its best feature was a sound bite at the end in which Clinton is heard saying, "There is a logical explanation for these things." It was a good ad, probably Bush's best, but Clinton was able to trump it with an ad that simply replayed the "read my lips" pledge.

Candidates seeking offices below the presidency must bear in mind that the public will form its image of them on the basis of far less evidence than what they have in the presidential case. Therefore, candidates must work all the harder to make sure that one clear, consistent image is portrayed. In the process, perhaps the best thing to bear in mind is that an image is a picture—a metaphor. In seeking a particular image, a candidate should know that the pictures of the campaign will speak the loudest—on television, in person, and in print. The pictures of the campaign should accurately convey the image defined in the image statement.

Issue Development and Exploitation

Bush's image problem stemming from the "read my lips" pledge illustrates the close connection between image and issue dimensions. The word "issue" has several different meanings in politics. We may say, for example, that the issue in the 1992 election was Bill Clinton's character, but in the analysis here, that is not an issue at all. It belongs in the preceding section about image. When we talk about issue development and exploitation, we understand the "issues" to be those policy questions upon which decisions have been made by the candidates in their antecedent public careers or questions that are pending for the office being sought. Among the important issues in 1992 were the economy, abortion, taxes, term limitations, congressional reform, government spending, health care, and crime prevention.

Some voters are one-issue voters—they feel so strongly about one issue that they will vote on the basis of a candidate's stand on that issue regardless of all other factors. Emotional issues such as abortion and gun control have generated many such voters, and government workers are unlikely to vote for a candidate who calls for spending reductions that would eliminate their jobs. To reach one-issue voters, paid media should obviously be closely targeted (suggesting the use of direct mail, or possibly radio, instead of television). Indeed, one of the important differences between image and issue media is that image media are essentially general (a candidate should present the same image to everyone) whereas issue media are essentially targeted (there is no point in talking agriculture policy to steelworkers in Pittsburgh).

Aside from one-issue voters, most Americans have an ambivalent relationship with regard to political issues. They will stoutly maintain that they cast their vote based on the issues and will berate others for not doing so. They will criticize the candidates for ignoring the issues and engaging in mudslinging instead. In truth, the voters themselves and their surrogates in the media ignore the issues. Postelection survey studies have consistently shown that only a very small minority (typically less than 10 percent) of the voters will name any issue when asked why they voted for their chosen candidate. A candidate can give an issues-laden speech to a local civic group, but what gets on the television news is far more likely to be his or her answer to a reporter's question about why he or she is trailing in the latest polls.

Candidates, understanding how the game works, therefore generally downgrade the issue content of their campaigns. Of course, they will deny this because one of the worst images a candidate can have is that of ignoring the issues, but in fact a candidate's issue stands generally bear little resemblance to the policies he or she will implement if elected. An example is George Bush's famous reneging on his "no new taxes" pledge, a very specific issue statement, but consider also that one of the first things Bill Clinton announced after his election victory was that he planned to convene a summit meeting of business leaders and others to get ideas for improving the economy. Clinton had campaigned for months on the basis of having a specific, detailed plan to improve the economy. If he already had a plan ("endorsed by 300 economists," one of his advertisements said), why did he need to seek new ideas? Within a few more weeks, Clinton had already backtracked on positions taken during the campaign on issues from gays in the military to the line-item veto. Such is politics, and voters have an intuitive understanding that campaign issue statements are indistinguishable from political promises and thus are unreliable predictors of what actually will be done.

There are other reasons why issues play only a subordinate role in voters' decisionmaking. One is that very few voters really believe they know the answers to the issues that trouble them. If you, the voter, are unsure of what the right course of action is to solve, for example, the problem of the federal deficit, you are highly unlikely to base your vote on someone else's proposed solution, even assuming you take the time to find out what that position is. You are far more likely to select someone who appears to be the kind of person you can trust to make wise decisions on such a matter. That, of course, is our definition of image. In addition, it is highly questionable that the issues that are most prominent on the first Tuesday after the first Monday of any given election year are in fact going to wind up being the most important issues during the course of the term for which a candidate has been elected. Neither Bush nor Michael Dukakis, for example, uttered a word in 1988 as to how he would react to the collapse of the Soviet Union. Of course not. Who knew?

In spite of their limitations, issue messages are important components of a candidate's media efforts: There are single-issue voters, issues do contribute significantly to image, and issues normally form the basis for the discussion of the differences between the candidates (see next section). If name identification is carried by the campaign's signs and headlines, and image by its pictures, issues are the body copy. Television advertising can convey issue messages as effectively as can radio. Direct-mail advertising is very good in this area as well. Newspaper advertising can have some issue impact, although, as always, it suffers from its inherent limitations.

Attack

Many people believe that politics is more negative than it used to be. This is a very debatable proposition, as a reading of the attack speeches of the great orators of the nineteenth century will show. However, there may be a sense in which it is true for recent times. Many important political decisions used to be made by "the big boys" in "the back room." Groups of such local political power brokers could literally vote a congressman in or out of office. One backroom meeting in the 1950s was called because the congressman in question had developed a serious drinking problem. The power brokers simply told him he could not run again, whereupon he retired. They then engineered the election of a successor, who went on to a distinguished career. The ordinary voters of the district never had any idea that their congressman had become a falling-down drunk.

Today, partly because of the television revolution, we no longer want the "big boys" making our decisions for us. The quid pro quo of that fact is that now we all have to know the things that previously only they knew, and sometimes those things are not pretty. Negative politics is almost universally decried, and yet it is an essential part of a competitive campaign. The simple fact is that the voters ought to know the good points and the bad points of the candidates who seek their support, and the logical source of information about the bad points of a candidate is that candidate's opponent. Often, the very same people who complain about negative politics are the ones who say they want more issue discussion. Yet it is difficult to imagine how a candidate could present a meaningful and understandable issue-based platform without contrasting the stands taken thereon with those taken by his or her opponent. Sometimes people will say they do not really mind issue-based attacks; it is just the "personal stuff" they object to—they do not like "name-calling," "mudslinging," and "dirty politics." However, what do these terms really mean? In fact, it is quite simple to separate the legitimate from the illegitimate campaign attacks. There are two tests: truth and relevance.

In both of these areas, the ultimate judges are the voters. There are some objective standards for truth. Did the member of Congress actually vote for the bill or not? Was his or her trip to Paris actually paid for by the taxpayers or not? However, there are also subjective aspects. Was the bill an example of wasteful spending? Was the trip a pleasure-filled junket? It is perfectly legitimate for a challenger to make these charges, but if the truth is stretched in the characterization, it may not impress the judges. Relevance is always subjective, although there would be widespread agreement on the relevance of some items and the irrelevance of others. The charge that a given candidate smoked marijuana when in college in the 1960s will be seen by most voters as irrelevant, even if true. Almost all voters, on the other hand, would find it relevant that a candidate was a current and regular user of cocaine. In the 1992 presidential campaign, research suggested that Bill Clinton's 1960s antiwar activities and his trip to Moscow were viewed as relevant by a fairly small percentage of voters. Far more, however, saw his subsequent contradictory explanations of those activities as indicative of a character flaw and thus relevant. The failure of the Bush campaign to exploit this aspect of the issue may be seen as a shortcoming of the campaign's attack function.

It should also be noted that the rules of attack vary somewhat by party. This stems in part from the proverbial media bias, but an equally important and often overlooked cause is the difference between the base voter groups in the two parties. In general, for example, sex-scandal attacks almost never work against Democrats, because the charges are regarded as irrelevant by large segments of both the intellectual elite and the low-income urban components of the Democratic base vote. Sex-scandal attacks almost always do work against Republicans, however, because the claims are regarded as relevant by large segments of both the Christian right and upper-income GOP base voter groups. The classic case is the 1983 sex scandal in which two congressmen were censured for affairs with teenaged House pages. The censured Democrat, Gerry Studds, was reelected easily in liberal Massachusetts; the Republican, Dan Crane, was defeated in conservative downstate Illinois.

In general, however, it is important to remember that committed voters will tend to believe attacks against candidates they oppose and reject attacks against candidates they support. Liberals, for example, tended to believe Anita Hill's charges against Clarence Thomas and disbelieve (or rationalize away) Gennifer Flowers's allegations against Bill Clinton. Republicans loved Ross Perot's "chicken map" and other statistical jibes at Clinton in Perot's final half-hour television show but discounted as manipulations the statistics he used to discredit Bush. In the final analysis, voters resemble referees in professional basketball—most of the close calls go against the rookies. It is very difficult to mount a successful attack against a very popular political figure; the facts must be new, self-evidently true, clearly relevant to a large percentage of the voters, and attested to by independent sources, such as the news media. Attacks against lesser-known or less popular figures, on the other hand, face far less stringent tests.

Radio is an excellent attack medium, and if appropriately targetable lists are available, so is direct mail. Television, of course, can do the job very well, but it should be noted that attack television commercials will invite much more vigorous third-party response than the other media. Direct mail is particularly good at delivering a message without raising the hackles of the news reporters.

Defense

Defense is not what the candidate is straddling; it is what he or she says when attacked by the opponent. One can, of course, ignore an attack. This used to be a very popular response, but today almost no candidate or incumbent believes in ignoring a serious attack. It is not really that anyone has changed his or her mind on the subject. It is just that most of those who believed in the "do not dignify that by a response" school were defeated, so their views no longer count. Of course, it can be a mistake to overrespond, but attacks will generally be believed if there is no response. This leads to one of the important rules of defense: If you are engaging in defense, you should do so in the same medium used in the attack and marshal the same degree of power as that with which the attack was made. If you are attacked in a news release, defend with a news release. If you are attacked with 500 gross rating points of television commercials, respond at the same level, on the same stations. The goal is to get everyone who heard the attack to hear your defense, without expanding the conflict to new listeners.

There are four categories of defense, which are presented here in descending order of their likelihood of success:[2]

Denial. Saying "I didn't do it" is the most effective defense, but it is also the least often used because the matter is seldom quite that simple. In order for someone to believe your denial, you must generally offer some evidence. One of the most successful recent uses of this defense was the complete and total denial of the Anita Hill charges by Clarence Thomas. Purists may argue that this was not an election campaign, and of course it was not. However, in a very real sense, Thomas was the first Supreme Court justice ever elected by the people; after the weekend of hearings, national polls showed people were more likely to believe

Thomas by approximately a 60-40 margin. Reverse those numbers and there is no way there are enough votes in the Senate to confirm.

Explanation. In the explanation approach, the most frequently used defense, the attacked candidate gives his or her side of the story. Clinton used explanation effectively when he was attacked on his performance as governor of Arkansas by both Bush and Perot. For every statistic they cited showing Arkansas was an ill-governed, backward, loser of a state, Clinton produced one showing it was an on-the-move, progressive state. The voters had no idea how to judge among the welter of numbers flying back and forth and generally disregarded the whole question, which is to say that the attack failed.

Apology. Research shows that the apology defense is inherently a very powerful defense indeed. It usually fails, however, because it is extremely difficult to convince the voters of the candidate's sincerity. Thus, George Bush's apology for breaking his "read my lips" pledge by supporting the 1990 budget deal was ineffective because it was not regarded as real. The general rule in utilizing this defense is simple—do it big. In Bush's case, it would have been far more successful to have issued the apology in the State of the Union message, when he could have portrayed the deal as the proximate cause of the recession and challenged Congress to admit that it too had erred and to set things right by undoing the tax increases. When Congress failed to act and the recession continued, he could have effectively pled not guilty. In all likelihood, Bush followed a different course for the same reason more politicians do not admit mistakes: They just hate to make such an admission. However, a tactical apology can be an extremely effective political weapon.

A few rules in utilizing this defense are that you cannot mix your defense with either of the first two tactics or use them serially (if you attempt to deny a charge and then apologize when additional evidence is revealed, you are doomed); you cannot plea bargain (such as when former District of Columbia mayor Marion Barry confessed to an alcohol problem when everyone knew it was a cocaine problem); and you generally cannot use the defense more than once.

Counterattack. When the first three defenses are unavailable, for whatever reason, the counterattack is called for. In essence, it involves ignoring the substance of the charges and attacking the source of those charges. When the source is one's opponent, in practice this defense amounts to accusing the opponent of dirty campaigning. When the source is some third party, the credibility of the source is drawn into question. Much of Bill Clinton's defense against the original charges by Gennifer Flowers was an attack on the *National Enquirer.* This defense also serves to discredit a third-party source if collusion can be shown between the source and one's opponent. Clinton, for example, referred repeatedly to "Republicans in Arkansas" as being involved in stirring up the various charges against him.

One of the most celebrated uses of counterattack was by Michael Dukakis in the 1988 presidential campaign. His defense in the so-called Willie Horton attack was not to deny the charge (which would have been an admission that he did not support the prison furlough program under which Horton was released) nor to explain his side of the issue (perhaps by showing other furloughees who had positive experiences). Nor did he apologize ("I thought it would be a good idea, but I can see now that it did not work"). Instead, he counterattacked by ignoring the substance of the charge and instead accusing Bush of mounting a racist campaign by using it. The defense was probably effective in motivating black turnout. Overall, however, Dukakis greatly overused the counterattack (Boston Harbor, Pledge of Allegiance), and it is, after all, inherently the weakest defense.

Response as attack. As stated earlier, no one medium is best for defense, and the rule is to respond in the same medium used in the attack. Note, however, that in some cases, the response to an attack is not really defense at all but rather an attack itself. In that case, the rules you follow and the media choices you make should be those indicated in the earlier section about attack. In order to tell whether the response is a defense or an attack, a media consultant should ask the following question: Is the goal to keep voters from deserting the candidate or to get new voters? An example of the latter occurred in a 1992 congressional campaign when a challenger attacked his incumbent opponent for junketing (the specific ad was done as a satire of *Lifestyles of the Rich and Famous*, a very popular 1992 genre). In the course of the advertisement, the challenger listed four destinations for the incumbent's travels. One of the four was "Arabia." The incumbent's campaign correctly perceived the challenger's error. "Arabia" was, of course, Saudi Arabia, and the "junket" in question was a trip to inspect troops during the Desert Shield phase of the Gulf war. In a scathing response, complete with photos of the (female) incumbent in combat gear talking to individual soldiers, the challenger was berated for not understanding the importance of showing support for our brave men and women in combat. The response reversed the incumbent's tracking numbers, which had been in free fall, and assured her reelection. It was a response, yes, but it was attack, not defense.

CONCLUSION

The careful application of the communications principles outlined in this chapter cannot guarantee a victory on election day. As Damon Runyon said, "The race is not always to the swiftest, nor the fight to the strongest"—although he also concluded that "the smart money bets that way." In a campaign, victory is more often than not found on the side of the candidate who best understood and applied the rules of political communication and knew when to amend them in light of extenuating circumstances.

NOTES

1. The five-functions analysis was formulated in 1975 by G. Norman Bishop and the author for a series of seminars sponsored by the Republican National Committee.

2. The four-defense analysis was developed by G. Norman Bishop and the author for the aforementioned seminars, and it was based on an earlier hypothesis by Paul M. Newman. It was subsequently (in 1982 and 1986) the subject of two extensive qualitative and quantitative research projects directed by Vincent J. Breglio, Charles F. Rund, and the author; in its current form the analysis draws from the conclusions reached by these projects.

8

Winning Through Advertising: It's All in the Context

STEVEN ANSOLABEHERE AND SHANTO IYENGAR

Today, television is the principal intermediary between politicians and voters. Candidates must master the art of impression management through media presentations in order to thrive at the polls. Understanding elections, however, requires more than a recognition of the primacy of broadcast media. No doubt, advertising and newsmaking are the staples of campaign communication, but voters also encounter relevant information from a multitude of alternative sources, including (in no particular order) conversations with friends and associates, talk and call-in shows, candidate debates, direct mailers, and entertainment programs (*Murphy Brown*, for instance). From a communications perspective, therefore, campaigns resemble kaleidoscopes; messages from a variety of competing sources interact to produce the voters' final image.

In this chapter, we elaborate upon the general overview in Chapter 7 by drawing on research that demonstrates how campaign advertisements, television news, and voters' prior beliefs jointly influence voter choice. Several discrete hypotheses have been formed concerning the nature of these interactions. The *riding-the-wave* hypothesis predicts that candidates will tend to reap greater returns by advertising on issues or topics "in the news." The *recirculation* hypothesis asserts that news coverage of campaign advertising energizes the advertisements under review. The *issue-ownership* hypothesis proposes that campaign messages (both free and paid) are most persuasive when they resonate with voters' stereotypes about the parties and candidates. Finally, the *competitive-advertising* hypothesis asserts that the impact of one candidate's advertising is contingent on the opponent's advertising. That is, political advertisers are interdependent rather than autonomous actors. Taken together, these hypotheses advance the argument that the prevailing information context is the crucial determinant of the effectiveness of campaign advertising.

EXPERIMENTAL TESTS OF ADVERTISING IN CONTEXT

We tested these four hypotheses during the 1992 presidential and senatorial campaigns in California. Our research was based on a series of experiments (conducted between May and November) in which groups of ordinary citizens watched particular combinations of advertising and news.

Given the stereotypes associated with experimental research, it is important to point out that our experimental design did not sacrifice realism at the altar of precision. Each study took place during an ongoing political campaign and featured real candidates (Democrats and Republicans, males and females, incumbents and challengers), all of whom were investing heavily in television advertising. Our experimental advertisements were professionally produced and, unless the viewer was a political consultant, could not be distinguished from the flurry of advertisements confronting the typical voter. Moreover, the experimental participants were a cross-section of southern California voters who, on election day, would have to choose between the candidates whose advertisements they watched.[1] In short, there is a world of difference between these experiments and the typical laboratory study of political advertising.

In addition to the use of real rather than artificial stimuli, our manipulations were also unobtrusive. The experimental advertisements and news reports were embedded in a fifteen-minute videotape recording of an evening newscast. Since candidates advertise heavily during news programs, the insertion of the experimental campaign advertisement into a local newscast was inconspicuous. When our studies focused on the joint effects of news stories and advertisements, the former addressed issues that were, in fact, newsworthy.

Finally, we minimized the aura of the research laboratory by showing the news tapes in an informal, living room–like setting. The viewing room was furnished with a couch, easy chairs, coffee table, and potted plants. Participants could snack on cookies and coffee while they watched the news, and in most cases participants came accompanied by a friend or coworker. In summary, our experiments were characterized by rigorous control over the flow of campaign messages and by considerable similarity to the real world of political campaigns.

When participants arrived, they completed a brief background questionnaire. They then watched the tape of the newscast. Depending on the flow of subjects, participants either watched the tape alone or in groups of two or three. Random assignment of participants to experimental conditions was used throughout. The thirty-second campaign advertisement was inserted into the first commercial break and appeared in the middle position of a five-advertisement break. In studies featuring two advertisements (one from each of the two major candidates), the second advertisement appeared during the second commercial break. In these two-advertisement studies, the candidates' advertisements were aired in random order.

On completion of the videotape, participants answered a lengthy questionnaire in which they indicated their opinions on current issues, evaluated the major candidates, and recalled particular stories and advertisements from the newscast. Finally, all participants were debriefed (the true purpose of the study was revealed) and paid $15.

THE INTERACTION OF ADVERTISING AND NEWS

Advertising on Newsworthy Issues, or How to Ride the Wave

Given the variety of information sources available to most voters, the major challenge facing the media consultant is the production of messages that do not get lost in this cluttered environment. For most candidates, inserting their preferred issues into the media agenda is an arduous task, and making the news is often a pyrrhic victory because reporters tend to provide interpretations that run counter to the candidate's. It is often easier (and less risky) for candidates to tailor their paid messages to themes that are currently regarded as newsworthy. In the context of American military involvement in Somalia and Haiti, candidates find it useful to dwell on their toughness or expertise in foreign policy. In the aftermath of the Los Angeles riots, candidates contesting local and statewide offices in California found it imperative to demonstrate their commitment to law and order.

The political logic here is elementary. The mass media—especially television news—set the public agenda by defining the issues that are particularly newsworthy. The public follows along (see Iyengar and Kinder, 1987; Rogers and Dearing, 1988). News coverage boosts the accessibility of political issues and also politicizes these issues (see Iyengar, 1991). Issues that achieve prominence on the public agenda are especially powerful determinants of candidate evaluation and voting preference (see Iyengar, 1993; Iyengar and Simon, 1993).

Clearly, it is in each candidate's interest to establish his or her credentials on the major issues of the day. In 1992, the public measured candidates Bush and Clinton against the dominant yardstick of the economy and found that they preferred Clinton. Unfortunately for former President Bush, the voters accorded little significance to those matters on which they actually preferred his abilities and positions (such as foreign policy expertise and personal integrity).

In general terms, the riding-the-wave hypothesis claims that advertising becomes more powerful when the candidate's message deals with the issues in the news. The hypothesis thus predicts that candidates should use their paid time in a way that the free channels can be expected to reinforce. Candidates should advertise on issues that are especially timely and newsworthy.

We tested this hypothesis using the issues of unemployment and sexual harassment. Given California's prolonged economic slump, unemployment was especially important in the 1992 election. Our first study examined the impact of an advertisement in which the sponsoring candidate pledged his or her support for job training programs and investment incentives. This advertisement was broadcast on behalf of all four of the major candidates running for the two Senate seats.[2] Half of the participants in this study also watched a news report (which appeared after the campaign advertisement) noting that California's unemployment rate was the highest in the nation; the remaining participants watched a news report that had no bearing on economic issues. Our prediction was that the advertisement would bear greater returns when reinforced by the grim economic news.

Gender-related issues were also prominent in California's U.S. Senate races. Both Democratic nominees were women (Barbara Boxer and Dianne Feinstein) who worked diligently to keep gender-related issues central to their campaigns. In addition, a significant amount of the news coverage accorded the Senate races was devoted to the novel phenomenon of two women running simultaneously and the prospects for a "year of the woman."

We produced an advertisement dealing with women's rights for both women Senate nominees and for presidential nominee Bill Clinton.[3] The advertisement showed scenes from the Hill-Thomas hearings while the announcer emphasized the sponsoring candidate's commitment to the cause of women's rights. For half the participants, the advertisement was followed by a news story on gender politics. This story focused on the efforts of a local feminist group to mobilize support and funds for female candidates.[4] The prediction, of course, was that candidates in general, but women candidates in particular, would prove more persuasive with advertisements dealing with women's issues when these issues are highlighted in the news.

The results varied by issue. In the case of unemployment, all four senatorial candidates gained support by running the advertisement; exposure to the advertisement increased the percentage of viewers intending to vote for the sponsoring candidate. The effects of the advertisement, however, were not strengthened by the presence of the news story. This pattern was reversed when the target issue was sexual harassment. For both women candidates, the interaction between news and advertising was statistically significant, indicating that the effects of the campaign advertisement were heightened by the news coverage. In contrast, when it was Clinton who advertised on gender issues, the interaction of advertising and news proved trivial. In sum, synchronizing campaign advertising with news coverage of gender issues did yield larger payoffs, but it was women and not men who could ride the wave.

Taken together, our results suggest that news coverage of issues is especially beneficial to issue advertising when the issue in question has achieved only a moderate level of public concern. At the time of our study, virtually all Californians acknowledged that unemployment was the state's major problem. They did not need news coverage to remind them of the state's economic predicament. The Senate candidates thus scored points with the audience by claiming to support jobs programs, regardless of whether the news focused on the issue. In the case of gender-related issues, however, the news reminded voters of the Hill-Thomas hearings and the oppression of women. The women candidates' advertisements were thus made more effective when paired with news coverage. The fact that the benefits of news coverage accrued to Boxer and Feinstein—but not to Clinton—suggests a higher-order interaction among news, advertising, and the credibility of the sponsoring candidate on the issue in question. We address the role of prior beliefs about the candidates in a later section.

Recirculation, or the Benefits of
Being Criticized by Reporters

Obtaining the attention of the news media is vital not only because the media lend much-needed credibility to campaign messages but also because they provide access to vast audiences at virtually no cost. One method of attracting news coverage is advertising. Increasingly, the national media have become preoccupied with campaign advertisements. A recent study found that 25 percent of all network news stories on the 1988 presidential campaign included some reference to the candidates' advertising (Kaid et al., 1993).

Not only has political advertising become newsworthy, but reporters have also appointed themselves as referees who scrutinize campaign advertisements for their accuracy and veracity. In the wake of the 1988 presidential election, there was widespread agreement within the journalistic community concerning the need for improved ways to cover campaigns. Distinguished journalists and analysts (e.g., Broder, 1992; Bode, 1992) suggested that the press should evaluate campaign advertisements on a regular basis and condemn those that distorted or blurred the record. The hope was to deter candidates from airing misleading or inaccurate claims. Thus, a new genre of campaign journalism was born, devoted to monitoring campaign advertising.[5]

By 1992, "truth-box" or "ad-watch" journalism had come into its own. Ad-watches appeared regularly on the networks' newscasts. The producers of CNN's *Inside Politics* program assigned a senior correspondent (Brooks Jackson) full-time to the task of inspecting and analyzing the advertisements aired by the presidential candidates. Today, ad-watch reports are standard fare in print and broadcast outlets at both national and local levels (see Otten, 1992; Wolinsky et al., 1991; Kaid et al., 1993).

One of our 1992 studies focused on ad-watch reports dealing with the presidential campaign. We designed this study to compare the effects of advertisements[6] and reports analyzing the advertisements.[7] If ad-watches actually exert the monitoring effect that the media intend, we would expect to find that exposure to an ad-watch should shift viewers' preferences away from the candidate whose advertisement has been scrutinized. On the other hand, if the ad-watch works to benefit the candidate, this pattern should be reversed. Our results indicated that ad-watches actually boosted the stock of a candidate whose advertisement was scrutinized.

In this study our experimental manipulations were limited to the Clinton and Bush campaigns; participants either watched an advertisement (from either candidate) or a CNN ad-watch report scrutinizing the advertisement. We found that the effects of the campaign advertisement on voting preference were trivial. Clinton enjoyed a huge lead (in terms of voting intention) among participants, and the size of this lead was unaffected by exposure to Clinton's or Bush's advertising.[8] The ad-watch reports, however, tended to move preferences toward the candidate whose advertisement was targeted for criticism. This effect was especially pronounced in the case of the report examining the Bush advertisement. Bush's deficit in the polls fell dramatically among voters who watched the ad-watch report on Bush's advertisement. The level of support for Bush in this condition differed significantly from all other conditions. In effect, the ad-watch that targeted the Bush advertisement had a substantial positive impact on voter preference for Bush.

These results suggest that ad-watches tend to benefit the candidate sponsoring the advertisement and that ad-watches are much more persuasive than the advertisements themselves. These results proved robust: They did not disappear when we controlled for voters' partisanship and past voting behavior (see Ansolabehere and Iyengar, 1993b). In short, the media's attempts to monitor campaign advertising may backfire and actually play into the hands of the image makers and consultants.

This unintended effect can be attributed to several features of ad-watch reports. The typical ad-watch report repeats the more controversial (or vicious) segments of the advertisement that is being scrutinized. By recirculating the advertisement in the guise of news, the ad-watch journalist may enhance the believability of the campaign's message. Iron-

ically, this sort of "bad press" is especially welcomed by political consultants. As Roger Ailes has pointed out, "You get a 30 or 40 percent bump
out of getting it [an advertisement] on the news. You get more viewers,
you get more credibility, you get it in your framework" (Runkel, 1989,
p. 142).

Ad-watches may also help the targeted candidate in other ways.
When a campaign advertisement is examined in an ad-watch, the media
analyst necessarily reinforces the targeted candidate's agenda by devot-
ing attention to the issue(s) on which the candidate is running. Ad-
watches may also elicit sympathy for the targeted candidate whose advertisement is being picked apart by a "hostile" media. Americans view
campaign-related news presentations with some skepticism anyway (see
Rosenstiel, 1993; Markle Foundation, 1993), and the singling out of a particular candidate for criticism can exacerbate perceptions of media bias
(Vallone et al., 1987). The public's skepticism is further fueled if it appears that the ad-watch was inspired by obviously partisan sources (such
as the opposing campaign).[9] Thus, for several reasons, ad-watches may
help the cause of a candidate whose advertisements have attracted this
form of media coverage.

THE ROLE OF PRIOR BELIEFS, OR WHY IT'S IMPORTANT TO CONFIRM STEREOTYPES

Obviously, the issues that preoccupy the media vary from time to time.
The ever shifting focus of news coverage represents a short-term or con-
textual determinant of advertising effectiveness. However, voter responses to campaign advertisements are also conditioned by longer-term
or dispositional factors. Long-held beliefs about the parties or candidates
are especially important (see Popkin, 1992; Petrocik, 1992). Although voters generally lack specific factual knowledge about issues, through years
of political experience and socialization they form impressions about
parties and candidates.

Research has shown that the accumulated body of political knowledge
held by the electorate includes expectations regarding the relative capa-
bilities of the political parties to deal with specific issues (for a summary,
see Petrocik, 1992). For example, the public generally considers Democrats more able than Republicans to deal with the problem of unemployment. Conversely, Republicans are seen as better than Democrats at fight-
ing crime.

These existing stereotypes are important filters for assimilating specific campaign messages. Our third hypothesis is that candidates are
likely to gain the most by advertising on those issues over which they can
claim "ownership." This hypothesis is based on the "confirmatory bias"
in information processing; this principle holds that people are more re-

ceptive to messages that confirm rather than disconfirm existing stereotypes. (For a review of this research, see Markus and Zajonc, 1984; Pratto
and John, 1991.) Accordingly, the hypothesis would predict that Democrats will be at an advantage by calling attention to the problem of unemployment. Alternatively, women will gain by advertising on women's issues, and men will be better off focusing on their maleness. In short, it is
expected that a candidate's advertisements will be more powerful when
they address issues on which the candidate enjoys a relative advantage.

In our studies on both unemployment and sexual harassment, we
were able to substantiate the issue-ownership notion. The effects of the
campaign advertisement on unemployment were generally more powerful when Democratic senatorial candidates Boxer and Feinstein (rather
than Republicans Bruce Herschensohn and John Seymour) ran the advertisement. The advertisement proved especially influential in increasing
the proportion of viewers who believed that the Democrats were supporters of government-funded jobs programs. The identical advertisement, when shown on behalf of Seymour or Herschensohn, produced no
change in the proportion of viewers rating these candidates as proponents of government jobs programs.

Parallel results were obtained with sexual harassment. This issue was
clearly "owned" by women. When sponsored by Barbara Boxer or Dianne Feinstein, the advertisement dealing with women's issues elicited a
sharp surge in the proportion of viewers intending to vote for Boxer or
Feinstein. When sponsored by Clinton, however, the advertisement in-
duced no change in Clinton's level of support. Similarly, viewers exposed
to the news story on the political mobilization of women became more
likely to vote for Boxer and Feinstein. No such benefits of news coverage
accrued to candidate Clinton.

These results suggest that advertising is interpreted within the context
of partisan stereotypes or existing beliefs about the candidates. A message on sexual harassment is more credible when it is a woman who calls
attention to the issue, and a call for increased job training programs
evokes particularly strong responses when used by a Democrat. Candidates are thus constrained by their reputation and image. Bill Clinton
would have been poorly served by advertisements extolling his personal
integrity, and George Bush was a laughingstock when he discussed his
plans to rejuvenate the economy.

COMPETITIVE ADVERTISING, OR IT'S MORE
LIKE TENNIS THAN GOLF

Traditionally, market researchers, consumer psychologists, and others
who study the effects of advertising have examined particular cam-

paigns in isolation. In effect, voters are assumed to respond to advertisements unilaterally, and each advertiser attempts autonomously to maximize its position vis-à-vis consumers with little regard for the strategies of other advertisers.

In the real world, there are few if any situations in which consumers encounter monopolistic messages from only one advertiser. The more general scenario is one of competition—Domino's and Pizza Hut vie for the attention of pizza eaters, Ford and Chevrolet for the loyalty of drivers, Bush and Clinton for the preference of voters, and so on. Accordingly, a much more realistic framework for assessing the impact of advertising would acknowledge that advertising involves a contest among multiple players whose actions interact.

To invoke a sporting analogy, the advertising game bears a closer resemblance to tennis than to golf. Golfers typically compete separately against a common course. Advertisers are more like tennis players who must not only take into account the "course" (playing surface, weather conditions), but also consider the particular strengths and weaknesses of the opponent.

Strategic considerations are especially important in the area of political advertising. As Jay Bryant points out in his discussion of offense and defense (Chapter 7), reactivity is an especially important element of advertising strategy. Candidates who are the targets of attack advertisements can either ignore the attack (Dukakis in 1988), air a prompt rebuttal (Clinton in 1992), use the opponent's attack as a basis for condemning his or her motives (both Clinton and Dukakis used this approach), or initiate an attack on a completely separate issue.

Which of the possible responses to attack advertising proves most effective will depend, of course, upon the circumstances and candidates. Our research examined the effects of different combinations of positive and negative advertisements. In several studies, we exposed voters to a pair of campaign advertisements, one from each of the candidates. We varied the tone of these advertisements so that some voters watched two positive messages, others watched one positive and negative, and others watched two negative messages. The results were as expected—there is no general rule that governs responses to attack advertising. Contrary to Roger Ailes's axiom of "once you get punched, you punch back" (Runkel, 1989, p. 164), we found that most candidates, but Democrats and females in particular, were better off ignoring the attack and maintaining a positive message (see Ansolabehere and Iyengar, 1993b).

The major implication of our two-advertisement studies is that advertising is competitive rather than monopolistic in its effects. The effects of any particular advertisement depend to a great degree upon characteristics of the opponent's advertisements. The effects of exposure to a particular advertisement do not yield much insight into why candidates choose particular advertising strategies. Campaign managers who rely on the marginal contributions of their own spots will pursue the wrong strategy. That is, campaign strategies based on the public's responses to one of the candidate's messages are likely to fail. Instead, campaign managers must design advertisements after anticipating the opponent's moves. Only then can they optimize the benefits of advertising.

CONCLUSION

Paid advertising is the critical ingredient of contemporary campaign communication, and most Americans rely heavily on the news media to keep informed. Candidates who have the funds to mount significant advertising buys and who successfully attract news coverage (while simultaneously controlling the message) benefit in several ways—they become well-known, they are able to set the public agenda and frame campaign issues in their terms, and they are able to convince voters that they possess the necessary prerequisites (such as integrity and competence) for holding elective office (see Ansolabehere, Behr, and Iyengar, 1992).

Most analysts of American campaigns differentiate between the paid and free channels of campaign communication. It is assumed that advertising and the news are two separate means of influencing voters. As we have suggested, however, the key to successful media campaigning is the orchestration of the paid and free channels into a coherent theme. When advertising and the news reinforce each other, the former generates added value.

A further element in the coordination of information is the degree of fit between campaign messages and voters' prior beliefs. Voters not only differentiate between candidates in terms of their attributes but also consider particular traits to be more or less important depending upon the party, race, gender, or other prominent characteristic of the candidate. As the preceding chapter suggested, old-fashioned morality is not considered a central trait of Democratic politicians; a more important characteristic may be that they supports civil rights. From a Republican's perspective, therefore, revealing that one's opponent belongs to an all-white country club may be a more powerful message than revealing instances of extramarital sexual activity. Campaign messages must resonate with popular stereotypes and expectations.

Finally, we have argued that campaign advertising fits a competitive rather than monopolistic framework. Each advertiser is able to condition the effects exercised by the opposition. Campaign strategists, recognizing that they are engaged in a dialogue, learn to anticipate the opposing campaign's moves. Only then can they optimize the benefits of advertising. In this sense, much of the trend toward attack advertising in American elections can be attributed not to mean-spirited candidates who attack for the sake of attacking but rather to rational candidates who seek to neutralize the efforts of their opponents.

NOTES

1. Using a weighted average of Los Angeles and Orange counties as the criterion, we closely matched our experimental participants to the local population in age, gender, percent white, and partisanship. Our participants deviated from the local population in two important respects—they included a higher percentage of African Americans and a higher percentage of college graduates.

2. For a variety of reasons, both of the state's U.S. Senate seats were open in 1992. The race for the short-term (two years) seat pitted Democrat Dianne Feinstein against Republican John Seymour. The long-term seat was contested by Democrat Barbara Boxer and Republican Bruce Herschensohn.

3. The selection of candidates was more a matter of necessity than choice. The nature of the message ("taking sexual harassment seriously") and the positions taken by the Republican Senate candidates made it impossible to run the treatment advertisement on behalf of them or President Bush.

4. The reporter noted the success of a local fund-raising event and interviewed several celebrities from the entertainment industry in attendance (including Barbra Streisand) who voiced their anger over the Hill-Thomas hearings and the treatment of women in general.

5. The pioneering efforts at scrutinizing televised spots occurred during the 1990 Texas gubernatorial campaign between Ann Richards and Clayton Williams. KVUE, an Austin television station, broadcast a series of highly critical reports on the content of both candidates' advertisements.

6. We used three advertisements in this study, two aired by the Clinton campaign and one for Bush. One of the Clinton advertisements was positive and the other negative. The positive message described his accomplishments as governor of Arkansas, with an emphasis on the state's economic growth and welfare and educational reforms. The Clinton negative advertisement attacked Bush's record on the economy by juxtaposing statements by Bush claiming that the economy was growing with gloomy economic statistics. Finally, the Bush advertisement was negative in tone and itemized a long list of taxes Clinton had enacted in Arkansas.

7. All three ad-watches were reported by Brooks Jackson of CNN. Each report began by replaying segments of the advertisement, then questioned the facts and assumptions, and concluded by rating the advertisement as accurate, inaccurate, or misleading. In the case of the Bush attack advertisement, for example, Jackson noted that Bush himself had raised taxes and increased government spending. Similarly, in analyzing the Clinton negative spot, Jackson pointed out that the economic statistics had been taken out of context and presented out of order.

8. Statewide polls taken at the time had Clinton leading Bush by as much as 26 percent.

9. In the case of the ad-watches done by the *Los Angeles Times* in 1992, nearly 50 percent of all criticisms emanated from representatives of the opposing campaign.

9

The Best Campaign Wins: Local Press Coverage of Nonpresidential Races

ANITA DUNN

One of the great ironies of the political process is that the higher the level of office sought, the greater amount of press scrutiny on the candidates. Paid media and communication with voters are less important for the campaigns, although the higher level of visibility for the race increases the amount of money that is raised. As so often seems to be the case in the American political process, candidates who don't need money get it, but those who desperately need it don't. For example, it is commonly believed that paid media coverage plays a relatively small role in presidential general elections because of the intensity of free (news) media coverage available to the candidates. Clinton's deputy campaign manager, George Stephanopolous, canceled a June 1992 half-hour television program that would have cost the campaign $3 million because of the number of free outlets available to Clinton.

Yet presidential campaigns are the only campaigns in the United States to receive federal funding in order to ensure communication with voters. Compare the plight of the typical challenger for the U.S. Senate with the incumbent's situation in June of an election year. The incumbent usually has at least twice as much cash on hand in the June 20 Federal Election Commission (FEC) reports filed at that time. Phil Donahue is not calling the challenger, and neither is Arsenio Hall. Nor are the local television stations or the political reporters for the local press expressing interest, except to ask the challenger to comment on the fact that given the underfunded state of his or her campaign most political professionals in the state and in Washington give the challenger no chance of winning. That is life at the local campaign level.

Just as there is a proportionately greater amount of coverage by the press as the level of office contested grows higher, so there is a proportionately greater amount of scrutiny given to the role the press plays in the campaigns. There is a significant body of literature and self-examination of the performance of the media in presidential elections following every campaign, and that discussion is an important one. But there is very little analysis about the role the press plays in campaigns below the presidential level—for senators, representatives, state legislators—and the very absence of that discussion, soul-searching, and scrutiny illustrates a significant problem of the coverage.

With some exceptions, press coverage of congressional races mirrors the worst flaws of what Paul Taylor of the *Washington Post* characterized as "gotcha" journalism and horse-race coverage, a reporting style that has evoked much criticism of the national-level press—but that is only when press coverage of these races has existed at all. This chapter addresses some of the typical problems I have observed during the past ten years of working on congressional elections and discusses the impact the coverage patterns can have on the races. This is by no means the kind of blanket indictment of non-Beltway press that the press applied to, say, the House of Representatives during the bank scandal. I have seen excellent political reporting on the local level during a number of races, and I hope the reporters with whom I have dealt and continue to deal know the respect I hold for them and their profession. But I believe it is necessary to raise some of the issues that I have raised with them over the years.

PRESS AS PACS: COVERAGE DECISIONS
BASED ON WINNABILITY

There is an argument to be made that the local press is the unindicted coconspirator in the alleged "permanent incumbency" that has given rise to the term-limit movement and other self-styled reform efforts. To those who work on campaigns, it often does appear that coverage decisions of races are made using standards similar to those used by PACs. PACs are criticized by the reform community for donating primarily to incumbents and to those they think most likely to be victors in races and for using poll numbers, overall strength of fund-raising, and the assessments of political professionals to determine viability of candidates.

The local press also makes early decisions about the competitive nature of the race, and those competitiveness decisions dictate press coverage. A vicious circle thus develops for challengers: If early in the race they do not have money, standing in the polls, endorsements, and the backing of political insiders, they—and the race—are written off, not covered, which means the likelihood of a competitive race developing is almost nonexistent. I illustrate this point first with an anecdotal example and then an analysis of the coverage of a 1992 congressional race that occurred in a major media market served by a major national newspaper.

In 1990 I was invited in my role as communications director for the Democratic Senatorial Campaign Committee (DSCC) to discuss the upcoming Senate elections with a group of news directors for public radio stations around the country. In my experience, public radio stations do a better than average job of covering politics and of covering the dialogue of local campaigns. In discussing the perception that incumbents never lose, I asked the news directors if they could name every challenger to every congressional incumbent in their listening areas. This was August, three months before the election. Not a single hand went up.

In 1992 there was a congressional race in Maryland's Eighth Congressional District, although readers of the *Washington Post*, a newspaper known for its concern about the advantages of incumbency in the political process, would never have known. The incumbent was Connie Morella, a liberal Republican considered by most political observers to be in step with the district and difficult to defeat. The primary was in March, and the *Post* took note of that with a February 27 article (its first on the race) profiling the Democratic candidates. The news caption was "This Crowded Field May Be Mostly Chaff; 8 Montgomery Democrats Seeking Right to Be Underdog to Morella." The article contained the requisite party insiders pronouncing the field of challengers to be "an embarrassment," ran through the electoral backgrounds of four of the candidates, picked a front-runner and quoted only a single candidate of the eight candidates who had filed for the office. In what appeared to be an afterthought, the paper listed the other people who had filed—all before pronouncing Morella unbeatable.

The next time the "chaff" surfaced was two days after the primary. One of the candidates whose coverage in the *Post* during the primary had consisted exclusively of having his name listed in the roundup article on February 27 had somehow won the primary by 600 votes over front-runner Pucs. The story began with the revelation that when Ed Heffernan had called a news conference to announce his candidacy, no one had shown up. After applauding the grassroots campaign Heffernan had run to win the nomination, the *Post* pronounced him a bigger underdog now than in the primary, gave a brief profile of his life, and detailed Morella's financial advantage in the race.

The *Post* next noticed the race on August 7, when Heffernan was identified as Morella's opponent in the final line of a story about Morella's testimony before a House subcommittee about a piece of legislation she had introduced that she freely admitted had no chance of becoming law. The pace of the campaign was clearly quickening, and the *Post* profiled Morella on August 9, 1992, as she prepared to go to the Republican convention in Houston to fight the majority of her party on the antiabortion plank in the platform. The article noted that she had been criticized for a lack of major legislative accomplishments, quoted Heffernan on the subject, but focused primarily on her image as a liberal Republican.

On September 24, in a story detailing the comparative fund-raising standings of all of the Maryland congressional races, the Post noted, in the thirteenth and fourteenth paragraphs of a sixteen-paragraph story, that Morella held a significant advantage over Heffernan and was heavily favored to win. On October 16, in another fund-raising overview of area races entitled "Incumbents Retain Lead in Collecting Campaign Contributions," the *Post* noted in the third paragraph that Morella had raised a great deal more than her "largely unknown" Democratic rival during the period.

On October 22, in a story appearing on page B-4 of the *Post*, Heffernan's 1986 experience with cancer was detailed. It was a sidebar to a longer piece appearing on page B-1 entitled "Queen of the Mountain; Heffernan Faces Long Odds Against Morella." That article was a profile of the race and discussed why Morella was perceived as unbeatable, although it did contain the nearest thing to a campaign dialogue to date. Heffernan criticized Morella for two specific procedural votes that he charged were attempts to weaken the overall legislation Morella supported in final passage, but the paper accepted Morella's explanation that "she was following her practice of voting with fellow Republicans for procedures that allow amendments to be offered on the House floor, even in cases where she supports the bill as it is." No explanation of the two specific votes was offered, nor did the reporter appear to question Morella on Heffernan's premise that she appeared to be trying to be on both sides of the issue.

Given the coverage to that time, it was no surprise when the *Washington Post* editorially endorsed Morella for reelection on October 25. It was also no surprise to read in the *Washington Post* "Maryland Weekly" section campaign wrap-up on October 29 that "Morella is running strongly despite the 8th District challenge of Democrat Edward Heffernan, a former congressional aide from Rockville" (last paragraph in a twenty-six-paragraph story). And finally, on November 4, it was revealed that Connie Morella "handily defeated" Ed Heffernan to win reelection, an outcome that should not have shocked *Post* readers whose sole knowledge of the race from the paper had been that Morella was unbeatable.

I picked this example because it illustrates several typical points of press coverage for the average "noncompetitive" congressional race. I generally tell challengers that they can count on only four stories in a campaign that the paper feels it has to cover: their announcement, their primary victory, a general profile at some point during the campaign, and their loss. Ed Heffernan's name appeared in the *Washington Post* ten times in the course of the election (and even his announcement was not covered). He was quoted in only three of the stories, including the one that detailed his bout with cancer. His substantive discussion of Connie Morella's record appeared once. Discussion of the issues he was running on, examination of his positions, scrutiny of his campaign claims—in other words, the kind of issues coverage that postelection convocations of journalists usually agree serves the public interest best—never appeared.

This was typical of the coverage of the majority of House races in the country and not unusual for some Senate races deemed uncompetitive as well. The decision is made (based on prior election results, money in the bank, general perception) that there is no story, therefore there is no coverage, and the initial decision becomes a self-fulfilling prophecy. The problems experienced by Ed Heffernan were by no means unique for a challenger, especially challengers running in areas within a major metropolitan area.

I worked on a congressional campaign in 1984 in the Philadelphia suburbs for a Democratic incumbent who won by 412 votes after a full recount. Our challenger was well funded, and the race was considered one of the top ten in the country. The campaign drew relatively little attention from Philadelphia media, although the television stations did carry half-hour joint appearances that were termed "debates," and a presidential appearance on behalf of the Republican challenger was, of course, exhaustively covered. The local paper (*Delaware Co. Daily Times*) gave the election daily coverage and did a credible job, but its circulation at the time was roughly 50,000 in a district where 250,000 people participated in the election at the voting booth. The race had never been perceived as being very close.

The media will say they have only a certain amount of space for politics, there is other news to cover, there is only a certain amount of air time, and the close contests must take precedence over the long shots. But it is important to stop and ask why a contest between two candidates with differing views, backgrounds, records, and philosophies to represent over a half million people in the U.S. House of Representatives is not in and of itself a newsworthy event in a democracy.

NEIL ARMSTRONG SYNDROME

Candidate A says the moon is a cold hard rock covered with craters. Candidate B says the moon is a huge chunk of green cheese with bites taken out of it. Local newspaper covers the exchange with a headline stating "Candidates Trade Charges About Makeup of Moon"—but no reporter calls Neil Armstrong to ask him what he actually found when he landed there in July 1969. Rather, Candidate A's evidence (scientific data, newspaper articles) will be cited but often given equal weight with Candidate B's evidence (whatever the campaign can find on somebody else's letterhead).

The "Neil Armstrong syndrome," as James Carville of Carville and Begalla, Inc. (Clinton's campaign management firm) used to dub this kind of coverage, is prevalent in local elections, particularly those that feature one or more candidates who have voting records in a legislative body. Reporters, when challenged on this, frequently defend themselves by saying their job is to report the news, not play the referee in the fight, and that citizens can make up their own minds about who is right and who is wrong. The problem with this line of reasoning is that without adequate objective information that logically should be provided by an impartial source (i.e., the press), voters can potentially be swayed by the loudest voice in the argument rather than by the accurate argument. Once again, the candidate with money gets the advantage in the local press.

There are several reasons arguments that should be factual end up being covered as charge-countercharge exchanges, and I by no means wish to leave the impression that one reason is some fundamental laziness of reporters who cover the races. From my personal observation, a significant factor goes directly to the editorial decision of who is assigned to cover local races. House and Senate elections occur in specific districts and states, yet the majority of the member's record is established in Washington, D.C., through votes, committee activity, and other achievements. This sets up a situation where many of the campaigns involving these officials are covered by political reporters within a state who have not covered federal issues and congressional activity and who bring a statehouse perspective to federal races.

In Congress, what appears to be a procedural vote is often the ball game for an issue. However, it is not always immediately apparent when that is the case. For example, the vote on the rule establishing a king-of-the-hill approach on contra aid in the House of Representatives was in fact the decisive vote on contra aid. It set the order of amendments in such a way as to guarantee the leadership's victory by letting moderate-to-conservative Democrats vote first for a larger amount of aid. Imagine explaining this in the heat of a campaign to a reporter who has three other assignments on deadline. In this situation, the vote for the rule was a vote for a smaller amount of aid (the last amendment), but it would have taken some knowledge, some digging, and some time to get to that reality. If Candidate A says he voted for the larger amount of aid (which he did, after voting for the rule) and Candidate B says that Candidate A voted to cut aid to the contras (which was the practical effect of the vote for the rule), the headline is likely to be "Candidates Trade Charges."

Most local media outlets do not have the resources to assign a single reporter to every race in their reader or viewership area, so one reporter often has responsibility for several races and several candidates. Again, the practical effect is more simplicity, less explanation of the complex truths that are the stuff of legislative records, and less coverage.

In 1986 a reporter for a large daily newspaper in Pennsylvania, assigned from the Harrisburg statehouse bureau to cover the Senate race, told me he did not plan to cover any exchanges based on voting records (in a race that featured a six-year Senate incumbent challenged by a twelve-year House incumbent). His reason was that votes were too easy to manipulate and distort. He had never worked in Washington—he did not have a bureau to research the records of the two candidates or to fill him in on the behind-the-scenes maneuvering that had produced a floor vote. He did not even have copies of the *Congressional Record* or *Congressional Quarterly*. Most reporters are not as brutally honest about their intentions, but the de facto outcome is usually the same. Substantive, intelligent coverage of the voting records of candidates, particularly incumbents, is sacrificed, an approach that leaves horse-race coverage and the cult of personality as the bulk of the information furnished to voters.

Timothy E. Cook, in his study of congressional coverage, observed (Cook, 1989, p. 114):

> Too much publicity in certain outlets is not a good thing. In fact, the less there is, the more the members themselves can use friendly weekly papers, newsletters, targeted mail, and the like to control the coverage. Put another way, even if the press does not give the member much coverage, this benign neglect ends up working to the incumbent's benefit. The irony of media strategies in the House is that more is not necessarily better.

Both PAC-like press behavior and the Neil Armstrong syndrome favor incumbents because incumbents generally have more money than challengers and both situations create a climate in which paid communication outshouts free media. But when the impregnability of incumbency is breached, the situation can be dramatically reversed, as the next section illustrates.

"PET ROCK" TIME: CHALLENGERS WITH MOMENTUM

Many political metaphors are war metaphors. Candidates go nuclear, outflank their opponents, set ambushes, and walk through minefields unscathed. Challengers are not even on the radar screen in many races—

but once they get on it, they are often guided in their attacks like a Patriot missile taking aim at a Scud, and guiding them is the local press. A challenger who gets "hot" suddenly becomes the beneficiary of celebrity coverage that I call "pet rock" coverage—the challenger is treated like a new fad.

Senate Republican leader Robert Dole complained in 1992 that the press had suddenly discovered "the year of the woman" when the Democratic Party fielded ten female Senate nominees, ignoring, in his view, the five extremely credible female Senate nominees in his party the previous election cycle. It is true that the coverage of the female Senate nominees, substantive women with records and things to say, often seemed as if reporters were shouting "They're new! They're different! They're women! They're mad about Clarence Thomas!" without drawing any distinctions between a Barbara Boxer with a House record of achievement and a Lynn Yeakel with years of community activism. But this type of coverage is not limited to women, nor was it uniquely a 1992 phenomenon.

In 1988 the *Today Show* ran a preannouncement profile of New Jersey senatorial challenger Pete Dawkins, a highly decorated veteran who had won the Heisman Trophy playing football for West Point. The profile lasted nearly five minutes—a biography piece that Roger Ailes, media consultant for Dawkins, could have run as an ad without editing. After the piece aired, an admiring anchor asked the correspondent if Dawkins had any flaws, and she responded that if he did she had not found them. Since the piece never looked at such Senate-race concerns as his knowledge of issues or of New Jersey (which he had only recently moved to, after allegedly "shopping around" for a state from which to run), her uncritical attitude can be forgiven. The most intense political scrutiny that Dawkins received was over the question of whether he ever planned to run for the presidency—nine months before he ever appeared on a ballot for any electoral office. (Dawkins was defeated by incumbent Frank Lautenberg and has not been a visible force in New Jersey politics since.)

WHAT GETS COVERED:
"PICTURES, MISTAKES, AND ATTACKS"

In the post-1988 presidential campaign forum at Harvard University, Roger Ailes put it best (Runkel, 1989, p. 136):

> Let's face it, there are three things that the media are interested in: pictures, mistakes and attacks. That's the one sure way of getting coverage. You try to avoid as many mistakes as you can. You try to give them as many pictures as you can. And if you need coverage, you attack, and you will get

coverage. It's my orchestra-pit theory of politics. If you have two guys on stage and one guy says, "I have a solution to the Middle East problem," and the other guy falls in the orchestra pit, who do you think is going to be on the evening news?

Ailes was talking about the presidential campaign, but the same rules apply to down-ballot races (races below the presidential level), with one exception—for the most part, pictures do not get covered. The campaigns must count on mistakes and attacks. Again, this plays into the strengths of the campaigns with the greatest resources because they can invest in the kind of opposition research that provides the best attack material and most evidence of opponents' mistakes.

Although it is repetitive, it bears repeating: Most news organizations do not have the money or personnel to do the in-depth investigatory reporting on candidates that one would like to see in order to make an informed decision. Campaigns, on the other hand, increasingly devote significant staff and energy to opposition research. The fruit of that effort is provided to the press—sometimes directly, sometimes anonymously, sometimes by a third party, but always most usefully when it is not traced back to the campaign but instead appears to be the product of individual reporting by a neutral press.

As communications director of the DSCC, I often was contacted by reporters from Senate-race states who wanted to know what our research showed about the opposition candidate, and I assume my counterpart at the Republican Senatorial Committee received the same inquiries. Likewise, campaigns often "shop" negative information developed by their organizations to find receptive reporters. In the 1990 U.S. Senate race in Iowa, information about incumbent Senator Tom Harkin's vacation home was offered to several reporters in the state before packages containing the same documents were mailed anonymously to reporters based in Washington, D.C.

But attacks and mistakes are fundamentally the way news is made in campaigns, beyond the furnishing of information about the opponent on a discreet basis. A policy speech is unlikely to receive much coverage unless it contains an attack on the opponent, and the more strident or negative the attack, the more likely it is to be covered. As former President Richard Nixon once observed, "A charge is usually put on the front page; the defense is buried among the deodorant ads."

In the 1990 Senate race in Oregon, the Democratic nominee was a businessman named Harry Lonsdale, an environmentalist and former president of a company called Bend Research. The race, which was written off by the Oregon press and particularly the Portland *Oregonian*, the dominant paper in the state, after Representative Ron Wyden decided against a challenge to four-term incumbent Mark Hatfield, received relatively little coverage until late September.

At that time, public polls showed that Lonsdale had pulled nearly even with Hatfield, and the race became a front-page story in the state. Hatfield, who had not waged a serious campaign up to that time, attacked Lonsdale on a number of issues, but the one most illustrative of the attack method was his call for an investigation of Bend Research on the charge of dumping toxic chemicals. The charge received exhaustive coverage not only the day it was made but during the crucial final phase of the campaign. The company's innocence was confirmed after the election.

There is a famous saying attributed to Lyndon Johnson: "Make him deny it." Making the opponent deny it—anything—is the surest way of getting prominent coverage in a local race.

SOUR GRAPES: VIOLATIONS OF
FEDERAL ELECTION LAW

Federal election law is complex and difficult. There are very few lawyers who are experts and no reporters who are assigned to it exclusively. State election laws vary, but the principle is the same: Few know it, fewer understand it, and no one covers it very well. But election laws are crucial to races, and in an era when ethics and issues involving money and politics have become decisive factors for incumbents at every level, it is worth looking at how these issues are covered.

On November 3, 1992, Georgia Senator Wyche Fowler won 49.6 percent of the vote in the general election (and was called the winner by many based on exit polling). Georgia law states that in order to win a general election, a candidate must poll 50 percent or above, so Senator Fowler was forced into a runoff.

A provision in federal election law sets limits on how much parties can spend in a Senate election. The limits are based on a formula that allocates $.02 per member of the voting-age population in a state. The National Republican Senatorial Committee (NRSC) had spent its legal limit on challenger Paul Coverdale before November 3, but the DSCC had roughly $200,000 in spending authority left on behalf of Senator Fowler. The FEC had ruled previously that there was only one spending limit to cover any election and a resulting runoff. But the NRSC asked the FEC to overrule that decision.

Whether one agrees with the FEC ruling or not (and I believe there is ample room for argument about the decision), the fact is that the Coverdale campaign and the NRSC made a conscious decision to violate federal law and spend far in excess of legal limits. Furthermore, this drew minimal attention from the state press corps when it occurred, although in an election decided by 15,000 votes it could have been key.

The DSCC filed a complaint with the FEC on the Thursday preceding the election (November 19, 1992) alleging that the NRSC had exceeded its spending authority by $225,405 in the race. This was covered November 20, 1992, on page E-11:1 of the *Atlanta Constitution*, the largest paper in the state, in a five-paragraph story in which Coverdell spokesman Bill Crane denied the NRSC was spending additional money in the state and seemed to acknowledge the problems surrounding additional NRSC spending by saying, "We would love to take more than we have taken, but we can't. We have been very careful about that." Subsequent news reports on the election indicated that the NRSC spent an additional $500,000 the final week of the election.

A reporter speaking to a DSCC attorney about the controversy, which became a story only after the election, asked him whether the complaints were not merely "sour grapes" on the part of Democrats who, had they had the funding, would presumably have spent above the legal limit as well. That is the typical press response to nearly every complaint filed, by candidates of both parties, so that the merits of the argument are ignored in the political analysis of the event.

Until the Georgia runoff, the classic case of party spending exceeding limits since modern federal election law was passed in 1974 had been the 1988 Senate race in Montana, where the NRSC had funneled money to the state party, which then spent it on behalf of its Senate candidate, again well in excess of federal law. (James Barnes of the *National Journal* [October 7, 1989, No. 40, p. 2471] did an extraordinary job of analyzing NRSC transfers to the state party and matching them against expenditures, an example of journalism rarely seen in this area.) The complaint, filed after the Republican challenger upset the incumbent, received little attention because "the election was over."

Of all the problems with local reporting on races below the presidential level, campaign spending is perhaps the most troubling in the context of the drive to legislate additional levels of regulation in the name of "campaign finance reform." Campaigns already know they can violate large sections of the code with relative impunity, because the reporters covering them (supposedly the watchdogs of the process) do not know the law, rarely in my experience make an attempt to learn the law, and view any complaints from the other side as either partisan politics or sour grapes.

Most violations of the law occur during the closing days of campaigns, when reporters are stretched thin, are traveling with candidates, and have little time or inclination to delve into the merits of an argument much less undertake independent research. Large sections of the law are already ignored by many candidates. For example, the disclosure requirements of occupation and employer on financial forms are not complied with by candidates across the board; in most cases, the press shrugs or wonders why the complaining campaign is so incompetent that its staff has not figured out some way to get around the rules as well. Once again, the advantage goes to the campaign with the resources.

CONCLUSION

The high level of cynicism currently held by American voters about their representatives in Washington is no accident. And although the editorial pages in this country are quickly filled with identified culprits—incumbents, PACs, political consultants, and some of the other usual suspects—I believe the press must take a serious look at the role it has played in the electoral process that has fed the cynicism.

What we have is a process in which voters are asked to judge which is the best campaign rather than to make a decision about the best candidate. The information voters are given—who has raised the money, who has the endorsements, who leads in the polls, who is seen as the likely winner, who has made the most mistakes—is composed of campaign judgments that often have little to do with what the candidates have said and done and are likely to do once in office.

To say that the process below the presidential level is stacked against challengers is to understate the case, because in many cases they are never allowed to enter the game to be dealt a bad hand. Many times their races are written off before they have begun, and even when candidates are awarded some coverage it is usually to note that they will not win. Those challengers who get to ante up at the table often resemble a pigeon playing a hustler. Too late, they discover that the audience has gathered to watch another sucker try to swim upstream.

To many candidates, press coverage of their campaign remains the greatest disappointment of their experience. They know the odds facing them when they enter the race—the money on the other side, the organization, the activists. They know they are underdogs. But they believe the odds can be overcome by their message if it can be heard, and many enter their respective races believing reporters can act as the great levelers in their races, so that even if the other side has more money (which is almost invariably the case when a challenger runs against an incumbent), the press will allow their message to be heard. Yet this is seldom the case.

The media say it is not their job to do the work of the campaign. Yet it is not clear what they think their job should be. Nearly all concede that the media have become key participants in the political process, not mere observers as their conceit once held, and so the question is begged: What

kind of participants? What is their job? The American political process
has evolved to one in which government is seen as a continuance of the
campaign, rather than the campaign being seen as a part of the dialogue
of governance. Because the emphasis is on smart politics rather than honest government, we can have a 1988 presidential campaign in which the
imminent collapse of the savings and loan system is never discussed (as
Howard Kurtz of the *Washington Post* outlined in his magazine piece of
November 29, 1992). Similarly, we can have five cycles of congressional
elections in which the budget deficit is never an issue for most voters.

Paul Taylor (Rosen and Taylor, p. 48) wrote that "with the decline of
political parties, journalists have increasingly become players in a political contest in which they also serve as observers, commentators, and referees." In describing campaigns to people, I have often drawn comparisons with trials, in which the incumbent is defendant, the challenger is
plaintiff, and the voters are the jury. Each campaign functions as a lawyer
for its candidate—presenting facts, witnesses, independent information,
and story lines. The role the press plays in this universe is that of judge—
deciding which information the jury gets access to, upholding or dis-
missing objections from either of the parties to the argument, and ultimately (through editorial endorsement) issuing its instructions.

That analogy is based on reality and does not represent a utopian view
of what should be as opposed to what is. The problem is that the American legal system works from a basis of law—there are reasons information is not allowed to reach the jury about prior conduct, for example—
but the press works from no established set of rules. Jay Rosen, associate
professor of journalism at New York University, argued that "to improve
their coverage of politics, journalists must do more than tinker with their
existing approach. They need to arrive at a vision of politics for which the
practice of journalism clearly stands" (Rosen and Taylor, p. 9). Rosen suggested the need for journalists to commit themselves to seeing their role
as promoting a public dialogue, which he called advocating a "public
politics." "In public politics, the activity that is most visible is discussion
and debate." Politics is seen as a continuing conversation, in which different rhetorics compete for influence, new debates arise and progress,
emergent facts are given various interpretation, and arguments interact
with events (p. 10).

In his first State of the Union address, President Clinton called on Congress to pass campaign finance reform, and legislation passed both the
House and the Senate, though in substantially different forms, in 1993.
But procedural fixes are not the only answer, or even necessarily the right
answer, to the cycle of cynicism and disengagement of the public. It is
true that money is the primary mode of communication in races below
the presidential level, but should not the news organizations that fail to

cover the candidates bear much of that blame? It is true that incumbents generally get covered on the news they want covered during their terms, but should not the news organizations that wait for the incumbents' press releases and news conferences share some of that responsibility? It is true that many challengers are not well versed on the intricacies of the offices they seek and do not have broad support at the beginning of their races, but should not voters be offered a dialogue about those representatives and offices and, ultimately, the opportunity to make the decisions themselves, rather than have the decisions made for them?

To close, I quote once again from the meeting of campaign decision-makers held at the Institute of Politics at Harvard's JFK School of Government December 2, 1988. The discussion was about the 1988 presidential campaign. The exchange that follows (Runkel, 1989, p. 136) is a summation of what smart politics has achieved on every campaign level.

> Roger Ailes: One thing you don't want to do is get your head up too far on some new vision for America because the next thing that happens is the media runs over to the Republican side and says, "Tell me why you think this is an idiotic idea."
>
> Judy Woodruff: So you're saying the notion of the candidate saying, "I want to run for President because I want to do something for this country" is crazy.
>
> Roger Ailes: Suicide.

10

Reporting Campaigns: Reforming the Press

JOHN R. PETROCIK

Contemporary students of elections, unlike our predecessors, are not very inclined toward reform. When we agree that something needs changing, it is often hard to develop a consensus about what constitutes a reform and not just a change. Examples abound. Voter turnout is low, but we cannot agree that low turnout is worth a lot of remedial effort or on how much turnout would increase if all the proposed reforms were instituted (see the various chapters of Crotty, 1991). Similarly, campaign spending has worried many, but not everybody agrees that candidates spend too much. It has also been hard to document many of the reputed evils (see, for example, Wright, 1985; Grenzke, 1989), and most proposals for change have flaws that raise the specter of still more problems (Alexander and Bauer, 1991, chap. 7).

THE PRESS AND ELECTORAL POLITICS

The mass media, like turnout and campaign spending, are part of the institutional environment of elections, and Anita Dunn's analysis of the elements of campaign coverage argues for reform in the volume and content of media coverage of down-ballot races (see Chapter 9). There are five specific problems she would like to see remedied. The first two deal with the amount of coverage, the second three with the content of the coverage.

First, the decline in press coverage from prominent to down-ballot offices is substantial, resulting in almost no press coverage of challengers for less prestigious, entry-level offices. Voters have little information about these races, no incentive to think about the choice, and a high probability of voting for the incumbent. Second, since voters do not know or hear much about down-ballot challengers, press coverage shapes a self-fulfilling prophecy. A candidacy deemed hopeless receives little cover-

126

age, and with little (or no) coverage, down-ballot challengers cannot achieve the recognition and credibility that are essential if they are to make their case before the electorate. It is the catch-22 of politics: Improbable challengers cannot raise funds or get attention for their campaigns, and challengers who cannot raise funds or get attention for their campaigns are improbable challengers—cause becomes effect becomes cause. Third, issue coverage is sparse and cynical, and most candidate assertions are taken at face value. There is no third-party refereeing by the press. Candidates are often allowed to misrepresent themselves, and voters, even conscientious ones, remain uninformed. Fourth, the press notices momentum and novelty, is often charmed by these aspects, and is inclined to produce puff pieces about candidates. It rarely publishes or broadcasts informed and sophisticated analyses of issues or a candidate's record. Finally, the press practices "gotcha" journalism that emphasizes mistakes, controversies, and attacks at the expense of issues and policy.

The point of this chapter is to put these "problems" in context. Anita Dunn's critique is persuasive. Her narratives ring true, and her objections to the conduct of the media could be repeated for elections many Americans have observed in their own cities and states. However, proposals to reform press coverage of politics and public affairs deserve the same cautious examination that we accord to proposals to remedy "problems" in any political institution. The press, we agree, spends a lot of time on nonpolicy and nonissue aspects of a campaign, and its pattern of coverage benefits incumbents. Does it follow that changing the operational code by which the press covers campaigns will reduce the incumbent advantage or improve the ability of voters to choose among the candidates? It might, but it might not. A press that is more attentive to campaigns and critical and searching in its stories about candidates might level the competition between challengers and incumbents; but it might only enhance the role of reporters in particular and the media in general, at the expense of the candidates, the parties, and party leaders. A critical and searching press might make voters more savvy and informed; but it might also only make them more bored by elections that already move many from inattention, to saturation, to annoyance within the short six-to-eight-week period that campaigns are visible to the public.

WHY ELECTIONS COME OUT THE WAY THEY DO

Before we accept Dunn's conviction that the media are a major influence on who wins, it is worth examining some of the systematic features of elections and politics that produce the process and outcomes that she has attributed, at least in part, to the media. I suggest that the most important determinants of election outcomes have little or no direct cause in the media. It is worth outlining what we know about a few of these non-media factors—partisanship, the issue environment of elections, and candidate recruitment—before we consider what the media might do better or not do at all.

Partisanship

The partisan predisposition of a voter is the dominating determinant of the vote, although a casual reader might be forgiven for believing otherwise. We have lamented the weakness of party identification in recent years and often pronounced its death, and some have treated it as a historical artifact. But it has been difficult to hold a funeral because the corpse keeps jumping up, running around, and muscling competing influences (Keith et al., 1992). Americans may not be the committed partisans that we tell each other they were 100 years ago, but neither are they indifferent to party. About 60 percent of the voters readily identify themselves as Democrats or Republicans, and after some hesitation, another 25 percent or so find no difficulty in confessing a preference for one of the parties. Further, most (about 75 percent on average) vote for the candidate of the party with which they identify in presidential and congressional elections.

These numbers have not been constant. There was a surge in independents in the late 1960s. Defection was quite substantial in the 1968, 1972, 1980, and 1992 presidential elections (the party vote was less than 70 percent), and three of these elections involved a third major candidate. On the other hand, party voting for president was higher in 1984 and 1988 (at 80 and 82 percent, respectively) than it was during the 1950s (at 77, 76, and 79 percent for the 1952 through 1960 elections). Congressional elections, examples of the low-level offices that escape much media scrutiny, repeat the pattern. They have been a bit less partisan since the middle 1960s (the party vote averaged about 81 percent through 1964 and about 73 percent since), but they remain contests in which about three-quarters of the votes are consistent with the partisanship of the voter (see Figure 10.1). We lack much systematic data for lower-level state and municipal elections, but what evidence we have indicates that they repeat the pattern observed for congressional elections.

Extrapolated to a county, district, or state, proportions such as those in Figure 10.1 become probabilities that fully explain why a candidate whose party matches the partisanship of a majority of voters is virtually assured of election and reelection.[1] The existence of residential patterns by social class, ethnicity, race, and religion and the correlation between

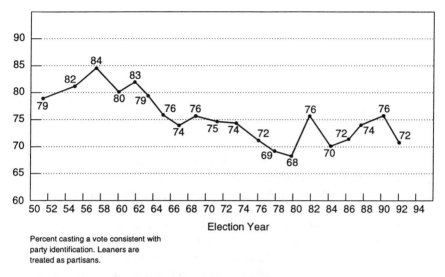

Percent casting a vote consistent with
party identification. Leaners are
treated as partisans.

Figure 10.1   Party Voting in Congressional Elections 1952–1992

these demographic differences and partisanship are the social and political facts that translate individual partisanship into majorities within districts. Historical inertia, individual preference, socially enforced conventions, and market factors have ensured that the political and social
heterogeneity of the United States is not uniform. Working-class and eth-
nic-minority Democratic cities abut white, middle-class GOP suburbs; a
Jewish or black south (or west, east, or north) side of town elects Democrats while an upscale Yankee north (or east, west, or south) side of town
consistently elects Republicans; and Republican rural sections of a state
compete with Democratic urban areas. This geographic lumpiness may
net out to a competitive electorate when viewed from the state or county
level, but it produces party bastions when geographical constituencies
coincide with partisan proclivities—and partisan and bipartisan appor-
tionments seek to ensure that they do.

The down-ballot elections that attract little media attention are particularly likely to be races in small constituencies in which reapportionment
has clustered like-minded partisans. Hard-to-defeat incumbents are the
result. A district (or a city, town, county) with a majority of Democratic
voters will elect a Democratic candidate while one with a majority of Republican voters will elect a Republican because voters overwhelmingly
vote for the candidate nominated by the party with which they identify.

Defection is possible and frequent but not common. We lack a complete account of the increase in legislative incumbency in the late 1960s, but the fact of incumbency has never been a mystery.

The Issue Environment

It took political scientists a long time to recognize that voters do have issue concerns in mind when they choose their leaders. They do not always care about all the matters about which they are quizzed in a survey, and they do not necessarily judge every candidate by every current public question, but policy choices and problems do shape candidate choice. Among the problems and choices that matter most are the condition of the public order as it is represented by the state of the economy, the reputed honesty and efficiency of the incumbents, and the citizenry's perception about whether the incumbents have handled problems well. Voters who are dissatisfied with the incumbent or feel that the country has not done well are, ceteris paribus, less supportive of the incumbent party and its candidates. These individual behaviors seem even more powerful in the aggregate, with election results strongly correlating with the environment of the election as it is indexed by such things as the approval level of the incumbent executive, the change in disposable personal income, or the level of consumer confidence (see Lewis-Beck and Rice, 1992, for a summary of much of this). Candidates of the incumbent party fare better when consumer confidence is high than when it is low, when the public approves rather than disapproves of the job performance of the incumbent president or governor, and when measures of economic health are positive.

Ambitious Politicians

Long before political scientists hung statistical estimators on these facts about voters and elections, the facts of partisanship and a "good (or bad) year" were not lost on politicians. In the American political system, as pursuing a career in politics has become even more common, this has had two important consequences. The first is that any officeholder taken at random puts considerable effort into ensuring his or her electoral security. He or she begins with a district drawn to partisan advantage and then works overtime doing whatever is necessary to enhance that partisan advantage and intimidate potential challengers (see Ehrenhalt, 1991, for case studies of ambition that make this point well; also see Loomis, 1988). The second consequence is that a politician with progressive ambitions, one seeking to move to a higher office, does not risk damaging his or her prospects by challenging an incumbent unless there is a reasonable chance of success (Schlesinger, 1966). In short, *politicians are long-term strategic players* on both sides of the incumbency divide. The incumbent anticipates a bad election environment in the future and protects himself or herself by acquiring and reinforcing every advantage—a favorable partisan base, a satisfied constituency, opinion makers who view his or her tenure positively, and so forth. Such incumbents will usually not draw a strong challenger since the most promising challengers cannot enhance their credentials by piling up losses (Jacobson and Kernell, 1983). The common and predictable result under these conditions is a lopsided victory for the incumbent.

Occasionally, the incumbent's advantages will diminish. When the incumbent's party is suffering from popular dissatisfaction with the state of the country, when redistricting has eroded the partisan base, or when a scandal has touched the incumbent, a challenger who knows how to campaign and how and from whom to raise money will perceive an opportunity. These opportunities arise idiosyncratically and systematically—idiosyncratically when a particular incumbent is weak and systematically when economic or governing cycles burden the incumbent party. But in contemporary American politics they arise with sufficient rarity that only a handful of challengers are accorded a reasonable prospect of defeating the incumbent.

THE PRESS KNOWS WHY ELECTIONS COME OUT THE WAY THEY DO

Political reporters also know that partisanship and good (or bad) years handicap candidates. There is, for example, no reason to treat a twenty-seven-year-old Republican lawyer with a small practice and a conviction that the incumbent's shortcomings have to be exposed as a strong competitor worth considerable news space when the incumbent is the Speaker of the House and from a district that is 60 percent Democratic by registration. Challengers of this sort can be applauded for standing up for their party and their beliefs, but no standard of newsworthiness dictates extensive coverage. There are many such hopeless challengers in any given media market, and one can understand why few reporters or editors would be prepared to give them much attention. Neither papers nor television stations have the space to report regularly on every election in their market.

How large could the reporting burden be? Very large indeed. Consider the example of Los Angeles in 1992: In Los Angeles County alone, there were 318 candidates—from the presidency (which had 6 candidates) down to local and special offices (which produced 159 candidates) and

40 propositions (which produced 80 different choices to be examined) on the November ballot. If we ignore county and special district offices and all candidates who were not running as Democrats or Republicans (but include Ross Perot), there were 87 state and federal candidates (seeking 43 offices) whose policy positions and record presumably merited some examination. On an average day the *Los Angeles Times* carries fewer than 40 headlined stories. Over the 63 campaign days from September 1 to November 3, this quantity enables the paper to print slightly over 2,500 new stories. If the *Times* had carried an average of three stories a day about the presidential election, one a day on the two Senate races, and, over the 63 days of the campaign, an average of five stories about each of the major national and state legislative races, it would have devoted almost 24 percent of its total editorial effort to elections. If the paper had spent any time with the thirteen state propositions on the ballot—and these things are very important in California, with advertising, charges, and countercharges that often drown out major candidate contests—election stories would have been almost 30 percent of all news in the paper.

For all this effort, municipal and county propositions, local elections, and candidates from the minor parties would have been ignored. Moreover, all the other state and national legislative elections occurring in the five-county metropolitan media market served by the *Times* would also have been ignored. National television news, which has even less news space (23 minutes each night) would have been overwhelmed by the demands of the election. The *Times* would have been the best source if it did as little as the preceding example suggests.

Moreover, the situation in Los Angeles is not unique, in kind or degree. Marquette County, in rural upper Michigan, has a population of barely 50,000, one television station, and one general newspaper. County elections accounted for about half the headlined stories on any given day, Marquette County had 20 offices and 56 candidates on the ballot in 1992, most of them down-ballot races (state legislator, county drain commissioner, county mine inspector). A news editor at the local paper (never mind the television station) with a commitment to reporting on candidates would have had to devote an incredible portion of his or her resources to elections (about 20 headlined news stories a day), more than could be justified unless nothing else of consequence were to happen during September and October.

But, of course, a lot of consequence does happen during these months, and news coverage cannot expand enough to report in detail on down-ballot races. No newspaper, not the *Los Angeles Times* or the *Marquette Mining Journal*, can commit 25 percent (or perhaps 50 percent in the Marquette case) of its hard-news space to elections, especially since the certain outcome of many of them limits their newsworthiness.

The Self-Fulfilling Prophecy

Challengers, especially those for less prominent offices, fail to receive the press coverage that might help them make their case against the incumbent. But that fact does not necessarily leave voters uninformed about important matters. The reason many races are ignored is that reporters, editors, and news executives are as knowledgeable as politicians and political scientists about the dynamics of elections, and they do not ignore their knowledge when making decisions about how to allocate scarce reporting resources. Someone who challenges a strong incumbent should not expect the media to aid that effort by repeating accusations and treating such candidacies as newsworthy. Editors can identify hopeless efforts, and they are unlikely to accord them a high priority for coverage because such campaigns do not produce news. When they do produce news—for example, the 1990 Hatfield-Lonsdale U.S. Senate race—the press quickly responds.

Does this approach consign many otherwise viable candidacies to sure defeat? I doubt that this is part of a self-fulfilling prophetic cycle in which the press predicts a likely winner and then proceeds to ensure the prediction by ignoring the predicted loser. This is not to argue that a candidate preference does not shape coverage and even contribute, if marginally, to the outcome. The point, rather, is that the volume of press coverage of a down-ballot race is, on average, only a minor influence on the outcome. The partisanship of the electorate, the political environment of the campaign, and the quality of the challenger are vastly more important than press coverage.

It is as hard to demonstrate the unimportance of the media as it is to document their influence unless there are systematic data—and we lack good systematic data. But the considerations outlined here do not lend much support to the notion that the press is a critical player in down-ballot outcomes. One way to see this intuitively is to examine the cases where challengers managed to "sneak up" on incumbents—as Lonsdale did on Hatfield in 1990. If candidates (like Lonsdale) are able to "come out of nowhere" with scant press coverage to boost them, why should we accept that the failure of a candidacy to develop any momentum is substantially caused by an absence of press coverage? It seems to me that the proposition that the press did it—that outcomes in scantily reported down-ballot races are heavily determined by the meager attention they receive from the press—is just not a proven proposition.

The Content of the Coverage

Issue coverage is quite sparse. Candidates spend most of their time talking about issues, their assets, and their opponent's liabilities, and the press devotes a majority of its resources to horse-race coverage, process, novelty, personality, mistakes, controversies, and attacks and counter-attacks. Why? The press behaves this way partly because of the definition of news and the behavior of the candidates and partly because of the characteristics of reporters.

THE CANDIDATES

Candidates are predictable. Figure 10.2 summarizes a measure of the attention paid to certain topics by the major party candidates in presidential elections from 1952 through 1988. The measure compares the emphasis the candidates placed on issues regarded as Democratic issue strengths compared to the emphasis placed on issues regarded as Republican issue strengths.[2] It is clear that Democratic candidates spent much more time raising Democratic than Republican issues; Republican candidates did just the opposite. Down-ballot candidates behave similarly. The result of this analysis is that if we know a candidate's party, we know the message—at least in broad outlines: Democratic candidates say things that Democratic candidates usually say; Republicans say things that GOP candidates usually say; a Democrat and a Republican rarely use each

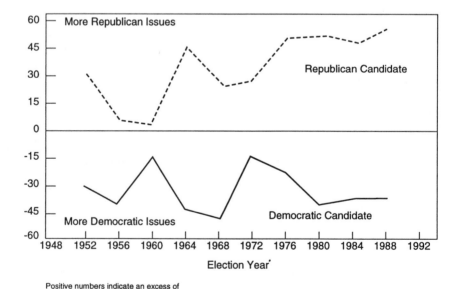

Positive numbers indicate an excess of
Republican over Democratic Issues. Negative
values indicate the opposite.

Figure 10.2   Candidate Issue Agendas in Presidential Campaigns: 1952–1988

other's lines. They rarely even talk about the same issues, since each is attempting to define the election as a struggle over issues at which his or her party is normally regarded as a better performer. Occasionally a candidate has an atypical position (a pro-life Democrat opposes a pro-choice Republican), but a candidate's speeches and commercials are primarily about the predictable issues and issue positions of his or her party (Petrocik, 1991).

Where is the news in this? After a couple of weeks of campaigning, the candidates are repetitive. Each talks about the same few issues repeatedly and, when asked, offers a position that is fairly similar to the median position of his or her party. Reporters have no incentive to cover such campaign activity because there is nothing new to report. If their stories are going to make the paper, if they are to satisfy their editors, they have to write something they have not written before—they need to report something new, not that the candidates continue to argue the same points over and over again (Semetko et al., 1991).

THE REPORTERS

The demands of the news cycle and the predictable and unchanging positions of the candidates partly explain the inattention to issues; the emphasis on momentum, charges, and countercharges; and the shift from puff pieces to exposé and from dismissal to rehabilitation. Momentum, accusations, candidate profiles, and antiprofiles that tell the reader about the "real" candidate allow the media to have something new but familiar to report every day of a campaign. Sometimes the competing and contrary stories lay out the differing viewpoints, issues, and personalities, but often they do not. However, they do provide something different for the next day's news.

But the news cycle alone does not dictate the coverage; the interests, knowledge, and capacities of reporters and editors are also important. The average political reporter knows a great deal of the lore of politics but is less well informed about the substance of policy and governing. The average American newspaper, even very large papers such as the *New York Times, Washington Post, Chicago Tribune,* and *Los Angeles Times,* does not, in my experience, have political reporters who are particularly knowledgeable about the policy issues raised in a campaign. They tend to be generalists who can quickly summarize what the candidates said about inflation, unemployment, the budget deficit, defense spending, crime, or education—not experts able to bring a sophisticated understanding to the candidates' comments. Usually they also lack a detailed knowledge of the history of legislation or the workings of the legislature, and this gap leaves them unable to contradict a dissembling candidate.

What they are able to do, in the post-Watergate age of skeptical journalism, is adopt a posture of belligerent neutrality. The belligerence is reflected in their cynicism about politicians and an inclination to regard all protests from political figures as self-serving. The neutrality is reflected in their inclination to define "evenhanded" as giving each candidate an equal chance to air accusations and complaints about the opposition.

CONCLUSION

The press is consequential because voters need information about candidates in order to make a choice that corresponds to their preferences. Limits on what a person can know and experience make the press the source of that information for most of us. It has been argued that the press fails to provide that information. Assuming this description is generally accurate, I would ask readers to keep the following doubts in mind.

First, I doubt that we have substantial evidence that the limited coverage of down-ballot races has a major effect on election outcomes. The determinants of voter behavior, candidacies, and the structure of elections leave only limited room for extensive press coverage to shift the outcome from what might be predicted given the partisanship of a district, the quality of the candidates, and the political environment within which the election occurs.

Second, candidates say and support predictable things, given their party, and they do so repetitively over the course of an election. Extensive coverage would reinforce the partisan proclivities of the voters since the press would be repeating largely partisan appeals by candidates who, for the most part, are backbenchers who cannot be expected to have independent positions of any consequence.

Third, reformers would have the press "promote a public dialogue." It is unclear how this would be done, although the clear implication is that the press would report each candidate's message and "require" responsiveness from the opposition. The limited space and time available to the press make this an unrealizable strategy for the score of down-ballot races that occur in every media market. Even if it could be implemented, would we want it? Is it a reporter's or an editor's task to tell a candidate what topics and issues must be dealt with during the campaign? Should the press decide when the answer is adequate? What theory of the democratic order confers such authoritativeness?

All of these matters need to be thought through in any plan to enhance the position of reporters and editors. We also need to anticipate the response of the candidates. Why would they cooperate? Candidates want to persuade voters, not defend themselves against a cynical and suspicious press that is able to dominate the information environment of the campaign. As it is, candidates feel that the press is imposing itself between them and the voters and either distorting or not communicating their messages. Their response in 1992 was to go on the networks' morning news and entertainment shows—*Arsenio Hall, Donahue,* the cable network MTV, and *Larry King Live.* This format reduced press editing of their messages to the voters and, overall, reduced press control over what they wanted to say to the electorate. Candidates want to debate their opponents. They want to be judged by their ability to dominate their opponents, not by how well they handle themselves in front of a constantly questioning press, which will always have the last word. It is unreasonable to think that candidates will acquiesce to a reporter's definition of the important issues and a satisfactory answer.

Finally, we should be cautious about demanding reforms from the media. Once the press reforms itself to the satisfaction of candidates, party leaders, campaign operatives, and interested observers, these same candidates, party leaders, campaign operatives, and interested observers will have implicitly committed themselves to satisfying the demands the press might care to make on them. The press is not characterized by the neutrality of the judge or the referee. Do we want the individuals and business entities that constitute the working press to serve as arbiters of our political process? That has not been their traditional role, and I have yet to see a compelling argument to give them this new status.

NOTES

1. The massive impact that a district's partisanship has on election outcomes can be observed by looking at a common wisdom about divided government in the United States. It is common to note how often districts diverge in their presidential and congressional vote. The figures have gone up, but the proportion of divergent results totaled less than 35 percent in 1988, and most of that came from the South. If the South is eliminated—and it probably should be, given that the region's massive partisan realignment has not yet eliminated the incumbent inertia of earlier Democratic classes—73 percent of the districts vote the same way for president and Congress. That figure is a triumph for partisan voting. Among the states that enjoy some of the most artful redistricting histories, the divergence in' results is even more modest. California, for example, had only 2 of its 45 districts vote inconsistently for president and Congress in 1988. Moreover, the two that split reelected their Democratic incumbents by small margins.

2. This analysis is based on a coding of issues in terms of whether they are normally regarded by voters as problems better handled by the Democrats or the Republicans. Problems better handled by one party are regarded as issue-handling strengths and give an advantage to that party's candidate when they are of concern to large numbers of voters. A brief version of the party system theory underlying this dynamic is presented in Petrocik, 1991. The theory is more fully elaborated and tested in chapters 2 through 5 of a manuscript in progress; see Petrocik, forthcoming.

11

Organizing the Field

WILL ROBINSON

It's four o'clock in the afternoon on election day. You're sitting in the campaign office drinking coffee, eating donuts, and worrying—but there is very little you can do this late in the campaign to impact the election. You can't buy any more television; you can't raise any more money, you can't even attack your opponent. Luckily it's also too late for your candidate to shoot himself in the foot—again. The success of your campaign will come down to your ability to get out your vote during the next three to four hours. If your campaign has a strong organizational operation working in the field, you may have thousands of people on the streets, hundreds of people working phone banks, and scores of election-day headquarters and turnout-control centers—all working to squeeze out two to four additional percentage points, and thousands of votes for your candidate, before the polls close. If your campaign doesn't have a field operation, now might be a good time to look for those lucky socks again. Although the candidate's schedule and the paid media portion of the campaign attracted most of the attention and almost all of the campaign's money, your field operation was probably the focus of most of your volunteers' and staff's time and may have taken months to set up—all in preparation for one day.

The purpose of the field operation of most campaigns is to do one or all of the following activities:

1. Repetitively move the campaign's message to key groups, areas, and individuals in an effort to persuade them to support your candidate.
2. Create programs to identify the key demographic groups, geographic areas, or specific individuals who are most likely to support your candidate.
3. Set up the structure and program to get those identified supporters out to vote on election day.

Members of the field operation may be assigned and execute other critical responsibilities within the campaign plan, including tasks such as getting the candidate on the ballot, raising money, recruiting volunteers, or staffing the candidate, but it is the completion of the field activities listed that will determine the ultimate success of the field operation.

VOTER CONTACT

Voter contact is the heart of the field operation. There are two types of voter contact: low intensity and high intensity. Low-intensity activities are not as individualized and are not high impact. Low-intensity voter contact programs can still impart information about the candidate and can still move voters, but these programs are not as persuasive as high-intensity programs, which are more individualized and more persuasive. Modern computer and electronic communication technology enables campaigns to communicate with voters in a very personal way. High-intensity voter contact techniques are often two-way communication. They give voters an opportunity to express their opinions about the candidate and the campaign. The voter identification programs—operations that organize staff or volunteers to talk to voters and ask them their candidate preference and their opinion on specific issues—are high-intensity programs. The voter identification programs give you information that allows you to contact voters in a more persuasive manner—such as sending a follow-up letter to all undecided voters from your phone bank discussing your candidate's position on the issue the undecided voter rated as most important.

You will probably concentrate the majority of your high-impact voter contact in areas where party performance is low. These are the areas where you have to do the most persuasion; you will also need to identify your supporters to get them out to vote. In high-performance areas you will be getting everyone out to the polls on election day, so you will not be doing much candidate preference identification before the push to get out the vote begins. These areas may be more suited for low-impact voter contact where the campaign does not need to persuade voters. The high-intensity contact in these areas will come during the get-out-the-vote phase of the campaign.

Low Impact Voter Contact

Literature distribution. Literature distribution—"lit drops"—is the most basic form of campaigning. Literature is placed securely on the door of houses in the areas or precincts that you want to cover. You do not want your literature blowing around the neighborhood. Be sure not to put any campaign literature in mailboxes; this is illegal. Volunteers usually do not knock on the doors or talk to voters during a lit drop. You can target literature by distributing it in persuadable precincts or by leaving it only at the homes of registered or target voters. Any type of literature can be left at homes during a lit drop, but literature left at the door is less likely to be read than anything sent though the mail.

Leafleting. This is similar to literature distribution, but the literature is distributed at public places such as shopping centers or college campuses. This approach is even less targeted than lit drops because you have little control over who is taking your literature or where these voters live. Leafleting is also volunteer-intensive. It does not require a lot of time or money, but it is definitely low impact.

Visibility. Visibility activities are those activities that get out the candidate's name and raise the profile of the campaign. There is usually very little message or issue information given out about the candidate with visibility items. You make these activities more effective if you add some message element to them. Include the slogan or a simple message such as "Cut Taxes—Vote for Smith" or "Bob Blowdry—Pro-Choice, Pro-Family." Some examples of visibility activities are buttons, bumper stickers, lawn signs, billboards, and human billboards. All increase the candidate's name recognition.

High-Impact Voter Contact

Door-to-door activity. This is one of the most traditional forms of voter contact and campaigning in the United States. A campaign or party volunteer or worker knocks on the door of a voter's home and talks to the voter. The volunteer often has been given an informal script to follow and usually leaves a piece of literature. This form of voter contact is also called canvassing and doorbelling. Often the canvasser attempts to determine the candidate preference of each household. This form of voter identification is not as effective as phone canvassing because voters are often unwilling to tell the canvasser negative information face-to-face. Door-to-door canvassing often produces a large number of undecided voters, but it is still a good way to identify supporters and recruit enthusiastic voters as volunteers. A larger amount of preparation and planning needs to be done for a door-to-door canvassing program than for a literature drop. The campaign needs to determine whether an area is canvassable and make sure that correct maps are found and the correct canvass areas are marked. The campaign also needs to create the correct voter list for the canvass area and create a system to identify and record candidate preference of each voter for follow-up and get-out-the-vote activity on election day. The door-to-door operation can be made more effective by concentrating on the more persuadable areas first and talking to only those households that have registered or target voters.

It is not necessary to have all door-to-door programs identify voters for candidate support at the door, especially if there are several canvasses planned or if the voters are to be identified through a phone canvass. In areas of high Democratic support, it probably does not make sense to identify individual voters, because the campaign will get everyone out to vote on election day. A few campaigns have used paid canvassers with some success, but issue-oriented organizations have had better success with paid canvassers. One of the first canvass activities a campaign may have to do is to go door to door in states where candidates must collect signatures on petitions to get on the ballot; this may be an early organizing task that should not come as a surprise. Door to door is a very high impact form of voter contact. It is a time- and people-intensive operation that can also cost the campaign some money for materials and staff.

Candidate activity. The most effective form of voter contact is the candidate asking someone face-to-face for his or her vote. In a race of almost any size, your candidate will spend a lot of time asking people for their vote. Even if your candidate is running for the U.S. Senate or even president, your campaign can use personalized direct mail, specialized canvasses, and targeted media buying to give voters the impression that they are being personally solicited for their vote. Still, the candidate's time, although one of the most valuable resources you have, is scarce. Obviously the most persuasive voter contact activity would be for the candidate to go to each voter, sit in the voter's living room, and personally make the case to the voter. Although this would be the most effective approach, it is impractical for all but the smallest races.

The best way to look at allocating your candidate's time is to think of what activities only the candidate can do or can do most effectively. Probably the most important activity the candidate can do is to raise money. A substantial part of the campaign schedule will be taken up with the candidate attending fund-raising events or making fund-raising calls.

The second most important activity of the candidate will be to generate free media. Even the most basic techniques for contact between the candidate and voters should be set up with this in mind. A candidate could speak to large rallies and shake thousands of hands and still reach only a fraction of the people who could see him or her on television. Even if the candidate is going door to door or holding a coffee hour, making sure a photo or story appears in the local weekly newspaper will make the event twice as successful. Be sure to bring a campaign camera to all events. Most candidate activity is time- and people-intensive, but the setup cost for some events can get very expensive. In addition to media events, some of the more basic contact activities for the candidate are to attend coffees and town meetings, go door to door, and appear at shopping centers, rallies, and main-street tours.

Precinct captains. The second most effective voter contact after direct communication by the candidate is for a family member, friend, or neighbor to tell a voter favorable things about the candidate. It is usually a very credible endorsement. The idea behind a precinct or block captain program is to get the volunteer to persuade the people he or she knows best to support the candidate and get them out to vote.

Direct mail. Over the last decade direct mail has become a very powerful campaign tool. As television and radio costs have skyrocketed, direct mail has become more cost-effective. Direct mail can be used to send longer targeted messages directly to target voters. It can be used as a follow-up to other voter contact activities. Direct mail can also be used to assist with getting out the vote by sending reminder postcards or Mailgrams to favorable voters. Direct mail has three advantages over other forms of voter contact. First, it can be extremely well targeted. Polling, electoral and demographic targeting, and a good voter file give you all of the tools you need to design a targeted message that can be sent to a specific audience. You can send an anti–property tax message to older voters who do not have children in the school system. You can send a pro-choice message to persuadable unmarried women. Second, you can inexpensively send repetitive contacts to the same audience. Some campaigns send seven to nine pieces of mail to targeted audiences. Not all of the pieces need to be personalized. The same tabloid can be sent to four or five different target groups. The final advantage is that direct mail is a "silent killer." It is very difficult for the opposing campaign to figure out when you sent a piece and to whom you sent it. It is very difficult to respond in kind to a negative mail piece.

You can also use the mail to shore up support in any group or area you need to work. For example, you could mail a social security piece to seniors. The major disadvantage is that mail is not necessarily read by the voter. It has been calculated that 35–45 percent of those who receive direct mail read only the headlines and the picture captions. Another 35–45 percent read only the headlines and the subheadlines. It is unlikely that all of the remaining 10–30 percent of the voters who read literature cover to cover contain all of your target voters.

In general, direct mail is expensive but cost-efficient and is less time-consuming than other forms of voter contact. Although most direct-mail programs are not volunteer-intensive, there are some provisions written into federal law that give federal candidates some advantages in using volunteers to assist in putting together direct mail. If you decide to put out direct mail on your own, you should also check with the post office to understand what is required to get reduced-rate bulk mail permits and what restrictions there are on size and weight of an individual piece. State and party committees can also send out mail at a greatly reduced rate in support of their candidates. You should check with officials of your state party or relevant party committee to determine what mail program, if any, they can create for your race.

Phone banks. Phone banks are one of the most commonly used forms of voter contact for voter identification and voter turnout. Phone banks can also be used to recruit volunteers, raise money, and build crowds for events.

MESSAGE

The previous section focused primarily on the mechanics of voter contact. The physical identification of supporters and the mechanics of moving them to the polls are critical, but the communication of the candidate's message is still the major function of the field operation. The paid media program has the primary burden of getting out the message, whereas the field operation reinforces the overall message and moves specialized messages to target voters and areas. The field operation also has the primary responsibility of getting out the candidate's message where the campaign has been unable to afford to buy television and radio. In addition, the field operation can contribute greatly in the creation of free media.

The best recent example of a campaign having message discipline and using the field operation to create free media is the Clinton-Gore campaign in 1992. A conscious decision was made by the campaign's field director, Michael Whouley, to use the field operation to create free media. Each week the campaign determined what the theme was for that week. Each state operation was sent a detailed memo outlining free media ideas. Each state was responsible for generating newspaper, radio, and television stories on the campaign message each day. "Our emphasis was on trying to speak with one voice across the country," said Simon Rosenberg, communication director for the state operation. A special effort was directed to generating free media outside of major markets. "It was difficult to get the media to cover events in a large city like Detroit, but the Detroit media market is only 45 percent of the state. It was much easier to get television and radio in Grand Rapids and Lansing," added Rosenberg (Phone interview, November 25, 1992).

The Clinton campaign was adept in two ways. First, it used modern technology very well. A computer network transmitted issue material and press information instantaneously to state campaign offices where it could be quickly rewritten into local press releases. The campaign also used radio and television satellite feeds in smaller markets very well. Second, the campaign was well integrated. The mail sent by the individual states contained the same message as was on the television commercials and reinforced what Bill Clinton and campaign surrogates were saying. A national grassroots-for-change program was set up that involved more than 10 million people through a precinct captain–type program that gave them a "doorstep kit"—basic campaign tools—and integrated them in the overall campaign.

VOTER CONTACT PROGRAMS

The campaign manager and field director must decide what types of voter contact programs are needed. This decision is driven by the strategic objectives of the campaign. If the candidate has low name identification, the campaign will have to spend its resources sending information to target voters about the candidate and the candidate's issues before any voter identification programs begin. If the campaign has financial assets, this can be accomplished by early purchases in media and a series of large or frequent mailings to voters targeted by polling information. If the campaign has less money, the campaign can organize a large number of volunteers to drop literature in targeted precincts. If the campaign has a large number of volunteers and sufficient time, a series of door-to-door canvasses can help raise name identification. If the campaign determines that it needs to attack the opponent, it can design a voter contact program using the same combination of techniques depending on the amount of resources available.

The sequence of these voter contact techniques is important. It is unlikely that you will have a successful phone canvass to identify support if your candidate has 5 percent name recognition. It is probably also unwise to attack your opponent without giving the same audience a reason to vote for your candidate. The proper sequence of a voter contact program will vary greatly from campaign to campaign. Most campaigns concentrate the early voter contact and voter identification programs in precincts that are low performance. Remember, there is no right or wrong way to organize a field operation.

Get Out the Vote

The success of the field operation depends on your ability to get out the vote (GOTV) on election day. All of the elements of the field operations should integrate into the final GOTV effort. Most field operations are divided into two parts: field operations done in low-performance areas and the operations done in high-performance areas. For the purposes of this section, a high-performance precinct is any precinct that has over 65 percent party support. A low-performance precinct is one that has less than 65 percent party support. The voter contact done in low-performance precincts is both high intensity and low intensity. The emphasis is on persuasion and on identifying individual supporters of the candidate through phone banks or door-to-door canvassing. The campaign should get only identified supporters out to the polls; getting every voter out on election day would bring out supporters and nonsupporters and would be counterproductive. The focus of voter contact in high-performance precincts is "showing the flag"—making sure the level of support is maintained and a structure to get out the vote on election day is set up. Very little persuasion is going on in high-performance precincts; the focus is to get out the vote on election day.

The types of activities used during GOTV differ depending on performance level of the precinct, but there are a few points that are important to review for both high-performance and low-performance precincts.

Absentee ballots. More and more states are allowing people to vote before election day through the mail by using absentee ballots or by going to early-vote locations—polls that are open days to weeks before election day. A number of states still require voters to be out of state or out of their home county in order to vote absentee. Others still have onerous absentee-ballot application guidelines such as requiring a notarized application, but the trend has been to liberalize the absentee-ballot process. In states like California and Texas, some regions have had 25–40 percent of the electorate vote by absentee ballot or through early voting. You need to check with your state and local board of election and research both the legal requirements and local traditions concerning absentee voting. If you decide that an absentee-ballot program is worthwhile, it should be integrated into your overall voter contact program. Some states allow the campaign to print its own absentee-ballot applications and mail them to large numbers of targeted voters.

Legal issues. All but a few of the elections in the United States are conducted in an honest and error-free environment. Still, it is worthwhile to prepare for the worst. You should have your legal team in place to assist in voting irregularities, machine breakdowns, and voter challenges. If you expect a close election, your lawyers should research your state's recount procedure, prepare fill-in-the-blank motions, and obtain the after-hours location and phone numbers of relevant election officials and judges. A few hours of preparation for a potential recount can make the difference between winning and losing. Your legal team should also speak at all election-day trainings to instruct the workers.

Mail. Your election-day mail must be planned weeks in advance of election day. You should send the mail with enough lead time that it arrives at the household the weekend before the election. Mail that arrives the day after the election is a waste. The GOTV mail pieces should be sent to known supporters and should be short and to the point. This is a time to motivate supporters, not persuade voters. If the mail can be computer matched, it should contain the location of the polling place and a number to call for a ride on election day. In locations where there are a large number of polling places, the campaign may want to have volunteers with precinct locators (books or printouts that match addresses with polling place locations) available on the election-day assistance line to help supporters figure out where to vote. The audience for your election-day mail should be your volunteer file, donor list, identified supporters in low-support precincts, and all voters in high-support precincts.

Food. Workers cannot be expected to be on their feet for sixteen hours without something to eat. All election-day workers should be fed. Food should be delivered to poll watchers and poll workers. A poll worker who is not delivered food may have to leave the polling place to eat, and there is a chance the worker might not return. Nothing is more disheartening for a worker than to see the opposition workers brought food and a drink during the day.

Training. The final element of your preelection activity is your training for election day. Formal training sessions should be held for each of your election-day worker operations. In addition, written instructions and materials should be prepared well in advance of election day for each of your election-day assignments. You should also put together election-day kits for assignments such as poll watcher or poll worker, especially when the worker will be out of touch with the campaign office for most of election day.

GOTV in Low-Performance Precincts

Precinct house. In higher-priority precincts, the campaign should locate a volunteer who lives in the precinct who is willing to let his or her house be used as a "precinct house" on election day. The door-to-door canvassing for the precinct is run out of the precinct house; in addition, some local GOTV phoning may be done from the volunteer's home.

Phones. Phone banks and at-home phoning are two of the primary ways the campaign will get out the vote in low-performance precincts. A simple GOTV script is prepared that conveys a sense of urgency about the campaign. Voters are reminded of their polling place and where there is a ride program if they need transportation. Some phoning is done from volunteers' homes in the precincts and some may be done from paid banks, but the bulk of phoning will probably be done by volunteers working out of phone banks. The campaign should look for law offices, labor unions, real estate offices, and other business offices that close at 5:00 P.M. to locate phones for the final GOTV push on election day. Locating these phones is an enormous task and should begin as soon as possible. It is not unusual for some large campaigns to use 300–500 volunteer phones on election day. The GOTV phoning may begin the weekend before election day, but all identified supporters should get a call on election day. Volunteers should not start making phone calls until after 10:00 A.M. The phone banks can be used earlier for other activities, such as 4:00–5:00 A.M. wake-up calls to election-day workers. The phones used for GOTV should not be the same phone lines used by the election-day workers to check in. A simple marking system should be developed to use with the GOTV lists. In some low-performance precincts, a duplicate alphabetical list of supporters is given to poll watchers inside the polling place. The watcher crosses off the names of supporters as they vote, and the list is then periodically picked up by a runner or phoned in to the precinct house or phone bank so that people who have not yet voted can be phoned or canvassed. This system allows you to avoid calling those who already voted.

Door-to-door activity. A large percentage of the door-to-door activity in low-performance precincts can be run out of precinct houses or local headquarters. The campaign uses a computer to print out the name, phone, and address of each identified supporter on a card. The cards are then organized into a number of "walking routes"—each route starts and ends at the precinct house. Sometimes the cards are put on rings or into small decks of cards. Depending on the size of the precinct, between three and five volunteers are given fifty to seventy-five households each. The volunteer walks the route three to four times during the day (for example, 10:00 A.M., 2:00 P.M., and 4:00 P.M.). The volunteer knocks on the door of each identified supporter along the route and encourages the person to vote. If a ride program exists, a ride may be offered. The supporter's card is removed from the deck when the person's name is crossed off the watcher's list or the person claims to have voted (be sure to double-check). This is a very efficient but time-consuming GOTV method. If there is no watcher, the volunteer canvasses every household; when voters tell the volunteer they have voted, the cards are removed from the deck. If there is no precinct house, the canvasser is sent to the precinct by a local headquarters. The canvassers start and end their walking routes at a central meeting place (usually the polling place.) Areas that are too rural may only be phoned. Sometimes the most effective GOTV method is to use both canvassers and phoners in key precincts. This requires time and personnel and is expensive, but it is the most effective form of GOTV activity in low-performance precincts.

Poll workers. Depending on election law and local custom, the campaign may want to place workers in front of individual polling places to hand out last-minute sample ballots. This is not a wise use of volunteers but is a political necessity in some areas. The poll workers should be pulled to do GOTV canvassing or phoning when possible. Workers in front of the polls may be more valuable in lower-ballot (low-information) races because of the falloff from voting for the top of the ticket. Poll workers are also valuable at the end of the day if the polls are crowded to keep people in line. This is not an expensive program, but it is time-consuming and volunteer-intensive.

Poll watching. Poll watchers have an important job in low-performance precincts. They keep track of which of the campaign's supporters have voted and report this to the campaign. The poll watcher may need a watcher's certificate issued by the county or the state. The residency and application requirements for a certificate may vary from state to state. While in the actual polling area, the watcher may observe and hear the voters call out their names, but the watcher may not engage in any electioneering. You may want to make sure the watcher has a chair and a clipboard. If the campaign is not checking voters, it is unlikely that a watcher will be needed all day. The watcher should check counters and seals on the machines or box in the morning and be present for the tally in the evening. All watchers and workers, especially paid staff, should remain in the area of their polling place until it looks as if the election is called. If they head straight for the victory party, they may have to be sent back to their area to do additional work in the case of a recount.

Ride program. Some campaigns may decide to offer rides to supporters. This can be done locally through the precinct headquarters or on a city- or regionwide basis with a central dispatcher. The campaign may print a central number to put on the election-day literature for an area or county. This is a good activity for volunteers who have cars and cannot canvass. The campaign should make sure each ride center confirms the address of the person who wants a ride along with a time and a phone number. The campaign should make sure that the drivers have well-marked cars (e.g., posters). A driver should also wear a campaign hat, button, or T-shirt so the supporter will know it is an official ride—and safe to get in the car. The campaign should check on the insurance liability involved in giving rides. The campaign may want to concentrate on giving seniors rides early in the morning on election day. These drivers can also be used to deliver literature, move election-day workers, and deliver lists and food. This activity is time- and volunteer-intensive and can be expensive if the campaign reimburses volunteers for gas or uses paid drivers.

Election-day volunteers. A special effort to recruit election-day volunteers should begin as soon as the campaign begins. Everyone should be recruited. Anyone who volunteers any time at all during the course of the campaign should be recruited to help on election day. The volunteer coordinator should make sure to have the correct name, address, and phone number of each volunteer. When possible, you should assign the volunteer an election-day task as the person is recruited. You should calculate the number of election-day shifts you will need and recruit twice as many people as you will need. You can always canvass a precinct twice if everyone shows up. The person who recruits the volunteers should also dispatch them when possible, because the volunteer recruiter can match ability or restriction (e.g., a problem walking) with the task. This is time-consuming and very volunteer-intensive and may still cost some money.

GOTV in High-Performance Precincts

Door-to-door activity. This activity differs in a high-performance precinct from in a low-performance precinct. In a high-performance precinct, every registered household is canvassed and pulled out to vote. Some campaigns use "flying squads"—volunteers who rapidly canvass the precincts that have the lowest turnouts. The flying squads are dispatched by the turnout control centers. The accuracy of the phone numbers in some high-performance areas is not very good, so the canvassing may be the primary form of voter turnout. If a precinct has habitually low turnout, a number of canvassers may be assigned to canvass a precinct all day, and they may be assigned rounds similar to canvassing in a low-performance precinct. This is a time-consuming and volunteer-intensive activity. It can also be very expensive if the canvassers are paid.

Poll workers. The duties of the poll worker are the same as they are in the low-performance areas. The high support of the precinct makes the presence of poll workers even more unnecessary; these volunteers and workers are better used to get the voter out in the precinct. This is a time- and volunteer-intensive activity and can be expensive if the workers are paid.

Poll watching. It is unlikely that high-performance precincts will need full-time poll watchers. Poll watchers and workers are still important at the end of the day if the polls are crowded to keep people in line. The watcher periodically checks on turnout figures and phones them into the turnout control center. The watcher also should check counters and seals on the machines or box in the morning and be present for the tally in the evening. The rest of the time the watcher should be phoning or canvassing. The same rules for watchers' certificates and for a recount apply to these watchers. This is a time- and volunteer-intensive activity, and it can be expensive if the workers are paid.

Phoning. Unlike in low-performance precincts, most of the phoning is done by phone banks. The order of the precincts called by the phone banks is determined by the targeting. On election day the priorities may change because of the turnout patterns. Election-day phoning is time- and volunteer-intensive. If paid phoners are used it can be very expensive.

Ride program. The program is similar to the one in low-performance precincts, although in high-performance areas the sound truck or van used to move flying squads may double as a ride van. The canvassers may offer immediate rides in the van as the canvassers move down the street. This is a volunteer-intensive and time-consuming activity. It can be expensive if the vans are rented, gas is reimbursed, or the workers are paid.

Sound truck. The sound truck is a traditional American GOTV device. It is a truck or car with a loudspeaker on top. A GOTV message with music is played over the loudspeaker to draw people's attention to the race and to remind them of election day. Obviously, the truck should be driven only in high-performance areas; you do not want to remind your opponent's supporters of election day. The efficiency of the sound truck can be improved by prerecording messages and music on loop tapes. This will allow the message to be played repeatedly over the speaker on a tape recorder and will eliminate the dangers of an open microphone. Each driver of a sound truck should be given a set of maps, each one containing a route for a target precinct. The driver should check in after completing each route and be reassigned to drive a route in an area that has lower turnout, in the same way as a canvasser. The is a time-consuming and expensive activity, but it is not very volunteer-intensive.

Radio. Purchasing GOTV radio spots is important if you have a targeted demographic group of supporters who listen to a particular station. If you have minority support, you can often work with local disc jockeys to assist you in raising turnout through nonpartisan announcements. This is an expensive activity but is not time- or volunteer-intensive.

Turnout control center. The turnout control center is the heart of a high-performance GOTV operation. Each region has a turnout control center that monitors turnout and reallocates GOTV resources (phones, canvassers, sound trucks) during the day to the precincts with the lowest turnout. A "reverse phone bank" is set up where the watchers or canvassers check turnout and phone in the total voter turnout at preset times. A phone is set aside for every seven to ten target precincts. The turnout figures are then calculated and resources are sent to those precincts that need them the most.

It is important to note that this is a worthwhile activity if you have the ability to shift workers between areas. If you do not have enough people to shift to priority areas, you should make your initial assignments and keep them there. It would be a waste of resources to set up a turnout control center just out of the intellectual curiosity of monitoring turnout. You should also not waste time sending groups of workers miles across cities to canvass areas far apart from each other. Depending on the size of the race, you may have from one to several dozen turnout control centers working high-performance precincts. This is a time- and volunteer-intensive activity. It can be expensive if workers are paid or large number of phones are involved.

CONCLUSION

The duties, structure, size, and budget of the field operation will depend on the strategy and objectives of the overall campaign. Some very successful campaigns have had no field operations, and even the best of field operations cannot overcome a twenty-point deficit on election day. In general, the more local the political office or the smaller the campaign, the more likely a field operation will be needed. But it depends on the situation. Senate and gubernatorial races in some of the largest states have been decided by very few votes, and many of these candidates won in large part because of their field operations.

12

Field Work, Political Parties, and Volunteerism

PAUL S. HERRNSON

Field work has traditionally been a major element of American election campaigns. Discussions of field work conjure up images of armies of campaign workers knocking on doors first to register voters and then to bring them to the polls. The topic also brings to mind a conception of politics dominated by urban political machines and corrupt party bosses. At the turn of the twentieth century, often labeled the golden age of politics, a well-heeled team of field workers who could assess constituents' needs and deliver their votes was a critical foundation for the power of any political organization or candidate (Sorauf, 1980). Currently, candidates and parties need more than a crack field staff to compete successfully in electoral politics. Nonetheless, field work remains an important campaign activity.

Campaign field work clearly does not capture as much attention in the press as do public opinion polls, television commercials, fund-raising events, and other contemporary election activities. Yet voter identification, registration, targeting, literature drops, and get-out-the-vote drives remain central components of modern elections. For many bottom-of-the-ticket elections, such as races for city council, the state legislature, and even a few House seats, field work remains the major activity of the campaign. Moreover, field work is one of the few areas of campaigning in which political parties and volunteers continue to play an important role.

Will Robinson's chapter (Chapter 11) is an excellent primer on campaign field activities. It demonstrates that although some of the techniques used to conduct field work have changed, the goals of these activities remain essentially the same as they were during the golden age, namely learning about, communicating to, and mobilizing voters. Robinson provides step-by-step instructions on how to assemble a field organization and develop and implement a field strategy. He also integrates the field operation into the total campaign organization, enabling one to envision how field work is related to campaign targeting, fund-raising, and communications. First-time campaigners and seasoned veterans should find the guidelines, tactics, and examples in Robinson's chapter useful. Campaign volunteers—who stuff envelopes, deliver campaign literature, and drive voters to the polls on election day—will get a broad overview of how the specific tasks they have been assigned fit into the overall campaign effort. Political scientists—who tend to be well versed on the influence that the economy, presidential popularity, candidate qualifications, and the distribution of partisanship among voters have on elections—will get a close-up look at another force that affects election outcomes: the campaign, particularly the nuts-and-bolts activities generally grouped under the heading of grassroots politics.

The main focus of this chapter is on three aspects of campaign field work: voter identification and targeting, campaign communications, and voter mobilization. First, I summarize how each of these activities is performed. Then, I discuss the impact that field work has on election outcomes. Finally, I consider the implications field work has for political parties and volunteerism in contemporary election campaigns.

VOTER IDENTIFICATION AND TARGETING

One of the first activities conducted by a campaign organization is voter research. Candidates and their campaign staffs must determine which groups of voters are inclined to support them, to support their opponent, or to be undecided. Voters have traditionally been categorized on the basis of geography, religion, ethnicity, race, income, education, profession, and party identification (Campbell, et al., 1960). More recent classifications are based on combinations of age, ideology, and lifestyle. Some of these include voters who are described using terms such as "yuppie" and "new-collar voter." In cases where issues form the core of a voter's political identity or are the primary motivation for an individual's political involvement, the issue itself may be used to define the group, as is the case with pro-choice or pro-life voters.

Once voters have been classified into relevant groupings, and it has been decided which groups are likely supporters, unlikely supporters, or "undecideds," campaign strategists seek to determine the intensity of each group's support. Strategists use historical data to speculate whether particular groups of voters are likely to cast their ballots for the candidate (or party) no matter what, or if their support is soft and in need of some reinforcement. If the latter is true, what can be done to solidify the bloc's support? Sometimes a group's loyalty is contingent upon a show of support for the group's position on a specific issue. Strong support for Israel, for example, is generally considered useful in shoring up strength among Jewish voters, just as a strong stand on civil rights has been help-ful in attracting the support of blacks.

In addition to group loyalties, campaigners also consider group size and turnout level when designing their targeting strategies (Axelrod, 1972). Obviously, it makes more sense for candidates to allocate scarce campaign resources in the direction of large groups that vote in relatively large numbers than to direct those resources toward small groups that have low levels of voter turnout. Building a winning coalition requires candidates and their campaign staffs to perform a kind of balancing act. Campaigners must consider the size, turnout, and loyalty of different segments of the population when deciding who their targeted groups will be. Once the target audiences are determined, the next step is to use demographic, geographic, and polling information to create a campaign plan that determines where voter mobilization activities will be con-ducted, the content of the candidate's message, and where and by what means that message will be communicated to voters.

During the golden age of political parties, field workers were largely responsible for gathering voter information, identifying the target audi-ence, and then implementing the campaign plan. At the lowest level of the party organization, precinct captains kept in touch with voters living in their neighborhoods and collected information about the size, proba-ble turnout, and loyalty of different voting blocs. They assessed the kinds of appeals (most of which were patronage-based) that could be used to win support and formulated a plan for communicating those appeals to voters. Their field work formed the foundation for the campaign plan. A summary of the information the precinct captains collected was commu-nicated to ward leaders, who used it to formulate their own campaign plan. Ward leaders used the information to allocate money, patronage jobs, and other resources among precinct leaders and to set a broader campaign strategy. Following this the ward leaders transmitted their campaign plans and a summary of the information they had collected from the precinct captains to city or county party leaders. These individ-uals, in turn, formulated their own campaign strategies and passed the information they had received up to state party leaders who used it to develop strategies for statewide races. Finally, the information made its way to the national level, where national party leaders used it to create a national campaign strategy.

Although all presidential, most congressional, and many state-level campaigns now develop their targeting plans using demographic re-search, polls, voter files, and computers, the field staff continues to play an important role in many campaigns. Local candidates, their support-ers, and, in some areas, party workers continue to traverse their neighborhoods knocking on doors and trying to learn about whether citizens intend to vote, whom they support, and whether they have any specific questions or concerns they would like the candidate to address.

MESSAGE AND COMMUNICATIONS

Getting the message out is a central part of any campaign. If a campaign is unable to define itself, it risks being defined by its opponents. Allowing others to define one's campaign, as Michael Dukakis's 1988 bid for the presidency demonstrated, is a recipe for certain disaster. Modern technology has furnished campaigns with a wide variety of tools for communicating with the electorate. The electronic airwaves, cable stations, videotapes, and the airplane have supplemented handbills, buttons, the railways, and the other campaign techniques of yesteryear. Nevertheless, the basic goals and strategies of campaign communications remain the same: to introduce your candidate to voters, to give them a reason to support that candidate, to discourage them from supporting the candidate's opponent, and to get them excited enough about the election to cast a ballot on election day.

Although most of the communications for presidential and statewide campaigns are created by political consultants cut from the cloth of Madison Avenue public relations experts, field work plays an important role in the two-way flow of communications between candidates and voters in virtually all elections. Personal contact with voters can be an important source of information about issues and a means for candidates to demonstrate to voters and news correspondents that they are in touch with people's wants and needs. Candidate-citizen interactions in the field allow for spontaneous learning and expressions of concern.

Candidates frequently weave the conversations they have with individuals they meet along the campaign trail into anecdotes that help them humanize the impact that economic trends, social conditions, and government policies have on ordinary people. Challengers use anecdotes about unemployed factory workers, farmers who have lost their land, homeless children, and other needy groups in order to dramatize the failure of policies that were enacted or implemented by incumbents and to indicate how their proposals would directly improve people's lives. Incumbents, not surprisingly, focus on success stories. They endeavor to direct attention to the entrepreneur who started a successful business using a low-interest loan made available through a government program that they introduced; to the school drop-out who earned a high school equivalency diploma through a literacy program that was their brainchild; or to some other person who benefited from their efforts. Incumbents, challengers, and open seat candidates for all levels of office make use of information gathered by field operatives and from face-to-face meetings with citizens in their campaign communications.

Field activities are also used to generate free media coverage. Even presidential campaigns, which make extensive use of paid television and radio advertisements, rely on field events to attract the media. Both the Clinton-Gore and the Bush-Quayle campaigns used road trips to generate free publicity. Bill Clinton and Al Gore crisscrossed the nation in a bus, tossed a football, and talked about their generation to emphasize their youth, outsider status, and commitment to change. President Bush sought to convince voters that the economy would soon rebound and that he understood the hardships caused by rising prices by visiting shopping malls. He also revived the "whistle stop" tour in order to remind voters of President Harry Truman's 1948 come-from-behind election victory.

Field activities are the major form of communications in most state and local campaigns and in some campaigns for Congress. Coffee klatches, town meetings, visits to shopping centers, and door-to-door canvassing by a candidate or surrogate campaigners are commonly used to introduce the candidate or publicize the campaign's major themes and issues. Visits to factories, hospitals, or pollution sites are designed to attract press coverage. Yard signs, posters, and bumper stickers are used to improve a candidate's level of name recognition. Literature drops enable a candidate to communicate issue information directly to voters without having to rely on the electronic media. Because they are labor-intensive, cheap, and easily carried out by volunteers, field activities play a big role in campaigns for state and local offices.

VOTER REGISTRATION AND
GET-OUT-THE-VOTE DRIVES

Voter registration and get-out-the-vote drives are key components of field work. By registering new voters who identify with their candidate's party or are likely to be favorably disposed toward the candidate, campaign field workers can affect the outcome of a close race. Computer technology, voter files, and precinct-level data have made it possible to pinpoint supportive electoral constituencies. Address lists, telephone numbers, and the mailing labels that many campaigns use to contact voters are usually furnished by party committees or purchased from private vendors. Providing these products has become a multimillion-dollar industry.

In some localities, campaign field workers can effectively walk from house to house registering likely supporters. In others, such as college campuses, it is more profitable to set up registration tables. Union halls, churches, and civic associations also make good locations for registering easily identifiable groups of voters. Voter registration drives that focus on well-defined populations can be very accurately targeted and very profitable for a candidate. Registration drives that are held in shopping malls or at fairgrounds, on the other hand, tend to be less well targeted and can result in the registration of an opponent's supporters. Indiscriminately registering voters may be good for democracy, but it can harm a candidate's election prospects.

Registering new voters is only half the battle in gaining their votes. The other half is making sure they go to the polls. Extensive follow-up is often needed to ensure that newly registered voters exercise their franchise. A well-run voter registration drive will record whether newly registered voters know the location of their polling place or if they will need a ride, a baby-sitter, an absentee ballot, or some other special assistance in order to vote. Newly registered voters and voters who have a history of inconsistently turning up at the polls may need to be contacted several times once the campaign begins its get-out-the-vote drive.

Get-out-the-vote activities are in many ways analogous to the sprint to the finish line that ends a closely run marathon. Both take place when the contestants are exhausted and have depleted most of their resources, and both can be decisive in determining the outcome of the race. For the politician, the final sprint takes place in the last one or two weeks of the campaign. By that time, the campaign has completed its fund-raising, finished most of its research and targeting, communicated its message, and stopped registering new voters. Campaigners principally focus on getting out the vote. Most campaigns use telephone banks, postcards, or foot canvasses to remind their supporters to go to the polls. Extra efforts are made to bring voters who need assistance to the polls.

FIELD WORK AND ELECTION OUTCOMES

What effect does field work have on who wins or loses an election? Field coordinators, the vendors of voter lists, and the individuals who volunteer to register and bring voters to the polls will typically report that field work is critical in separating winning candidates from losers. Most campaign consultants would readily agree. The tens of millions of dollars per election cycle that national and state party committees spent on their coordinated campaigns during the last decade further suggest that party leaders also consider field work to be an important part of campaigning (Herrnson, 1992). Although personal anecdotes and financial reports may be useful for measuring a campaign's field effort, they are limited in terms of what they tell about the impact of that effort on voters and election outcomes. More systematic research is needed to assess the impact that field activities have on votes.

Studying the impact of field activities on election outcomes is a complex task. Ideally, researchers would collect information about the activities that were conducted in conjunction with a particular election and disentangle the effects of field work from the effects of the other campaign efforts. A study that fully isolates the effects of field work would be extremely difficult, if not impossible, to conduct. Nevertheless, political scientists have rigorously studied campaign field work and found that it does, indeed, affect election outcomes. Party canvasses have been found to increase voter turnout and affect the division of the two-party vote (Krassa, 1988; Huckfeldt and Sprague, 1992). This suggests that campaign field activities play a bigger role in swaying voter preferences than in bringing voters to the polls.

FIELD WORK, POLITICAL PARTIES, AND CAMPAIGN VOLUNTEERS

In this era of money-driven, professionally run, technologically sophisticated campaigns, field work remains an area of campaigning that can draw on the resources of party organizations and the efforts of ordinary citizens. Most field activities are labor-intensive and can be carried out by volunteers. Individuals who are efficacious, active in civic groups, and familiar with their neighborhoods make excellent field workers. Local party committees, where they are vigorous, can be an excellent source of field assistance and campaign volunteers.

A study of congressional elections conducted in 1984 showed that candidates for the House of Representatives and their campaign staffs found party organizations to be a significant source of assistance in field-related election activities. Thirty-two percent of the campaigns reported that local party committees played a moderately to extremely important role in collecting information about voters, and 40 percent stated that local parties played a moderately to extremely important role in carrying out voter registration and get-out-the-vote drives. State party committees were also a significant source of voter information and provided substantial assistance in voter mobilization.[1] National party organizations, however, were helpful in areas of campaigning requiring technical expertise, in-depth research, or connections with political action committees, political consultants, and other Washington operatives (Herrnson, 1988).

The area where political parties were the most helpful was in recruiting campaign volunteers. Fully 52 percent of the campaigns reported that local party committees were moderately to extremely important in this area. Interest groups were ranked next, with 35 percent of the campaigns ranking them moderately to extremely important. In general, Republican House candidates relied more heavily on their party committees for field assistance than did Democrats, who were able to call on labor unions and other interest groups for campaign assistance. Similar findings were reported for campaigns for the U.S. Senate. The preliminary results of a study of the 1992 congressional elections indicated that local party committees were continuing to play an important role in campaign field work (Herrnson, 1994).

Field work is important for reasons beyond the impact that it can have on election outcomes or for the opportunities it provides for parties to assert themselves in the political process. Because campaign field work seeks to enfranchise new voters and ensure the participation of those who have voted before, and because it is conducted by volunteers, it is good for democracy in the broadest sense. Campaign field activities help increase levels of political participation, efficacy, and support for government by encouraging people to get involved in politics.

The experiences of campaign volunteers are especially telling. Most volunteers have little knowledge or campaign skills when they first get involved in politics. No previous training is required for most field activities. Through canvassing their neighborhoods, erecting yard signs, and bringing voters to the polls, volunteers learn that they can influence politics. They discover that in addition to controlling their own votes, they can influence the votes of others through working in a campaign.

Most campaigns for lower-level office and some campaigns for Congress afford campaign volunteers the opportunity to meet with field coordinators, the campaign manager, and the candidate. Usually the candidate and the professional consultants who work in the campaign will periodically hold short briefings with volunteers to boost morale and motivate them to work harder. These briefings give volunteers a chance to learn how the campaign is progressing, become informed about the relevance of the tasks they are performing, ask questions, and make suggestions.

Although it is uncommon for many volunteers' suggestions to be adopted, the exchanges that take place at campaign briefings are useful to both the paid staff and the volunteers. The staff members learn about issues that are on the minds of those volunteering, and thus gain insights into what people outside the campaign are concerned about. The volunteers have an opportunity to find out more about how campaigns are run and how government works. Discussions of why only selected issues are presented in the campaign's literature, why certain appeals are targeted to specific demographic groups, and why some events are held only in particular neighborhoods serve as practical lessons in representation and coalition building.

The give-and-take that occurs between campaign staffs and campaign volunteers and between campaign volunteers and the citizens they contact in the field can give the volunteers a feeling of empowerment and engender loyalty to the political system. Other aspects of contemporary elections, such as television commercials, political action committees, fund-raising events, and mass mailings, do little to increase the ties that common citizens have to the political process. These activities do not allow for the elite-mass interaction that is at the heart of grassroots politics.

CONCLUSION

Field work is an important element of campaign politics. Even though contemporary campaigns, particularly those for high office, rely heavily on the electronic media, polls, "spin doctors," and other modern electioneering techniques, field activities continue to be important in voter identification and targeting, message development and communications, and voter mobilization. Anecdotal as well as systematic evidence demonstrates that field activities can influence election outcomes. Moreover, field work is an area of campaigning that frequently relies on the efforts of political parties and volunteers. In this sense, field work provides latent benefits to the political system. The exchanges that occur between field workers, candidates, campaign staffs, and ordinary voters are an important part of the dialogue of democracy.

NOTES

1. Candidates and campaign officials were asked to rate party committees, unions, political action committees, and other interest groups as not important, slightly important, moderately important, very important, or extremely important in campaign activities ranging from mass media advertising to voter mobilization. These findings are from survey data collected in "The 1984 Congressional Campaign Study." For information about the study, see Paul S. Herrnson, *Party Campaigning in the 1980s* (Cambridge, Mass.: Harvard University Press, 1988), especially the appendixes.

13

Political Polling: From the Beginning to the Center

WILLIAM R. HAMILTON

In 1983, the ever precocious Democratic pollster Pat Caddell is purported to have said before a congressional hearing, "Today, the opinion pollster has become the strategic center of most campaigns." In 1984, Republican pollster Chuck Rund sat before a monitor flashing up different electoral vote scenarios based on Dick Wirthlin's state-by-state polling for President Reagan's reelection and said, "Gee, I feel like a voyeur into the American political psyche." (Interview with author, January 1988.) In 1992, *Newsweek* reported on an opinion research project designed and driven by Bill Clinton's campaign pollster, Stan Greenberg, along with general strategic consultant James Carville and media maven Mandy Grunwald, that was destined to change the public's perception of Bill Clinton—and ultimately lead to his election as president.

Clearly the art and science of modern political polling have become the major influence in strategic decisionmaking in modern U.S. political campaigns. This uniquely U.S. profession was not always at the center of our election campaigns. The importance of analyzing the electorate via public opinion polls has grown as the need for direct feedback from individual voters has intensified. Political parties have become less influential; the power of traditional interest groups has atrophied; and television, telephone, and mail technologies have improved and begun to dominate direct communication with the voters.

The polling profession has improved over the past twenty-five years because of the steady buildup of experience gained by pollsters provided by the numerous, frequent elections in the United States. As experience was gained, improvement in communication technology, which was changing political campaigning in general, was also increasing the opportunity to use polls in this dynamic milieu. To understand how polls eventually moved to the epicenter of American campaigns, it is necessary to trace political polling's short but dynamic history.

161

POLLING BEFORE 1967

In the beginning there was George Gallup, the ultimate psephologist. His disciples were Elmo Roper, Arch Crossley, and Hadley Cantril. But soon there came a generational split, led for a short time by Louis Harris and followers like Oliver Quayle, John Kraft, and Charles Roll.

This description succinctly outlines the pre-Columbian history of American political polling. As most people acknowledge, the *public* pollster (now called media pollsters) preceded the *private* political pollsters by nearly thirty years. In the early 1930s, George Gallup believed that his desire for direct democracy called for public information and policy evaluation that were not filtered through the economic elite. Gallup first applied this new concept of going directly to the voter by polling for one of his mother's elections for local office in Iowa. Shortly thereafter he began to apply his new technique to predicting the results of elections for dissemination by the public media.

Throughout the 1930s and 1940s, Gallup and two or three breakthrough social scientists conducted numerous polls for media while keeping their new businesses afloat with marketing research studies for private companies and advertising agencies. Although a number of the new pollsters tried to interest candidates and political parties in using polling as a strategic tool for campaigns, most of the opinion polling remained public, paid for by the media for general publication. Then came 1948 and the year of "President Dewey."

Contrary to most accounts, the highly publicized "miss" by Gallup and others in 1948 did not automatically discredit polling after the Truman-Dewey era. The technique had proved so accurate in other instances and so enlightening to business and political decisionmakers that there remained a market not only for polling about products but also for public polling on public policy issues. However, parties and major political candidates continued to use polling only idiosyncratically and even then not for strategic purposes.

In the early 1950s, most politicians continued to show little interest in using political polling. A few political players would hire a pollster to conduct a quick poll late in the campaign just to "see how things were going," but the technique was peripheral to actual campaign operations.

During this postwar period of consumerism, however, some marketing researchers were beginning to apply psychology to their commercial studies and help marketing departments plan strategy. The clients in the political field were slower to move in this direction, but a few pioneers kept trying—Roll with Crossley and Roper and his employees, Harris and later Quayle and Kraft.

Harris left Roper shortly after the 1956 Democratic convention to begin his own research company, and one of his first clients was U.S. Senator John F. Kennedy. Harris continued working with the future president up through the successful 1960 primaries and general election, bringing with him Quayle and Kraft from the Roper organization.

On the Republican side, Charles Roll had a small New Jersey firm going but was handling only a few clients. George Romney's executive assistant Walter DeVries, later of *The Ticket Splitter* fame, was working with the Market Opinion Research firm (MOR) to help GOP candidates in Michigan. But it was Harris who truly spawned a new industry or profession in 1960 with the publicity surrounding his polling for the new president. Two years later, however, Harris announced that he was eschewing private political work and would, from 1962 on, conduct only public polls (for his newspaper column) and private marketing polls.

By 1964, Democrats Quayle and Kraft had left the Harris organization and begun what was to become a powerful and influential cottage industry in American politics. They were followed by a number of smaller operations on both sides of the partisan fence, including me. In 1965, supporters of Ronald Reagan asked an economics professor from Utah, Richard Wirthlin, if he could conduct polls to help the former actor in his campaign for governor of California.

In the mid-1960s private political polling began to take hold. In 1964 my firm's first client (and only client at the time) wanted to run for statewide office in Florida. After two polls, I suggested it was an uphill race against the entrenched incumbent, and he finally quit the race. The firm struggled for a few months until we picked up our second statewide client—a state senator running for governor in a six-way Democratic primary.

Our client's plan was to run second in the primary and win the nomination (tantamount to election) in the runoff. In Florida and much of the South, this was the traditional strategy of moderate-conservative candidates—to get the liberals and ultraconservatives out of the race early and narrow the contest to a head-to-head one with a single moderate-liberal urban opponent. The number two finisher in the primary, often the "legitimate" moderately conservative Democrat, usually won these runoff elections before 1966.

The first primary poll showed our candidate running third—behind the moderate-liberal favorite as expected but also behind the big-city, ultraliberal mayor from Miami. When I presented the predicted third-place finish to the candidate-client, he strongly questioned our sample of respondents, promptly rose from his chair, left the room. I never saw the candidate himself again during the primary campaign, though we continued to poll for the public relations company handling his campaign. Our polls showed him a likely fourth, which was the election outcome.

After the primary, the candidate called me to his office and the first words out of his mouth were, "How'd you know that . . . ?" A new convert for using polling in campaigns had been made, but more important, the publicity of our accuracy had helped to launch a new polling firm.

Other pollsters from this prepubescent period have similar stories, usually told with different accents—from New York to Pennsylvania to California. But the stories generated the same questions: How can you challenge the existing party or political elite's structure and thinking about a campaign? How can a poll be so correct? And how can it help a campaign win?

In 1966, now-veteran consultant Joe Napolitan polled for Milton Shapp and helped an unknown millionaire defeat an entrenched Pennsylvania Democratic machine for the gubernatorial nomination. In the same year, Dick Wirthlin used the new technique to help fashion the Reagan gubernatorial victory in California. Regular polling helped that ultraliberal from Miami, Robert King High, knock off Haydon Burns, a sitting governor in the Democratic primary, and DeVries continued to use MOR's surveys in Michigan to reelect George Romney.

There was not a cataclysmic event that caused political polling to catapult forward to dominate the political dialogue in American election campaigning. It was, rather, a series of fairly compressed events during the middle political cycles of the 1960s—when communications technology was changing the face of the politics of America—that caused polling to become necessary and critical to the operation of a modern campaign. It was at the end of this period that polling became a required line item in the campaign budgets of many major races, but many of us (pollsters) were still arguing with candidates, campaign managers, and fund-raisers to allow our data to help guide the strategy of the campaign rather than have us simply evaluate, too late, the impact of key campaign decisions.

In 1960, Bobby Kennedy was reported to have cut Lou Harris short during one of his analytical poll presentations and said, "Just give us the numbers, Lou." The movement from number cruncher to strategic counselor had changed little during this prehistory era of the polling profession. But polling was on the political map.

The change in U.S. pollsters' role from last-minute evaluator to early strategic initiator was to begin soon enough—during the first true era of modern campaigns (1967–1978). In the second era (1979–1988) polling was to become the strategic centerpiece of the modern American political campaign. In the 1990s the polling industry is continuing to refine its strategic research techniques to meet the changing needs of American political campaigns—but not without some conflicts and controversies.

POLLING 1967–1978

During most of this early era of the 1970s, there were only three or four national polling firms conducting most of the polls for candidates of each major political party. This was partially because a fairly large infrastructure and network were necessary to conduct the type of polling used in those days and partially because the market was not yet producing enough dollars to support many additional research firms.

During the early part of this period, only about half of the top-of-the-ticket races (U.S. Senate and gubernatorial) were using pollsters, and less than a fourth of the congressional candidates commissioned polls for their campaigns. Very few legislative contests or local races even considered polling. Near the end of this era, however, most of the federal and all of the gubernatorial candidates were using pollsters extensively. Accordingly, major political research firms grew in size and influence.

The pollster and polling function during the early 1970s still served largely as the "provider of a unique set of numbers and data" to the media consultants and direct voter contact functions in the campaign. But the polling function had won a seat at the strategy table by the middle of this era, which allowed it to become increasingly more central to campaign decisionmaking. As many have often said, and rightly so, "information is power."

However, polling in the early and mid-1970s was largely conducted using in-home, face-to-face interviews. This procedure, although it produced extensive in-depth data for analysis and assistance in developing a campaign plan, was relatively expensive, very slow, and not as accurate as the telephone polling to come. Thus, numerous polls with the quick turnaround (time from beginning of interviewing to reporting of numbers) needed to manage strategy at midcampaign and endgame were costly, impractical or untimely. This was one of the main reasons pollsters and their product did not move to the center of strategic decisionmaking sooner. At the same time, there was less need for an increased volume of data on a quick turnaround timetable. Media producers were still shooting 16mm film that took time to transfer and edit, television stations could not (or would not) change spot traffic daily, Federal Express was in its infancy, and there were no satellite feeds or broadcast FAXs—yet.

Near the end of this era, however, polling in campaigns began to change. Patrick Caddell, polling for presidential candidate Jimmy Carter, and Robert Teeter, polling for Jerry Ford, both used some telephone surveys at the end of their presidential races, and by 1978 most of the statewide contests were at least using the telephone for trend polling or panel-back surveys and were just beginning to conduct rolling-average tracking polls.

POLLING 1979–1988

In the initial two election cycles of this period, there was an explosion of central telephone facilities with 20–100 telephone stations at which large sample surveys could be completed in a short time. Some of these were built by the major pollsters themselves, and some were run by independent contractors hired by pollsters who had no phone bank. By 1980 most initial benchmark surveys were being conducted by phone as experience was gained with the different questioning techniques used on the phone and as the in-house interview became even more impractical—travel costs rose, the independent interviewer network atrophied, and some urban (and rural) areas became completely inaccessible to the survey researcher.

These basic improvements in technology either directly or indirectly changed the polling industry and how polls and pollsters were used in political campaigns.[1] First, more frequent polls were conducted by major campaigns (all statewide and congressionals), but down-ballot campaigns (such as mayors, judges, and statewide constitutional officers) could also now afford polling.

During this period, the campaign committees of the U.S. House and Senate became volume purchasers of polls for their targeted candidates. And, to a lesser degree, major PACs began commissioning polls for their favorite candidates.[2] Finally, during the late 1980s the leadership of major state legislative bodies became volume purchasers of polls for their marginal districts as part of a new mode of centralized strategic planning and operations for these campaigns.

Second, the increased availability of telephone interviewing facilities meant that establishment of new, independent polling firms was more feasible than in the past. Experience in questionnaire construction, minimal knowledge of analytical techniques, and a personal computer were all pollsters needed if they could purchase samples, interviewing time, and data-entry services. During the 1980s many of the younger people, who had built some years of experience at the six to eight established firms that had previously controlled much of American polling, established their own firms. This trend was augmented when a number of young academics, who had been teaching at a university and doing some consulting on the side, saw an opportunity to work in this exciting field full-time—and with little financial investment. So the number of national firms doubled and then tripled in this decade—not to mention the introduction of a number of excellent state or regional polling firms.

Third, the increased use of telephone interviewing, a technique that produces mainly quantitative data, brought about the need for a more qualitative, "touchy-feelie" type of arrow in the researcher's quiver. So, during the late 1970s, focus groups were initially borrowed by the political pollsters from the market researchers.[3] It was in the early 1980s, how-ever, that the use of focus groups expanded dramatically, and they were often a required companion to the telephone benchmark poll. In most cases, the principals in the polling firm took on the role of focus group moderator and analyst. Although some may argue these pollsters lacked training to conduct this research function, this argument is offset by the pollsters' full understanding of a client's political situation and knowl-edge of what was needed to improve the more quantitative research phase to follow.

The combination of a larger, more diverse and competitive polling in-dustry paired with the rather quantitative style of the telephone survey led to more analysis and development of research techniques during the 1980s. In short, more professionals were searching for a competitive edge—not only in marketing themselves but in helping defeat their cli-ent's opponent, who was also using opinion research techniques.

During the latter part of this era, different research products were be-ing thought about and tested: pre- and posttests of on-air television, the dial-measured focus group, testing of radio spots over the phone, content analysis of verbatim responses for message development, and more re-fined statistical techniques in data analysis. As private political polling moved into its third decade, many of these techniques would become standard.

One other development during this period had a significant impact on both the polling industry and U.S. campaigning in general. That was the expansion of *public* polling during campaign periods—not only the na-tional polls but the conduct of multiple polls during state election cam-paigns by a single media outlet or a consortium of outlets. Not only did it make everyone (the public, press, and politicians) more aware of polls, sampling, and questioning techniques—which in turn demystified the "black box" concept of a pollster's analysis—but it also made the pollster even more important to campaigns in order to interpret and help manage the impact of the media polls.

This decade-long combination of events and developments placed the pollster at the center of campaign decisionmaking. The speed and rea-sonable cost of polls brought their increased use as planning tools for strategy and message development as well as the monitoring of tactics. Focus groups and other polling techniques became the standard tests for expensive media products. Most of the pollsters had extensive experi-ence drawn from numerous campaigns over a number of election cycles. And the increased use of polls by the media had forced campaigns to account for and monitor public opinion.

Caddell's remarks in his 1983 congressional testimony were rather prescient, and it is now clear, based on reports of polling work in the

Clinton presidential campaign, that the pollster (polling) function is at the center of strategic planning and tactical decisionmaking in most major campaigns in America.

POLLING IN 1988, 1992, AND BEYOND

This trend toward the polling function (and the pollster as a personification of it) being at the strategic center of campaigns is not likely to be reversed. Although no longer the only campaign professional with access to and understanding of data, the pollster can still best interpret the opinion research data and has the most varied experience in helping campaigns determine the strategic imperatives for a campaign to win.

Questions have been raised about whether there is an ethical concern or conflict of interest in the pollster helping develop overall strategy while providing the initial data on which the strategy is based and then monitoring how well the strategy is working. My answer to these questions is no, mainly because the job of building strategy is never the pollster's alone. Strategy is derived from a number of different data bases (the polling data base is probably the most important) and is a product of a campaign team—among others, the candidate, campaign manager, a media consultant, and often a fund-raiser. Furthermore, it would seem unwise to discard the input of the most analytical and often most experienced member of a campaign's inner circle.

It is possible, however, for a pollster to become so enamored of or involved in the consulting aspect of the campaign that his or her attention is diverted from designing and executing the most creative and rigorous research design for the client's campaign. As an experienced counselor to the campaign, the pollster is also the best instrument for producing specific and accurate opinion research data for that unique campaign; anything that causes the pollster to lose focus on this task is dangerous. This potential problem, of course, can be partially solved by expanding the size of the research firm (while maintaining quality), the dollar size of the contract, or both.

Regardless of how integrated the pollster is into the campaign team and regardless of what level of election (presidential or state representative) is involved, every modern campaign demands that the pollster provide major input to two critical questions:

- What is the most persuasive *message(s)* for this campaign?
- What is the definition of our key *target* group of voters?

There are other important questions on which some of the more experienced pollsters provide advice (What are the best channels to use in communicating with our targets? What intensity, weight, or emotionalism do we use in communicating with the targets?), but targets and message are the critical elements that modern American campaigns need to address in order to develop a winning strategy. In other words, *in order to win, what must be communicated directly to which group of voters (most of whom are not seeking the information) with a limited budget?*

POLLING IN PRESIDENTIAL CONTESTS

Is this responsibility for message and target the same for a pollster working for a presidential candidate as it is for one working at any other level of election? The answer is yes. After that, the pollster's role (like the role of many other campaign professionals) is very different in a run for the presidency. First, this contest is for the leadership of the strongest, most influential country on earth; neither a governor's race in California nor a prime minister's contest in Canada is even close in terms of the raw power of the office. The knowledge of the potential power of the office being sought affects all political participants, of course, not just the pollster. Second, the campaign operates in a fishbowl with more constant and total press contact than any other American election contest. Third, more powerful people are interested in the race—the top leaders of all special interests want to help or hurt you or your candidate. Finally, the campaign is geometrically larger than any other contest that any first-time presidential pollster has ever dealt with. And that is just the general election campaign.

The presidential primaries are different and in some ways more difficult for pollsters of the leading players. In these primaries, a pollster may do very little specific polling unless the candidate is wealthy but still may be required to provide the campaign with advice on message and targets. If polling can be afforded in a primary effort, the pollster must be prepared to help keep the national message focused while providing the campaign with message and target direction for three or four different, ill-defined state primary electorates. Next week, the tasks will be the same but most of the states will have changed.

After the primaries decide the candidates, the polling firms then have the largest set of clients they will ever have—in theory, 50 different state elections and a national campaign (in reality, usually only 15–25 states are in play in a given election). The pollster not only must help the campaign devise and operationalize its national communication strategy but also must develop a research plan and execute it for at least the target states; this means helping each state campaign develop a campaign plan and then tracking the effects of each state's execution of the plan.

Although it has been different for Democratic and Republican campaigns over the years, general election polling since 1980 has usually taken on a structure that puts the main polling firm (and winning) pollster at the center of all polling, with special responsibility for national message (and possibly a few key states) and that then divides data collection and first-cut analysis duties among other party pollsters—the tracking to be conducted according to a predetermined plan. The secondary pollsters would feed their data and analysis to the major pollster, who would usually advise the state coordinators and put the actual data in some type of large model or simulation. In short, techniques are the same regardless of election level, but the volume of work and the pressure are unique to a presidential race.

POLLING IN MOST U.S. ELECTIONS

All American electoral contests today attempt to use some type of public opinion research technique to gauge the mood or collective mind-set of the electorate. This information and proper analysis are simply essential to success in the present American political system. Most campaigns with more than 10,000–15,000 voters and more than $50,000 in campaign funds to spend will use some type of professional, modern research technique to guide them in developing or refining their campaign strategy.

Virtually all gubernatorial and U.S. Senate campaigns now rely heavily on the pollster as one of the two or three major consultant-operatives of their campaign brain trust. These campaigns require significant amounts of personal consultation (time) from the pollster as well as use of many of the different research techniques in the pollster's repertoire. This cost to the campaign is usually 5–10 percent of the total campaign budget.

Most congressional contests also now use polls—often to determine whether they need to mount a campaign in what is often considered to be a "safe" district. In only about 15–20 percent of the congressional districts is there some degree of competitiveness where a true campaign is run, although in 1992 the Democratic Congressional Campaign Committee (DCCC) reported nearly 150 districts "severely in play" following scandals, redistricting, and retirements.

These competitive congressional contests use the polling function much as do their statewide counterparts, except they usually have a smaller budget and therefore less need (or ability to pay) for the varying types and volume of data used in a statewide contest. Most of these congressional races conduct early benchmarks and some type of trend or tracking polls, but often the frequency of their tracking is less than in statewide contests, and often they do not use all of the specialized techniques and studies. For example, only about 25–30 percent of the targeted congressional races used focus groups in the 1992 election cycle; even fewer used any of the new ad-testing techniques. These techniques remained, however, the standard fare of the larger budget, statewide campaigns.[4]

State legislative races are similar to congressional races except their budgets are even smaller, and therefore marginal, competitive races are even harder pressed to afford these modern research techniques and the advice of an experienced pollster. Yet even in many of these "little" legislative races there are changes occurring that will impact these contests in the future.

The cost of these different research techniques (and other campaign services) is leading state legislative leaders (house speakers, senate presidents, minority leaders) to set up separate funds, raise money, and provide campaign services, including polling services, to the critical group of marginal districts they deem might make a difference in partisan control of these legislative bodies. In some of the larger states these state senate and representative races now use all the same polling techniques and advice provided to a major statewide campaign—except they use them more as do party leaders in a parliamentary system of government.

Local races—mayor, county commissioner, county treasurer, and so on—have expanded their use of polling techniques to help plan and operate their campaigns. The variation in use remains fairly wide, however, based on the size of the campaign budget and partisanship in the community. Clearly, mayors' races in all major cities use polling in their campaigns, but the techniques and advice are too expensive and could not be used effectively in a county commissioner's race in Saline County, Kansas, with a campaign budget of $4,700.

CAMPAIGN PHASES

Most American political operatives and consultants think of modern U.S. election campaigns, whether major statewide efforts or local races, as divided into three particular phases: *early*, when the campaigns are getting organized, strategy is developed, staff is hired, and the candidate is reviewing his or her issue material, but the vast majority of voters are unaware of any candidate or campaign activity; *midcampaign*, when the candidates attempt to improve their recognition and popularity and each one begins to position himself or herself for the final run; and *endgame*, which is the period in which the campaigns spend most of their communication dollars, the voters begin to pay attention, and the candidates compare each other and each other's records while "asking for the order."

During each of these campaign periods, the pollster is a vital participant in campaign decisionmaking but plays a slightly different role, often using different techniques in each period. This relationship of activity to the campaign has changed little over the first two previous eras of political polling, but in all three time phases the pollster's activity level and importance to the process have intensified. As voters have continued to drift from the anchors that provide consistency in voting behavior, someone is needed to interpret which way they will drift—and whether the tide or the wind will have the most influence on that direction.

The Early Phase

Early in the campaign the pollster attempts to become immersed in the campaign itself—reviewing clip files, studying electoral and demographic targeting, reading any previous strategy memos, and often conducting a series of structured interviews with friends, fund-raisers, party officials, and existing campaign or office staff. A most important element of this early period is for the pollster strongly to urge the campaign to conduct what is called *opposition research* if this process has not already been started.[5] This prepolling process is an effort to (1) provide the campaign with a discipline that *information must precede decisions* and (2) allow the pollster to become thoroughly familiar with the candidate's record, family and background, and staff, as well as his or her party's officials, opponent, and constituency, in order to conduct the best benchmark poll possible.

Often the pollster is the first one on board a campaign who has both a gestalt view of the process and a penchant for data-driven decisionmaking—and who therefore has no unique personal agenda within the campaign. This immersion process is critical to moving a campaign at the correct pace and in the right direction. When this process is shortcut, it is usually to the detriment of the benchmark poll and campaign plan.

All of this activity is pointed toward developing, executing, and analyzing a *benchmark poll* for the campaign that is enhanced both by the pollster's experience in other election campaigns and also by sensitizing him or her to the uniqueness of this particular race in this particular constituency. Often a set (two to four) of focus groups will also be conducted before the benchmark. These are designed to listen to the voters brainstorm about the issues, candidates, and their relevance to their lives and to test competing hypotheses or assumptions that have arisen in the immersion process. At a minimum, these focus groups will be used to determine how best to measure the voters' priorities among a number of different competing arguments, messages, and hypotheses regarding strategy.

The benchmark poll is the major research product in this early phase. This is a lengthy poll (90–100 items or questions) usually conducted with a fairly large sample—500–1,200 likely voters in statewide races and 400–500 in congressional races, depending on the size and heterogeneity of the constituency. After execution of the survey, which includes both open-end and fixed-answer questions on mood, personalities, issues, partisanship, and candidate choice, the polling firm provides a detailed analysis and makes a full presentation to the key players in the campaign. This is usually the most expensive single research project in the campaign. The next sections highlight some trends in products and types of research designs that are or will become a part of the pollster's research repertoire.

Future trend 1. Because "early" in some campaigns means twelve to eighteen months before an election (an incumbent U.S. senator, for example), a number of professionals, including Tom King, a Democratic media consultant, and Rob Schroth, a Democratic pollster, believe that this is too early to conduct such an expensive poll—that it is too far in advance of when the campaign is developing communication products for the voter. They suggest that conducting a minibenchmark early with a slightly smaller sample and shorter questionnaire would be sufficient for early strategic planning. The larger benchmark then would be conducted closer to the initiation of actual campaign communication and therefore closer to the time the voters will be paying attention. The cost saving can be as much as one-third the cost of the benchmark. Everyone, however, agrees that some form of benchmark poll is necessary as early as possible in a campaign.

Future trend 2. Some pollsters, including myself, have developed programs using the content analysis technique on voters' actual responses to open-end questions including both quantified analysis and the display of actual verbatim quotes by message element; the program is a substitute for early focus groups. Although in this process the pollster cannot view the interaction among voters, it has the advantage of a quantified measure, spreads the investigation across a larger portion of the constituency, and is less expensive than a set of separate focus groups because it is a by-product of the benchmark poll.

The pollster's input to the campaign plan at this early juncture is vital. The existing benchmark poll and these new techniques will guarantee that the campaign plan will be based on the most sensitive analysis of voters' opinions about a particular race and set of candidates.

Midcampaign

The midcampaign phase is usually the longest period in the campaign. It begins after a campaign plan is written and discussed and implementation begins. Over this period of time there are three different roles the pollster plays in the campaign: *a constant adviser* or "reality check" on all campaign decisions that in any fashion might have an impact on the voters (and this does not leave out much in a modern political campaign); a *monitor*, through trend polling, of the success of the campaign's tactics in achieving its strategic goals, as evaluated at separate time phases of the campaign; and an *evaluator* of different communication elements the campaign produces, from the candidate's stump speech to a tabloid to a television spot.

As already noted, the pollster is a key member of the campaign's strategy team. It is during this building period that the pollster's regular advice on how specific decisions can affect the electorate is critical. Should we attend the teachers' convention or not? Should we return the National Rifle Association questionnaire (not what answers to give)? Should we hire an out-of-state operative to do press relations? Should we push the existing budget bill to the floor of the legislature for an early vote? These are the types of questions that come up during midcampaign. The pollster should not be the last word on these questions but should be consulted for insight on how the voters react to the various options posed by these questions. Finally, the pollster often serves as the disciplinarian in the campaign—the force that attempts to keep the focus of the campaign on the messages set forth in the basic strategy plan and to keep the campaign from being thrown off track by any of the myriad of decisions that campaigns are forced to make. In major campaigns the pollster is usually in daily contact with the campaign leaders; in congressional or lower-level campaigns it is usually the campaign manager or candidate who brings the pollster in on key questions.

The pollster or polling firm usually conducts one or more *trend polls* during this midcampaign period. A trend poll usually uses a similar sample size as the benchmark, but the questionnaire is much shorter—usually 25–35 items or questions—and thus the analysis is more direct and brief. The purpose of each trend poll is (1) simply to measure what basic changes have occurred since the benchmark, (2) to "go fishing" in case some issue, mood, or message is beginning to move within the electorate, and (3) most important, to test the progress toward the goals of the campaign during the interim since the last poll—goals that specifically relate to the voters' (or the targets') opinions. When the trend poll results are combined with evaluative measures on other matters—fund-raising goals met, staff hired, volunteers in place, endorsements achieved—the campaign can make a full self-evaluation.

The second aspect of this evaluator role is the polling firm's ability to work closely with the communications director and the media consultant. In an ideal case, the benchmark analysis, open-end comments, special message analyses, focus group reports, and targeting information have provided the creators of communication with the initial input on voters' opinion and feelings that they need to design persuasive media. The next step is to test voters' reactions to the concepts, copy, symbols, and specific messages the media producers have operationalized for the media. In the early era of polling in campaigns, this was not a function performed by the polling firm, but when focus groups came into use in the early 1980s, one use of the technique was to test the potential effectiveness of ads—at least to have group members catch glitches or the ambiguities of a symbol or slogan before that communication piece went out to other voters. Focus groups were helpful, but they were still a qualitative tool that was not wholly satisfactory to the pollsters or media producers, and political polling has begun much innovation in this area.

Future trend 1. In 1988 Lee Atwater used standard focus groups in New Jersey to figure out that crime was an underlying fear among many voters, that Democrats were perceived as weak on the issue, and that racism still existed in America. If we forget morality for a moment, it should not have been difficult to put that analysis together using these basic focus groups. In 1992, the Greenberg-Carville-Grunwald team faced a more difficult problem for Bill Clinton, and the team used a new technique that allows a group of preselected voters (about 50) to push a seven-digit dial every ten seconds to demonstrate their feelings while watching a piece of video about the candidate. By later superimposing a quantified trend line on the video, the analysts were able to determine what symbols, issues, facial expressions, and body language of the candidate were most pleasing (and not so pleasing) to these voters.

No one should deny that in early June 1992 Bill Clinton faced a much larger problem with his personal image than even George Bush faced during June 1988. Stanley Greenberg, who had seen this research product used very occasionally in the preceding cycle, knew that the sensitivity it added to the measurement and analysis of a candidate's problem was what was needed. This technique will see expanding use in major statewide campaigns.

Future trend 2. I have adapted a technique from marketing research that entails testing television spots while people view them in their homes. This requires recruiting a panel of 100 voters to watch a particular television show on the following evening—an inexpensive buy of some rerun program on an independent station. The campaign has placed the spot(s) to test in that program. The panel members are not told the purpose of the survey but are asked four or five commercial-product questions and two or three political questions as a baseline.

Immediately after the program airs, the panel is recalled and asked a number of "cover" questions about the program and other ads that ran in the program and then a series of questions on the candidate's ads. This allows campaigns to choose between two different styles of ads, find duds, and determine which of two symbols better triggers the message desired. And it is done with voters who viewed the ad in a natural setting.

Future trend 3. A number of polling firms, with Republican pollster Bill McInturff in the lead, have begun to test radio spots or the audio track from television spots during a telephone interview. The interviewer introduces the poll, asks a few key "pre-ad" questions, and then has a computer play the spot for the voter over the telephone. Follow-up questions are then asked in order to measure the voter's reaction to the spot and the potential impact on the candidate and the overall dynamic of the race. This also allows the viewer (listener) to receive the stimuli in a natural setting. As a by-product of a trend or track poll, the technique is not overly expensive.

Future trend 4. Near the end of this midcampaign period many pollsters are recommending specialized polls that include very few questions and very large sample sizes. The purpose is largely to increase the campaign's ability to target more precisely. Although early electoral and demographic targeting and benchmark polls have provided some guidance, using enhanced lists (or geodemographics) late in this midcampaign period allows the pollsters to bring current opinions and issues into the targeting formula and to be much more specific in terms of demographics, lifestyles, and life cycles.[6]

For example, it is important to know that a Republican candidate should target white men in his or her communication, but it is even more important to know whether these should be younger or older, well off, not so well off, or across the board in income. These smaller subgroups of white men respond to different messages, live in different parts of town, and watch different news programs and television shows. Using this increased precision in targeting research greatly improves direct-mail strategy, broadcast buys, cable buys, and radio segmentation.

The increasingly lower cost of data collection and the shortness of the questionnaire make this modification of a trend poll very feasible for large campaigns with a heterogeneous electorate, and it will be used more frequently because media consultants are requesting it.

Endgame

As voters begin to focus, campaigns begin to communicate—or vice versa. With four to eight weeks to go, positioning and image development are usually over in most campaigns, and both party's candidates go into what media guru Bob Squier calls "rock and roll."[7] This is the period when both candidates are firing their best shots at their soft voters and the pure persuadables—not to mention firing at each other. These groups of voters obviously overlap for both candidates, and that is where the communications collision exists.

Years ago, the soft vote for each candidate and the pure persuadables accounted for only 10–15 percent of the vote. With the exception of a few races (especially urban mayors' races), this is no longer the case. Now, 45–50 percent of voters report they made up their mind for whom to vote in October or within five weeks of election day. Most preelection polls show undecideds in the 5–20 percent range, but both candidates' soft vote, in most competitive races, usually runs the totally malleable electorate upward to 50 percent.[8] One of the key functions of the polling firm during this period is to define the persuadables in order to pinpoint final targets for the campaign. The other key function is to determine which way the persuadables are moving—and why.

The volatility at the end of a campaign results largely from the lack of strength of party identification in the United States. Party loyalty and strength of commitment to one's party have tended dramatically downward in the past twenty-five years, and now there is only minimal structure to most campaigns. Thus there are plenty of voters for whom political party identification has little or no meaning. That is why money is spent on repetitive communication at the end of a campaign and why tracking polls have become one of the most important tools of modern-day campaigns.

In the 1960s, when party identification meant more, there was less need for tracking, but political leaders would not have done tracking anyway. In the 1970s, the in-home personal interview was too expensive and surveys could not be turned around quickly enough to have an impact on last-minute decisionmaking. However, improving technology has continually increased the speed of communication.

With the advent of central facility telephone interviewing, completing large samples in one, two, or three days became commonplace. In most contests in the 1970s, tracking usually meant conducting a poll once a week for three or four weeks and reporting on each poll once a week. At the end of the decade, however, tracking came to mean *rolling averages*, continuous tracking that was more costly but provided a more stable trend line and was able to measure the effect of virtually every event or media mix during endgame.

Rolling-average tracking means interviewing a set number of likely voters every night, cumulating the number of nights that would provide a full sample, and then tabulating the results. For the next track, the oldest data would be discarded and an equivalent amount of new data from the most recent night(s) would be added—thus rolling the new data over the old data while keeping the middle data constant. Each wave of data is weighted by a model or demographic estimate of the electorate developed by the pollster in order to hold down variances caused by sampling error on critical demographic variables. This concept was introduced in Mississippi in 1978 (by Lance Tarrance for Republicans) and Louisiana in 1979 (by William R. Hamilton for Democrats).

There are numerous variations of the rolling-average technique, but major U.S. political campaigns were never the same again. In the early 1980s, campaigns with major budgets used this technique with its twice or thrice a week, and occasionally daily, reporting of poll results to help traffic specific television spots, change the candidate's schedule, determine how to respond to an opponent's charge, determine where to spend extra television money, or measure the impact of a debate. In contrast to a number of specific polls that were three and four days apart and might miss measuring a specific event or media wave, rolling-average tracking is available instantly—it is like the Dow-Jones average of the campaign.

Future trend. Rolling-average tracking will only increase in use by political campaigns. As data-collection costs drift downward, it will become available to lower-level campaigns, and major statewide campaigns will increase their sample sizes and receive more frequent updates.

The product itself is unlikely to change dramatically over the next decade; it will retain the two major determinants—rolling in new data in place of old and weighing each wave of results by a predetermined model. What may change is that some of the future trends noted earlier, principally testing of the television or radio spots, might be grafted onto the tracking system.

There is one caveat, however. Although we live in an instant-information world, it is difficult to think of American voters as being so enthralled with politics that they are changing and responding to every little media modification a campaign or its opponent makes. It is possible that with daily tracking a pollster will get movement that is not real but simply a research artifact; sample surveys of people's opinions can be only so accurate. If, however, due caution is taken by an experienced pollster and major attention is given to the trend line rather than to daily changes, the polling profession in America has an immensely powerful tool.

CONCLUSION

Pollsters are at the heart of this information system—they create it, execute it, and develop the reporting and analytical format. This provides the pollster with the potential for enormous influence over both creative and spending decisions at the endgame of a campaign.

There is no doubt that public opinion research has become the central nervous system of the modern American political campaign. Increasing cynicism, alienation, and information overload have created a disconnection between voters and their government. Voters thus must be polled, probed, and repolled if we are to stay abreast of what they are thinking and how they are thinking about it.

The charges that polling stifles leadership, creates rather than measures opinion, or helps promote mostly negative campaigns pale compared to the positive attribute of citizen feedback to public officials—officials who would have very few other ways to obtain this fuel for our democracy.

In this chapter, I have personified the function of the pollster, largely because that is the way it is. Almost all strategic research done in the United States is done by small to medium-sized independent research firms, each of them headed by one or more established researcher-gurus. This personified function is not likely to go away now that it has found the center of the campaign.

NOTES

1. The technology continued to change through the 1980s, which made central telephone interviewing more important to modern campaigns. Examples include the AT&T breakup, which kept toll rates low; least-cost, computerized routing systems; computerized speed dialing of samples; and computer-assisted telephone interviewing (CATI).

2. PACs took advantage of an FEC loophole that allows an independent entity to conduct a poll for a candidate, hold the results for fifteen days, and be held accountable for only 50 percent of the cost of the poll in attribution to the candidate. In other words, a PAC could conduct a $9,500 poll for a candidate and remain under the $5,000 maximum contribution limit for a federal candidate.

3. Focus group research is the technique of bringing ten to twelve voters together to discuss campaign issues and candidates. The voters are encouraged by a moderator to talk among themselves on topics of interest to the campaign. These groups are videotaped and then analyzed.

4. According to assistant political director at the DCCC, Rob Engel, interview with author, August, 1992.

5. Opposition research has come to mean more than searching for negatives in the opponent's record, business, or personal life. It means applying the same research task to your candidate and researching the key issues in your constituency.

6. Geodemographics is the combining of a number of demographic variables with geography in terms of defining a voter and where he or she lives. I first used this type of voter segmentation in political polling in a winning Missouri referendum campaign in 1978. The results of this research provided state-of-the-art guidance to a successful phone and mail campaign coordinated by political consultant Matt Reese.

7. Obviously this occurs in primary campaigns also—usually over a shorter period of time but often with the front-runners (and targets) shifting back and forth.

8. Based on results of postelection surveys I conducted in 1986, 1988, 1990, and 1992. Results for presidential and congressional vote are averaged.

14

The Promising Adolescence
of Campaign Surveys

RAYMOND E. WOLFINGER

Before survey research became commonplace in the United States, candidates for elective office who were trailing in the polls had an easy demagogic way to cast doubt on the bad news. All they had to do was ask this rhetorical question of a sympathetic audience: "How many of you have ever been interviewed in one of those polls?" The truthful answer was that precious few people had been respondents in a survey, and the politician had an encouraging, if fallacious, rejoinder that might reassure the more uncritical activists and potential contributors.

By the late 1980s, of course, such a rejoinder was no longer possible. Few people would deny having ever been a respondent in a survey about politics or vacuum cleaners or life insurance or whatever. One consequence of the growth of surveys may well be increased popular acceptance of their validity.

EXPANSION OF SURVEY RESEARCH

The Growth in Nonacademic
Survey Research

The tremendous expansion of campaign surveys has been matched, if not exceeded, by an explosion in the use of survey research by newspapers, television stations, broadcasting networks, and the like. In 1988 an astonishing total of 259 political surveys were conducted by just eight major media organizations.[1] Yet these national surveys were just the tip of the iceberg. Eighty-two percent of all newspapers with circulations over 100,000 were "substantially involved in news polling" at the end of the 1980s, as were 56 percent of all television stations (Ladd and Benson, 1992).

Much of this growth results from the development of telephone interviewing and all of its ramifications and refinements. But a less technological invention—exit polling—has also played a part. Surveys, whether by phone or in person, are an essential component of campaign planning. Exit polls, on the other hand, are an after-action technique useful almost entirely for instant explanations of election outcomes. Although they have obvious drawbacks as instruments for measuring public opinion, exit polls are clearly superior to the person-in-the-street interviews that used to clutter local as well as network election-night coverage. Because exit polls require little fancy equipment or expertise, they can be done almost anywhere. Fully 69 percent of the nation's television stations reported that they conducted exit polls in 1988, and the proportion in 1992 doubtless was even greater (Ladd and Benson, 1992).

Survey Research in Campaigns

The preceding chapter discusses two main uses for attitude research in political campaigns. One is to find the most persuasive messages for the campaign. The other is to identify the key target groups. Yet I think there is a third and equally important purpose—namely, to help the campaign staff understand its candidate's image. For example, in Chapter 17 Samuel Popkin describes the discovery by Clinton's campaign planners that their candidate's background was widely misperceived by much of the electorate. Because Clinton went to Georgetown University, to Oxford, and to Yale Law School, millions of Americans thought he was a rich kid whose background may not have been much different from George Bush's. When polling results revealed the misperceptions, the Clinton campaign instituted a major advertising campaign to tell the American people about the hardships of Clinton's early life. This advertising campaign culminated in "A Man from Hope," a biographical film shown at the Democratic National Convention.

Comparing the use of survey research in the Clinton campaign to the use of survey research in campaigns twenty years ago reveals how far politicians have come in their acceptance of quantitative research. In 1970 most of the academic election specialists in the San Francisco Bay Area were consultants to Jess Unruh, then the speaker of the California Assembly and eventually the Democratic nominee opposing Ronald Reagan's reelection as governor. A genuinely creative legislator, Unruh was responsible for many innovative policies in California, as well as for raising the state legislature to a new level of professional competence. However, Unruh had a dreadful public image. Part of the problem was his appearance; he was short and fat. Another part of the problem was his proclivity for maxims such as "Money is the mother's milk of politics," which led to his unfortunate nickname: Big Daddy. Consequently, groups that had benefited from Unruh's policy leadership and suffered from Reagan's had a distressing, from Unruh's perspective, tendency to support the governor.

If ever a candidate needed in-depth quantitative research to uncover the various elements of his public image, it was Unruh. A number of professors in the Bay Area who were consultants to the Unruh campaign convinced the campaign to do professional, quantitative interviewing in order to ascertain Unruh's quite astonishing negative image, even in the face of apparent issue agreement with many of the constituencies that were important in California. A research program was worked out in biweekly meetings with a series of campaign managers (the Unruh campaign went through two campaign managers and one campaign outside consultant in the first four months of 1970). The first phase of the survey was on the point of going into the field when the campaign manager of the month was told that in a few days he would get a bill from the research company that was to conduct the interviews. The concept of a bill introduced a note of reality that evidently had been lacking in previous discussions with the campaign, and the campaign rapidly backed out of the deal.

Clearly, much changed in the acceptance of survey research as a necessary tool in political campaigns between the late 1970s and the early 1990s. As the previous chapter points out, by 1990 no federal or statewide campaign would proceed without survey research, and many state and local races used polling as well.

Differences Between Academic and Nonacademic Survey Research

As the discussion in the previous chapter illustrates, academics lag behind practical researchers when it comes to data-gathering techniques. People meters and ad testing are largely unknown in the academic survey research field. Yet because the focus of academic survey research into elections differs from practical research, academics have used surveys to explore assumptions about political attitudes and behaviors. Whereas campaigns use survey research to help predict and thus shape the vote on election day, academics use survey research to help explain election outcomes. The previous chapter illustrates this point in the discussion of the fading of party identification, with respect both to the proportion of Americans who identify with a party and to the importance of this identification as a factor in vote choice.

A common assumption among many scholars and journalists is that party identification has little or no meaning as a predictor of an individual's vote. Hedrick Smith spoke for a great many political observers in concluding that "the most important phenomenon of American politics in the past quarter century has been the rise of independent voters who have at times outnumbered Republicans" (Smith, 1988, p. 671).

Survey research, such as that done in most campaigns, seems to confirm this view. More people identify themselves as Independents today than they did twenty-five years ago. Yet academic survey research enables scholars to explore this seeming decline in party identification in more detail.

Two points are at issue here: (1) To what extent are citizens who consider themselves Democrats or Republicans becoming a smaller proportion of the electorate? (2) Is the relationship of these partisan identifications to voting decisions weakening?

The answer to the first question turns on how one interprets findings from the National Election Studies (NES), the University of Michigan's nationwide surveys. This forty-year body of data is the fount of our understanding of party identification: a long-standing attachment to one or the other major party. The series of NES questions about party identification begins with, "Generally speaking, do you usually think of yourself as a Republican, a Democrat, an Independent, or what?" People who call themselves Independents are always asked, "Do you think of yourself as closer to the Republican Party or the Democratic Party?"

Since the inception of the Michigan research, most people initially calling themselves Independents—who as previously mentioned, have become much more numerous since the late 1960s—concede that they are closer to one of the parties. If answers to the second question are ignored, as they often are in campaign polling, then the country is indeed in the grips of "dealignment"; Independents are now as numerous as Democrats and far outnumber Republicans. But if one pays attention to the acknowledgment of "closeness" to one or the other party, the story is very different, because the proportion of respondents denying that they are close to either party was only a few percentage points greater in 1988 and 1984 than in 1956 or 1960.

One might think that defining Independents was a simple problem that would be settled by trying both definitions and comparing the results. For a long time, however, most analysts of the NES data (which is to say most academic students of elections) evidently chose to overlook the question about closeness to a party. The result was the inclusive definition of Independents that fostered the conventional wisdom about dealignment sweeping the country.

A very different interpretation of the last quarter century results if one distinguishes between respondents who are adamant about their independence and those who concede closeness to a party. Those putative Independents who say they are closer to the Democratic Party are very similar to outright Democrats. The resemblance includes not only their voting habits but also their views of the two parties, their attitudes on issues, the stability of their affiliation, their participation in presidential primaries, and indeed, virtually any measure of behavior or attitude. The same pattern holds for Independents who are closer to the Republican Party (Keith et al., 1992).

In short, the vast majority of self-defined Independents are not neutral but partisan—a bit bashful about admitting it, but partisan nevertheless. Once this is recognized, the proportion of the electorate that is truly neutral between the two parties is scarcely different now from what it was in the Eisenhower era. Moreover, because these "pure Independents" now are less inclined to vote, their share of the voting population is, if anything, a bit smaller now than in the 1950s and 1960s.

So much for a decline in popular affiliation with the parties. What about the significance of this affiliation when it comes to casting a ballot? No one ever said or suggested that party identification was the only predictor of vote choice. Indeed, that would have been highly implausible when one considers that the first elections studied by the Michigan researchers were marked by decisive Republican presidential victories produced by votes for Eisenhower by millions of Democratic identifiers. Of course, there are always some defections in any presidential election; people vote for the other party's candidates without abandoning their long-term identification as Republicans or Democrats. In fact, sometimes defections are quite asymmetrical, as when one party or the other manages to nominate a particularly unappealing candidate, such as Barry Goldwater in 1964 or George McGovern in 1972. Although the level of presidential defectors varies from one election to the next, there is no long-term trend. From 1952 through 1988 there was no significant increase in defection by any category of party identifier, and the proportion of defectors in the total population of presidential voters was, if anything, lower in 1988 and 1984 than in 1956 and 1960.[2]

The 1990 elections in New Jersey also support the proposition that parties are still meaningful electoral guides. In 1990 the newly elected Democratic governor, James Florio, pushed a $2.8 billion tax increase through the legislature. This achievement was met by a truly spectacular outburst of popular rage, a mood that wholly dominated the November election. Florio was the villain, being widely and accurately perceived as the cause of the impending jump in most citizens' taxes. But Florio was not a candidate in 1990, so the voters had to vent their fury elsewhere. Not surprisingly, voters took out their anger on the Democratic ticket. This must mean that an important connection was made between Florio being a Democrat and other candidates being Democrats. The most interesting near-victim in 1990 was a candidate who had no responsibility for state taxes, Senator Bill Bradley. Just being on the Democratic ticket in 1990 was enough to jeopardize Bradley's reelection. Challenged by an obscure Republican whom he outspent by a ratio of over 11 to 1, Bradley squeaked through with less than 51 percent of the vote, an object lesson of the enduring power of party labels.[3]

This view of party identification does not mean that all election outcomes are determined by the balance of Republicans and Democrats. To say that party identification is durable and important is not the same thing as saying that all elections come out the same way. Common wisdom suggests that in any given election, about 40 percent of the votes are likely to go to the Republican Party's candidate and 40 percent are likely to go to the Democratic Party's candidate, leaving about 20 percent of the vote undecided. Yet academic survey research has enabled students of elections to go beyond the current conventional wisdom to demonstrate the continuing importance of party identification in the vote decision.

THE PUZZLE OF THE VOTE FOR ROSS PEROT

One common way that political scientists have approached the problem of understanding elections might be called *fundamental analysis*. Fundamental analysis suggests that party identification will determine most of the votes in an election and that the main dynamic factor is the health of the economy, unless there is a large scandal or a war that has continued for some time with an uncertain outcome. One implication of this sort of analysis is that, for example, the people who elected Ronald Reagan in 1980 were not endorsing anything he had said or done but were expressing a lack of confidence in Jimmy Carter. By the same token, Americans did not so much vote against Walter Mondale in 1984 as vote for the man who had brought them "Morning in America." In other words, when Reagan was the challenger, stagflation elected him, and when he was the incumbent, prosperity kept him in office.

To apply such an analysis to the 1992 presidential election would predict a victory for Bill Clinton. In summer 1992 there was fairly widespread and apparently durable unemployment, coupled with job anxiety. The economy was nearly stagnant. The incumbent president, running for reelection, was fairly unpopular, particularly among women infuriated and energized by the Anita Hill–Clarence Thomas hearings and the Bush administration's dogged hostility to abortion. Starting from this position and behind in the polls, the president launched his campaign with a convention that provided lavish attention to his vanquished intraparty opponents and managed to give particular offense to working women, racial minorities, homosexuals, and pacifists, in a declared "cultural war." By October, Bush had abandoned even his presidential dignity, most notably in calling Al Gore "Ozone Man." Most observers, including most Republicans, agreed that from a technical standpoint as well, the Bush campaign was simply dreadful.

In contrast, the Clinton campaign conducted what most political observers believe was an excellent campaign. Not only was the Clinton campaign vastly superior to the Bush campaign, but Democrats still outnumbered Republicans. The puzzle, given the assumptions of fundamental analysis, is this: Why did only 5 percentage points separate Clinton from Bush in the popular vote, when party identification and all the familiar short-term forces were in Clinton's favor? With everything going for him, how could Clinton manage just 43 percent of the vote?

The answer seems to be Ross Perot. The assumption is that absent Perot's candidacy Clinton would have ranked with such recent landslide winners as Reagan, Nixon, and Johnson. This conclusion is consistent with fundamental analysis, which sees the state of the economy and presidential popularity as the major dynamic variables and predicts that as either declines, so will the incumbent's votes. Ordinarily, votes lost by the Republican incumbent go to the Democratic challenger. However, if there are two alternatives to the incumbent, then the opposition party may not benefit in proportion to the incumbent party's loss. Hence Clinton had to split the anti-Bush vote with Perot.

The intellectual puzzle is what led Ross Perot to get 19 percent of the popular vote in the 1992 election. Before 1992 third-party candidates fell neatly into one of two categories. More numerous and less successful were the standard-bearers of sectarian parties based on some ethnic, issue, or ideological perspective. A number of these are on the ballot every four years and draw a handful of votes for their special outlook. In contrast to these fringe candidates, occasionally a major political figure, his ambitions disappointed in a major party, will attract considerable attention and millions of votes by running for president outside the two-party system in which his career had hitherto been spent. Before Perot, a half dozen such frustrated notables had run for president in this century. The first one, Theodore Roosevelt, with 27 percent of the vote in 1912, was the most successful. He was also the only one who had any effect on the outcome, splitting the Republican vote and giving the White House to Woodrow Wilson.

Perot fits into neither of these categories. Whatever else one might say about his policy views, they clearly did not reflect a sectarian outlook. Like the frustrated notables, he ran as the candidate of a party that was no more than a vehicle for his ambitions. Unlike them, his first venture into electoral politics was his presidential campaign. Also unlike them, he may have more staying power, if only because of his wealth.

What can be said about his success? For one thing, of course, he was the first third-party candidate at least since Roosevelt who had no worries about funding his campaign. Perot's immense fortune surely made his campaign possible. Having said this does not, however, relieve one of the need to explain the issues and voters that made him the most successful third-party candidate since a former president who was also a world celebrity, a war hero, and a winner of the Nobel Peace Prize.

The demographic correlates of vote choice in 1992 are fairly inscrutable. Perot voters looked much like white Christian America; blacks, Hispanics, and Jews all were underrepresented in the survey respondents who said they voted for Perot. There was a faintly curvilinear relationship between choosing Perot and both education and income. Eighteen percent of voters without a high school diploma said they voted for Perot, compared to 20 or 21 percent of everyone else except people with postgraduate training, only 15 percent of whom did so. The relationship of income to Perot voting was a pale shadow of this already pale relationship. Previous research has found that third-party candidates are most appealing to younger voters.[4] This was true of Perot, but the only clear dividing line was at the advanced age of fifty-nine, above which Perot won just 12 percent of the votes. From there down to age thirty he averaged 20 percent and got 23 percent from voters under thirty.

For the first time since 1964, Democrats exceeded Republicans in loyalty to their presidential candidates. Seventy-eight percent of them voted for Clinton, compared to 72 percent of Republicans who voted for Bush. Equal proportions defected to the other party's contender. The difference was in voting for Perot, which was done by 13 percent of Democrats and 18 percent of Republicans. By the same token, Perot did a bit better among respondents who said they voted for a Republican House candidate. Another indication that Perot's appeal was catholic in the terms customarily used to analyze elections is the finding that almost equal proportions of self-defined liberals, moderates, and conservatives voted for him.

The analysis of past third-party candidacies by Rosenstone, Behr, and Lazarus is a useful guide to political scientists trying to explain Perot's appeal. Some past candidates emerged and drew votes because of "neglected preferences"—that is, a popular point of view on a salient issue that was ignored by the major-party candidates (Rosenstone, Behr, and Lazarus, 1984). Offhand, this does not seem apposite to 1992. Fertile soil for third-party candidates also is provided by "neglected issues" (Rosenstone, Behr, and Lazarus, 1984). Perot launched his campaign as a crusade to awaken Americans to the $4 trillion national debt and the need for strong fiscal discipline, exemplified by his proposal for a fifty-cent increase in the federal gasoline tax. However, after his reentry into the campaign, Perot diversified his themes and seemed less interested in preaching a doctrine of bitter fiscal medicine. Survey data suggest that "budget deficit" may have been something of a mantra to Perot's followers. When asked, "Which issues mattered most in deciding how you voted?," 21 percent of all respondents in the exit polls conducted by Voter Research and Surveys (VRS) in 1992 mentioned the deficit, and of these, 37 percent voted for Perot. On the other hand, Perot voters were not notably supportive of lower spending or higher taxes. Nevertheless, it did seem that neither Bush nor Clinton paid more than lip service to fiscal discipline, so one might speculate that this issue was important to Perot's popularity.

Third-party candidates also flourish when the major parties "seem to mismanage the economy or nominate unqualified candidates." (Rosenstone, Behr, and Lazarus, 1984, p. 181). It is not difficult to understand why voters would have flunked the Bush administration's record of economic management. The puzzle is why so many of them failed to think it was time to give the Democrats a chance. Fifteen percent of voters who said their families were better off than in 1988 voted for Perot, compared to 18 percent who reported no change and fully 25 percent who said they were worse off. The answer may be that some voters, reacting to the barrage of assaults on Clinton's character, felt uneasy about him. Yet Clinton was attacked as a draft dodger and adulterer, not for economic mismanagement. Many voters may have come to be uneasy about Perot's character also, but once again, no serious questions were asked about his talents in the world of business. It is possible that Clinton's inability to profit fully from Bush's apparent failure occurred because he was competing for the votes of the disillusioned against a rival whose business success gave him an aura of economic competence.

One of Perot's favorite promises was that he would go to Washington and do something to get results: "get under the hood and fix it." It might be thought, then, that his followers would favor arrangements to promote action on the Potomac, such as an end to divided government. Sixty-two percent of the VRS respondents said that it was better for the country that the president and Congress be from the same party; only 28 percent preferred the alternative. Perot received a quarter of the votes from the latter group, those who supported divided government, compared to 18 percent from the majority who wanted just one party in charge.

This finding is consistent with the belief that Perot appealed primarily to citizens who are suspicious of "the system," represented by the politicians, campaign contributors, lobbyists, and consultants to foreign governments whom he denounced throughout the campaign. It is also consistent with Rosenstone, Behr, and Lazarus's finding that people who mistrust the government and government officials are more likely to vote for third-party candidates (Rosenstone, Behr, and Lazarus, 1984).

It may seem strange that the most successful populist leader of the postwar era was a billionaire who made much of his money from government contracts. Equally surprising is that this leader's appeal lacked even a veneer of prescribed remedies and was mainly complaints. This largely negative tone may represent not so much Perot's personality as his calculation about the most promising way to gather support. If he made such a calculation, perhaps it was based not on inspired guesswork but on surveys of the public.

CONCLUSION

Interpretation of Ross Perot's support in the 1992 election is frustrated because the vote choices that different categories of voters made in 1992 do not add up to any sort of coherent explanation. There is a genuine intellectual puzzle of how, with everything in the world going for him, Bill Clinton managed to get only 43 percent of the popular vote. Why would people vote for Ross Perot as the alternative to a failed incumbency? Some people argued that voters supported Perot because he was an outsider, yet the other alternative to the incumbent was the governor of a small and obscure state. Ross Perot made his billions on government contracts and arguably was much more of an insider than Bill Clinton.

The outcome of the 1992 presidential election suggests that there are some serious intellectual puzzles about how campaigns work that have not yet been solved, neither through the brilliance of the National Election Studies, nor through the human intelligence plus the technological skill of the campaign polling enterprise.

NOTES

1. Everett Carll Ladd and John Benson, "The Growth of News Polls in American Politics," in Thomas E. Mann and Gary R. Orren, eds., *Media Polls in American Politics* (Washington, D.C.: Brookings Institution, 1992), p. 19.

2. Bruce E. Keith, David B. Magleby, Candice J. Nelson, Elizabeth Orr, Mark C. Westlye, and Raymond E. Wolfinger, *The Myth of the Independent Voter* (Berkeley: University of California Press, 1992), pp. 70, 202. For a similar conclusion about the continued predictive power of party identification by a scholar who rejects the Keith et al. definition, see Warren E. Miller, "Party Identification, Realignment, and Party Voting: Back to the Basics," *American Political Science Review* 85 (June 1991):557–568.

3. The then obscure Republican, Christine Todd Whitman, ran for governor of New Jersey in 1992 against James Florio and defeated him.

4. Steven J. Rosenstone, Roy L. Behr, and Edward H. Lazarus, *Third Parties in America: Citizen Response to Major Party Failure* (Princeton: Princeton University Press, 1984), pp. 113, 116, 119, 176–178. This was notably true in 1968 when young people, with the most liberal views on civil rights of any age group, were at the same time the most likely to vote for the segregationist third-party candidate, George C. Wallace. See Philip E. Converse et al., "Continuity and Change in American Politics: Parties and Issues in the 1968 Election," *American Political Science Review* 63 (December 1969):1103.

15

The Ethics of Political Campaigns

WILMA GOLDSTEIN

But so far as I know, he has never been remotely involved in anything illegal—just unethical.

This observation was made by Gideon Page, an attorney for the office of public defender in *Expert Testimony*, a recent work of popular fiction by Grif Stockley. Page had been assigned by the court to defend an indigent mental patient who had been accused of murder. Page made the remark when he heard that his client's psychologist had just been arrested and charged with hiring Page's client to commit the murder in question. This particular psychologist was known to the attorney as someone who often testified as an expert witness on matters of sanity in cases Page was involved with. Gideon Page, portrayed in the book as a caring person with a strong sense of right and wrong, makes this remark implying a distinction between legality and ethics, in a casual, offhanded manner. This serves as a good introduction to the issue of ethics, because it is that very distinction that adds to the confusion surrounding ethical issues and so often leaves them unresolved.

LEGAL VERSUS ETHICAL

Where then should we begin the effort to discuss, define, and offer some conclusions on the topic of political ethics? A full examination of any topic usually begins with a definition of terms. The definition of the term "legal" has some usefulness, but the definition of "ethics" leaves many aspects of the term somewhat less than clear:

Legal: 1) of, created by, based upon, or authorized by law; 2) in conformity with the positive rules of law; permitted by law (a legal act); 3) that can be enforced in a court of law (legal rights).

Ethics: 1) a system of moral principle; 2) the rules of conduct recognized in respect to a particular class of human actions of a particular group, culture, etc. (e.g., medical, Judeo-Christian); 3) moral principles of an individual; e.g. his ethics forbade betrayal of a confidence; 4) that branch of philosophy dealing with values relating to human conduct with respect to the rightness and wrongness of certain actions and to the goodness and badness of the motives and ends of such actions.

Even an initial look at these two definitions helps to explain the problem. There are parameters and specificity to the definition of legal that do not exist in the definition of ethics. The very words used in the definition of that which is legal, such as "rules," "permitted," and "enforceable by a court of law," make it clear that there is some sort of standard by which to determine right and wrong and some way to take action if a wrong has been committed. On the other hand, the words used to describe ethics are vague, such as "system," "conduct," "rightness and wrongness," and "goodness and badness." Nowhere in the definition is there a way to establish compliance with these somewhat arbitrary standards. At best, we can use the definition of that which is legal to help us try to understand the parameters and limitations of ethics.

In an attempt to narrow the definition, we can look at the words used within the definition of ethics, such as "moral," as well as some of its suggested synonyms. The definition of "moral" goes beyond that of ethics in pointing out that to be moral is to be able to make the distinction between right and wrong, as well as to be "truthful." "Truthful" is a concept that may be useful here; it may not always be possible to determine if someone is telling the truth, but there are times when an investigation can determine if the truth has not been told. As well, "virtuous" is suggested as a synonym for ethical, and the definition of virtue connotes a morally excellent character and that a moral person is virtuous in such things as sexual matters. It thus quickly becomes obvious that defining ethics is no easy task and that most definitions are open to subjective analysis.

Another question that might be asked is why we should be concerned with the ethical practices of elected and appointed public officials and the professionals who help them to gain their positions. The answer perhaps is that it would seem we should expect people whom we trust to make major decisions about our lives to have good motives, be able to distinguish between right and wrong, and have a system of moral principles.

THE CHANGING DEBATE OVER POLITICAL ETHICS

There has been an increasing amount of attention given to ethical matters, both in and out of politics, over the past several decades. Watergate was undoubtedly a line of demarcation in contemporary political ethics, and it was a unique event for several reasons. It led to the first resignation of a sitting president of the United States, and it changed the way political issues and politicians were covered by the media. Prior to Watergate there had been limits and some unspoken rules about the crossover between a person's public and private lives. American history is full of documented and undocumented scandals about public figures going as far back as Martha and George Washington: allegations about debilitating illnesses, extramarital affairs, out-of-wedlock children, and homosexual relationships. Until Watergate, however, they were rarely part of the public discourse, at least not until the person was out of office and more often not until after the person's death. Watergate and, undoubtedly, the increase of tabloid journalism in this country seem to have changed the rules. Since Watergate, we have been treated to steadily increasing amounts of information about the lifestyles of political figures.

This kind of political coverage probably reached its zenith during Senator Gary Hart's second attempt to win the Democratic nomination for president in 1988. Rumors about Senator Hart's lifestyle had circulated for years. In 1984 he mounted a strong challenge to former Vice President Mondale, and when Mondale was defeated by President Reagan, Hart became the front-runner for the Democratic nomination in 1988. In 1988, after Hart was suspected of spending the night in his Washington townhouse with aspiring actress and model Donna Rice, Hart became the first presidential candidate ever to be asked in public if he had committed adultery. His refusal to answer the question directly, based on his notion of privacy, kept the issue at the level of high drama for many weeks. Hart left the race for the presidency, rejoined it, and finally took himself out of contention. However, for a very long time afterward, having "the Gary Hart problem" became a way to describe marital fidelity issues.

THE 1992 ELECTIONS

The 1992 election and the year leading up to it certainly provided a great deal of fodder for those who follow and cover politics and are concerned with ethical issues. It began with the now infamous Hill-Thomas hearings before the Senate Judiciary Committee. As the entire world watched the proceedings on television, attorney and law professor Anita Hill accused then nominee and now Supreme Court Justice Clarence Thomas of sexual harassment. During the course of the 1992 elections, two U.S. senators were accused of rape; four were accused of sexual harassment. A former beauty queen went public with allegations that she had an affair with a U.S. senator and documented some of the times they spent together. The same senator also had to defend himself against charges of bugging the telephones of the governor of his state, a person with whom he had a well-known rivalry.

The U.S. House of Representatives contributed to the body politic with its own series of ethical and legal abuses. In late 1991 it was discovered that the House of Representatives "bank" was a great deal more lax than traditional banking institutions about cashing checks for members of Congress who did not have sufficient funds in their accounts to cover the checks. Despite efforts by the House leadership not to disclose the names of the abusers, eventually the list was published. It was virtually impossible not to see the list in some newspaper in America or watch it displayed on television. In some instances the amounts were small and the overdrafts few. However, in other cases it was obvious that checks for amounts as much as $50,000 were written at times when they could not be covered and also at times that coincided with major purchases of property, houses, or automobiles. Shortly after these disclosures, a drug operation was uncovered in post offices located in congressional office buildings, and it turned out that postal employees were selling more than stamps between the hours of nine and five. In addition, these employees were allowing members of Congress and some of their staff to cash checks at the post office, a practice not available to the general public.

Finally, ethical questions surfaced in the presidential election. Bill Clinton was accused of marital infidelity, dodging the draft during the Vietnam War, using marijuana, and going to Moscow at the height of the Cold War. Somewhere during the course of this campaign, discussions about ethics became discussions about telling the truth. Early in the race "character" was used interchangeably with ethics, but gradually "telling the truth" became the way to talk about ethics. As we have seen, because it is difficult to define ethics, the issue easily lends itself to new synonyms.

MEDIA SCRUTINY OF CAMPAIGN TACTICS

Campaign tactics have also come under particularly close scrutiny in the two decades following the Watergate incident. One reason for this is the virtual explosion of reporters who now cover politics for the media since that watershed incident in American history. The increased coverage is made more possible by the number of students who enrolled in journalism schools during the 1970s and 1980s, hoping also to become famous by covering politics.

Many reporters claim that their intense focus on campaign tactics is due to the shift in campaigns away from personal appearances and toward carefully crafted messages delivered through paid media. In the period between the 1988 and 1992 elections, syndicated *Washington Post* columnist David Broder, often referred to as the dean of political journalists, encouraged his colleagues across the country to print and analyze the messages in paid advertising in their local newspapers. Many reporters have taken up this challenge, and verbatim scripts for political ads, usually accompanied by a photograph from the ad or a file photo of the candidates, are now seen regularly in newspapers across the country. The reporter attempts to validate the claims or accusations made in the advertisements and usually adds her or his own analysis of the implications and imagery created by these messages.

Television programming has also played a role in the increased amount of attention given to the process of campaigning. In addition to the increased coverage of candidates and campaigns, traditional broadcast television often includes present and former campaign operatives as political commentators and analysts on the nightly news as well as on morning and weekend talk shows. There are a growing number of television programs that use permanent panels of political journalists and invite campaign practitioners, candidates, and elected officials on as guests.

Public television has contributed to this expanded coverage of politics as well. Intimate portraits of campaigns done by following candidates around for weeks, even occasionally throughout entire campaigns, appear later in cinema verité format. Most of the dialogue consists of verbatim comments in scenes with candidates, campaign staff, volunteers, and voters; the dialogue is then surrounded by the reporter's perspective. Public television has also begun covering seminars around the country, often on college campuses, in which the participants tend to be political practitioners. The projection that there will be 500 or more television channels by the end of this century will undoubtedly produce even more coverage on all aspects of politics.

There are now three cable television channels that cover the proceedings of the U.S. House and Senate, along with breaking news stories at the White House, the State Department, or the Supreme Court. Local cable channels often cover the proceedings of state legislatures, city and county councils, and boards of education. For better or worse, the American public now has the ability to know at least as much about campaign and legislative political practices as it knows about candidates. If current polling data are to be believed, and there is little reason to doubt the data, neither the practitioners of politics nor politicians themselves are held in particularly high esteem by most Americans.

DEFINING WHAT IS ETHICAL

Discussions among campaign operatives on the issues surrounding political ethics can be almost as confusing as the attempts to define the term itself. Although another outgrowth of Watergate was the regulation of political fund-raising for federal campaigns, accompanied by similar legislation at the state level, there are other aspects of political campaigning for which there are neither ethical nor legal guidelines or remedies when alleged abuses are uncovered. Debates in both formal and informal settings tend to conclude by pointing out that there still seem to be more questions than answers about the ethics of politics.

Is it ethical or unethical, for example, for a political management consultant and a vendor who sells direct mail to a campaign to have an additional financial arrangement between them based on either earnings or potential earnings from that campaign? Those who believe these arrangements to be ethical usually describe them as "finders' fees" or "commissions." Those who believe these arrangements to be unethical tend to describe them in more emotionally charged words such as "kickbacks." In reality such relationships do exist, and even though they have been discussed in public forums of political operatives and written about in newspapers, no action has been taken to stop them, either formally or informally.

Do these special arrangements cross the line into unethical behavior depending upon whether or not the candidate is aware of them? That such arrangements exist at all would seem to beg the "rightness-wrongness" dimension of the political ethics question. Whether or not the candidate is aware of such relationships would seem to concern itself with the "truthfulness" element of ethical questions. Many who believe commissions and finders' fees are an acceptable way of doing business in politics think that if the candidate is unaware of the arrangement, ethics have been breached. For those who have already decided that these extra monetary relationships are unethical, the candidate factor serves only to compound the issue. And, for those who might try to establish ethical guidelines for the practice of politics, such questions tend to make the whole issue even murkier.

The questions most often asked about political campaigns revolve around the nature of the messages in paid advertising and the verbal exchanges between candidates when they appear jointly. "Dirty politics," "too negative," say those who think what they see and hear is more hard-hitting than is necessary. Simply a matter of "contrast" say those who believe in the more aggressive nature of these kinds of actions.

Where do those who accept strong contrasts in campaign messages draw the line? Many will tell you they believe the line is crossed when the accusations move from job-related to personal. They accept the aggressive nature of certain political messages because they believe it important for potential voters to know about such things as poor voting and attendance records and certain position switches, known in the political vernacular as "flip-flops." They would usually add that they might even overlook some of the harshness because candidates are never going to highlight their own inadequacies, so it is legitimate for their opponents to do so. When the issue turns to more private matters, such as marriages, divorce, fidelity, substance abuse, or the behavior of a candidate's family members, often even those who accept the harsher messages believe the ethical line has been crossed. Complicating the issue even further is existing research that shows people tend to remember negative information for longer periods of time than they do positive information, and even when they find the information and delivery style distasteful, it can become a factor in their final voting decision.

At least once in every campaign a situation arises in which there is a discussion about a loyalist from one camp signing on as a volunteer in the opposing campaign so she or he can observe what is going on and report back. Most often these "opportunities" are generated by overly enthusiastic volunteers who assume all political campaigns have a cloak-and-dagger element to them. That these offers get made is, to some, the sign of an unfortunate mythology about campaigning. When these offers are accepted by campaign staff, then the issue takes on ethical considerations.

IS IT TIME FOR A CODE OF ETHICS?

Anyone who reviews some of the literature on ethics in fields such as business and education will find that one of the first recommendations made is the need for a code of ethics. Many professions, such as medicine and law, do have codes and oaths that help set the expectations for right and wrong behaviors. Once a person is elected to political office, there usually is a code of ethics, such as those that exist in Congress and most state legislatures. However, there is no code of ethics for candidates or for that group of people described as political operatives or practitioners. There are rules and reporting requirements for certain aspects of campaigns at both the federal and state level, mostly regarding the raising and spending of money. However, when it comes to a general code of conduct for candidates and campaign operatives as they interact with each other, a code does not exist.

There have been occasional attempts to discuss ethical issues and the need for a code in certain settings when operatives gather, but no conclusions have emerged. It is difficult even to get agreement on what kinds of questions need to be asked and answered. In addition to such issues as those raised previously in this chapter, there are a host of other matters that might be discussed. Would it help if there was a code that stated what kinds of information the public has a right to know about candidates for public office? What does a campaign operative owe the candidate, and what in turn does the candidate owe a campaign operative? Should a consultant be told about every skeleton in the closet? Is it ethical for a campaign consultant to work for candidates of different parties? Does it make a difference if it is in the same campaign year or in the same geographical location?

The pursuit of a code of ethics for the profession of politics would be a worthy endeavor. There are, however, certain obstacles to overcome in order even to begin the process. Who is eligible for the title of campaign consultant? Although many political consultants are well-known, usually because they work in high-visibility races, there are probably three to four times as many who provide services to campaigns in local races, and these consultants would be difficult to locate. There is no reliable registry for people who practice politics; there are fewer than ten schools that graduate people with a degree in political consulting. Even if one used a list of those who subscribe to popular political publications, it would be difficult to come up with an accurate cross-section of the wide variety of people who are involved in the business of politics. It would then be even more difficult to get them to agree on what they consider ethical questions and abuses, what to include in a code, and even more important, who would evaluate practices for a possible breach and what actions would be taken if such a breach were determined. Although I have never been one to promote excessive regulation, I question whether it is possible for such a disparate group of people to police themselves. It might make sense for the final development of a code and a set of regulations to be determined by a bipartisan commission, similar to the one that now exists to guide presidential elections. Its membership includes party chairs from both the Democratic and Republican Parties, and its mission has included offering policy recommendations as well as resolving certain controversies as they arise during campaigns.

CONCLUSION

The debate on a code of ethics might be lengthy and difficult, but the result might help restore some respect to a profession that has been in a state of ill repute for the past several decades. One of the major American political polling firms added the profession of politics to the list on a question that has long been asked in social and political research. It requires respondents to rank-order certain professions as to such qualities as reliability and trustworthiness. Political operatives were ranked below those who had previously been at the bottom of the list namely, used-car salesmen and televangelists. Politics is a noble pursuit, and those of us involved in it believe that to be true. Obviously we have a long way to go to gain the trust of most Americans.

16

Campaign Ethics and Political Trust

LINDA L. FOWLER

When Ronald Reagan was campaigning for the presidency, he used to tell a story about two hikers backpacking in the mountains. As they trudged along the path, they heard crashing noises as if a large animal were moving about in the brush. Soon, the noises got louder and closer, and they caught a glimpse of an irate grizzly heading in their direction. At that point, one hiker sat down by the trail, quickly pulled off his heavy boots, and began to lace on his sneakers. "Hey," said his companion, "what are you doing? You know you can't outrun a grizzly bear." "That's right," the hiker replied as he tied the second shoe. "But I'm not going to outrun that grizzly—I'm just going to outrun you."

Since Reagan told that story, I have often repeated it as an allegory about the ethics of political campaigns. Like the hikers, candidates find themselves in a zero-sum situation in which one of them must lose. What behavior is acceptable for two such rivals? Do the ends of getting elected justify whatever means ensure victory? Is it ethical to throw one's political opponents to the grizzlies?

Political scientists seldom ask these questions. Our professional neutrality as scholars moves us to explain what *is* rather than what *ought to be* in politics. We see our role as observing politicians, not prescribing codes of conduct for them. We also have not given much attention to election campaigns because until quite recently the conventional wisdom in our discipline held that campaigns were relatively unimportant influences on the vote. In our collective view, elections have been decided by voters' long-term identification with a particular party and their response to short-term stimuli, such as the performance of the president, the state of the economy, and the personal attributes of individual candidates. We had little cause for concern about campaign ethics so long as we regarded campaigns themselves as insignificant.

However, several trends suggest that our profession can no longer ignore campaign ethics. First, scientific detachment notwithstanding, many political scientists worry about citizens' growing cynicism and dissatisfaction with the nation's electoral process. Historically, citizens have approved of individual officeholders and expressed pride in governmental institutions, although they disdained the campaigning and bargaining so characteristic of politics generally. However, citizens' increasingly low regard for electioneering has helped sour their opinions about most politicians and many institutions. For example, the eroding public confidence in established political leaders was evident during the 1992 election in the passage of term limitations in many states and in the strong showing of independent presidential candidate Ross Perot.

Second, political scientists' research methods and results have contributed to the widespread use of manipulative advertising and negative campaigns that have antagonized voters toward election politics. For several decades we have promulgated a view of the electorate as ignorant and apathetic—easy targets, in effect, for unscrupulous candidates and their consultants. We have refined the survey techniques that enable politicians to manufacture issues and distort opponents' weaknesses. Although our profession does not condone ads like the one that featured convicted rapist Willie Horton in the 1988 presidential race, we surely bear some responsibility for facilitating the use of such racist tactics.

Third, political scientists now have a considerable body of research that challenges our previous conclusions about the unimportance of campaigns. Largely because of the rise of personalized elections, the candidates' organizational skills and political messages matter more today than in the past. The intensity of campaigns, in terms of the level of candidate spending and the amount of press coverage now has a decided effect on the final vote.

Granting that political scientists have incentives to pay attention to campaign ethics, do they have anything useful to say on the subject? Our profession claims no special expertise regarding ethical standards for campaigns, but we do have substantial experience watching politicians grapple with the pressures of electioneering. We can clarify how ethics in politics differs from ethics in private life, and we can establish why ethical conduct is more difficult to define and enforce for candidates in election campaigns than for public officials in office. Given these distinctions, we can perhaps derive some modest rules of thumb for judging the appropriateness of behavior in contemporary elections.

ETHICS IN POLITICS AND
ETHICS IN PRIVATE LIFE

Public concern about the ethics of campaign investigations into politicians' private lives is part of a larger debate in society—in business, in medicine, in education, and in private life—about moral values and individual obligations for the general good. Many professional schools, for example, have instituted courses that attempt to sensitize future doctors, lawyers, and accountants to ethical conflicts and to help them define suitable norms of practice. Similarly, many corporate executives and board members confront changing liability rules that hold them personally responsible for the wrongful actions of their organizations.

Amid this widespread examination of appropriate standards of conduct, however, the ethical requirements of politics stand somewhat apart. The issues are different because the public sphere of politics demands a higher standard than the private sphere of the market. They are different because voters tend to equate private morality with public responsibility. These distinctive aspects of political ethics not only have fostered more stringent standards of behavior for public officials than for ordinary citizens but also have created an environment in which the appearance of wrongdoing can often be as serious as the fact of wrongdoing. Furthermore, the uniqueness of political ethics provides a justification of sorts for the public's intense scrutiny of politicians' personal finances and private lives.

Some critics argue that such a double standard is hypocritical, and others contend that it deters talented people who want to protect their privacy from seeking public office. Yet we need to recognize that public beliefs about political ethics are deeply rooted in the American political culture, which contains contradictory views about the nature of political leaders. On the one hand, the U.S. democracy was founded on a pessimistic view of human nature that did not expect public officials to be virtuous. As Jefferson observed, "Whenever a man has cast a longing eye on offices, a rottenness begins in his conduct" (Auden and Kronenberger, 1981, p. 304). On the other hand, the nation has a strong puritanical streak and an idealistic view of its place in history that lead to highly moralistic attitudes toward public life. The chronic mistrust of political ambition that citizens inherited from the framers thus coexists with their desire for a higher-order politics that reflects American exceptionalism.

Even without the moralistic tradition of American politics, the very nature of representative government prompts public insistence on ethical standards that are stricter for public officials than for private individuals. Unlike the direct democracy one finds in town meetings and classical Greek city-states, republican government vests enormous discretion in elected officials to act on behalf of citizens. Citizens entrust their representatives with the authority to make decisions that they cannot make themselves, and in delegating so much power, they create two sorts of risk: (1) that representatives will pursue their own views and interests instead of those of their constituents; (2) that representatives will make unacceptable trade-offs requiring sacrifices from particular individuals or groups in order to promote a particular vision of the collective good. Representative government thus entails an enormous act of trust on the part of citizens and properly requires that elected officials be worthy of that confidence.

Consider briefly the nature of the responsibility that citizens confer on their representatives. First is fiscal responsibility—the power to confiscate citizens' wealth through taxes and allocate these public monies among competing demands. Second is regulatory responsibility—the power to prohibit particular behavior and punish infractions through fines, imprisonment, or even the death penalty. Third is warmaking responsibility—the power to conscript young people into the armed services, to send them into battle, and to inflict havoc on the declared enemies of the state. Given these awesome grants of authority, citizens are entitled to ask that their representatives be men and women who are honest, trustworthy, and decent and that they set an example of civic-mindedness for others to follow. A representative system of government may not require the classic civic virtues of the Greeks and Romans, but it does demand character in its elected officials.

This is particularly true when one considers how difficult it is to monitor and evaluate the performance of politicians in office. Issues are complex, information is spotty, and consequences are imperfectly understood. A citizenry far more attentive and knowledgeable than the American public would be hard-pressed to figure out what politicians were up to and whether or not they had made the right decisions. In our democracy, the horse-race mentality of the press and the weak position of the parties make the task of obtaining consistent and reliable information about politicians' performance nearly impossible.

Given the very real obstacles citizens confront in holding elective officials accountable, therefore, the intense public scrutiny of politicians' private lives becomes something more than mere nosiness or prurience. Citizens compensate for their ignorance by employing past private acts as predictors about future public acts. For example, if a husband cheats on his wife, perhaps he will deceive his constituents. If a woman misuses Medicaid funds to pay for a relative's health care, perhaps she will play fast and loose with the public purse. If a male harasses female employees for sexual favors, perhaps he will be hostile to the needs and aspirations of female voters. If candidates are unscrupulous in seeking campaign contributions, perhaps they will make shady deals in smoke-filled backrooms. Given the preoccupation of the press with personal behavior, obtaining such information is relatively easy and cheap compared to the costly business of examining campaign records, committee hearings, and roll-call votes.

The personal conduct of politicians is also pertinent in voters' eyes because the consequences of individual wrongdoing are magnified in the public arena. Instead of a single injured party, politicians have the capacity to damage many citizens or even the whole society. In this sense, citizens' weighing of private acts is an attempt to avoid serious public consequences. Suppose, for example, that the probability that an unfaithful husband will turn out to be a dishonest legislator is quite low. But suppose that a dishonest legislator imposes substantial losses on the public in terms of squandered revenue and diminished governmental effectiveness. Put the two calculations together and the prudent citizen might reasonably decide that even a small chance of incurring a very large cost is unacceptable. The corollary to this cost-benefit calculation is that the greater a public official's capacity for inflicting harm, the greater the weight citizens will place on relatively small violations of ethical norms. Hence, infidelity in a potential president is judged more severely than the same behavior in a governor; alcoholism in a future secretary of defense is less tolerable than in a senator.

Rightly or wrongly, then, the public generates predictions about politicians' behavior in office from their myriad private activities. Social scientists call this type of calculation "satisficing"—that is, making a less than optimal decision on the basis of imperfect information. Given the difficulty of getting better data and the extraordinary investment of time and energy necessary to adopt other, more politically relevant criteria, citizens are likely to persist in their scrutiny of politicians' private lives. Such a strategy is undeniably distasteful to many public officials; it leads to excesses in the news media that can be painful or grotesque; and it drives good people out of the public arena. One wonders, for example, whether Franklin Roosevelt would have been a four-term president had voters known about his extramarital affairs. Nevertheless, the public's tendency to equate personal ethics with governmental performance, though overly simplistic, is far from irrational.

Citizens consequently regard personal conduct as a legitimate subject of debate in political campaigns. Candidates stress their own family backgrounds and reputations in the community because voters want to know what kind of people they are entrusting with the public welfare. They point out the personal failings of their opponents because voters attach great importance to any evidence that a politician might abuse the discretion vested in public office. Negative advertising works, in short, because voters use it as a simple, low-cost cue for estimating a candidate's future behavior. It works because it speaks to citizens' very real concerns about the trustworthiness of prospective officeholders.

But the political relevance of candidates' personal conduct raises its own ethical questions. Assuming that voters do not need to know everything about elective officials, where do we draw the line in examining politicians' personal lives? Who defines the boundaries separating their private actions from publicly relevant behavior? When does a candidate's effort to exploit an opponent's personal weakness itself become unethical?

Obviously, the norms governing the political treatment of private behavior have changed radically in recent years. Changing standards in the news media about what constitutes investigative reporting have broadened the scope of activity that is now subject to public scrutiny. Increasing cynicism among the citizenry has created a receptive audience for scandal-mongering by the press and misleading advertisements by candidates. If Americans in the past were too trusting and credulous about public figures, they now seem too inclined to believe the worst. Such a climate of opinion invites abuse, particularly at the height of a hard-fought campaign. Candidates so far seem content to let the press do the dirtiest work by maintaining silence on the subject of their opponents' sexual activities. But just about everything else seems to be fair game.

The 1992 New York Democratic primary for the U.S. Senate nomination offers a telling example of the ambiguities that arise when a candidate's private conduct becomes a campaign issue. In this case, both the alleged transgressor and the accusers became embroiled in controversies over ethical norms in politics. The race involved New York State Attorney General Robert Abrams, former U.S. House member and 1984 Democratic vice-presidential nominee Geraldine Ferraro, Queens County District Attorney and former U.S. House member Elizabeth Holtzman, and African American community activist, the Rev. Al Sharpton. The prize was the opportunity to run against incumbent Republican senator, Alfonse D'Amato, who had been investigated in 1991 by the Senate Ethics Committee on charges that he had permitted his brother to peddle influence from his office on various governmental contracts. The committee cleared D'Amato of any complicity in his brother's dealings, but it strongly criticized his judgment. Previously, D'Amato had also been implicated but never convicted in several Suffolk County investigations regarding favoritism in federal housing programs and kickbacks to the local Republican Party organization.

The primary was essentially a three-way contest with Sharpton initially playing a largely symbolic role. Abrams started out as the front-runner, having won his statewide office by large margins and having won many of the counties that D'Amato had also carried previously. But a lackluster fund-raising effort and poorly run campaign left him vulnerable to Ferraro's media appeal and aggressive style. Holtzman, who had lost narrowly to D'Amato in 1980, had difficulty raising money and shaking off the image that she would lose again. All three were committed liberals who agreed on most major issues, so they clashed over who could best capitalize on D'Amato's tarnished ethical image.

Late in the race Holtzman attempted to revive her flagging campaign by charging Ferraro with two types of misconduct: accepting a large campaign contribution in the late 1970s from a business associate of her husband who subsequently was reported to have connections with the Mafia; and profiting from rental property that was occupied by a tenant who trafficked in child pornography. The first charge assumed that Ferraro knew or should have known her contributors and their source of funds. The second charge centered on the fact that the real estate firm headed by Ferraro's husband did not act vigorously enough to evict the tenant and actually raised the rent after the unsavory nature of the business became known. These issues were similar to those Ferraro had dealt with in the 1984 presidential election—her level of involvement with her husband's convoluted financial transactions. Ferraro could not accept responsibility for behavior that was largely beyond her control; but she could not claim ignorance of her husband's finances without suggesting that she had been either too calculating or too naive in not knowing about her husband's allegedly shady dealings. Her defense was to claim that she did not know the campaign contributor or have dealings with him after her election to Congress and to argue that her involvement in her husband's real estate dealings were negligible and that New York City's procedures for evicting tenants were so cumbersome that it took him four years to get rid of the pornographer. She charged Holtzman with distorting the facts and engaging in ethnic slurs against Italian Americans, and she condemned Abrams for complicity in the mudslinging.

In what New Yorkers will remember as one of the nastiest campaigns ever visited on the state, the charges and countercharges led to a barrage of negative advertising that left the voters feeling all three participants were unethical. Enough suspicion stuck to Ferraro to cost her the primary, and enough disgust at Holtzman's seeming opportunism landed her in last place behind Sharpton. Abrams subsequently lost to D'Amato in the general election because large numbers of Democrats resented his participation in the attacks on Ferraro and refused to cast a ballot for any senatorial candidate. Many independents and Republicans who disliked D'Amato ended up supporting him because of his reputation for bringing federal money into the state. "Senator Pothole," as he was dubbed in the press, for all his questionable connections, ended up looking no worse on ethical grounds than the alternative.

The New York Senate race suggests that the standards for political behavior have become so broad and vague that neither the candidates nor the public understands what they mean. Image can be as damaging as behavior; rules can be applied retroactively. The charges against Ferraro entailed improprieties rather than illegal actions, and they involved alleged misdeeds by her husband rather than by the candidate herself. Ferraro's alleged sin was poor judgment about political appearances—in failing to appreciate how a campaign contribution from an alleged Mafia associate would look to the public (assuming that she did know about the contribution and its donor's history) and in being insensitive to the connection, however remote, with the business of child pornography.

The New York case further indicates how ethical posturing can supersede issues as the stuff of campaigns. The allegations against Ferraro did discredit her, even in the eyes of voters who thought that Holtzman had been wrong to raise them. Arising so late in the primary season, when the press and the uncommitted voters were just starting to pay attention to the race, the charges consumed the remainder of the campaign. As is so often the case in tight races with low turnout, this one was decided at the margins by defections that proved fatal to Ferraro's candidacy.

Yet Holtzman's fourth-place showing and Sharpton's improved standing in the polls, suggest that the public judged the accuser almost as harshly as the accused. Ironically, Sharpton's aplomb amid the namecalling made voters forgive his own checkered background as a tax delinquent and agitator for questionable causes. New York's experience thus demonstrates how the politicization of personal conduct introduces a new element of volatility into American elections and leaves the electorate extremely ambivalent about its choice of public officials.

ENFORCING ETHICAL STANDARDS IN CAMPAIGNS

Although the public sets higher standards of conduct for elected officials than for private citizens, it is in a relatively weak position to enforce these expectations during an election. Campaign norms tend to be implicit rather than explicit, and they operate primarily through electoral or informal sanctions rather than through the legal system. Politicians operate in an ethical environment that is largely self-policing, subject to intermittent oversight by the press and the electorate.

Even when the rules have been codified, as in the case of the campaign finance regulations, enforcement is largely through voluntary compliance. The Federal Election Campaign Act (FECA) passed during the 1970s relies on regular reporting of campaign contributions under the theory that abuses would be minimized by the threat of public exposure and that political opponents would be more zealous prosecutors of corruption than would government bureaucrats. The Federal Election Commission therefore has minimal investigative resources and punitive powers, and it usually confines its role to providing technical support for candidates' compliance efforts and collecting data on contributions and expenditures. Consequently, candidates differ widely in their adherence to the letter of the law, and they enjoy numerous loopholes to circumvent the spirit of the law.

The very nature of political campaigns, moreover, impedes the enforcement of uniform ethical standards. Some obstacles are endemic to electioneering, and some result from the highly decentralized electoral system in the United States.

Campaigns are short, episodic, often intense events. Despite the lengthy presidential primary process every four years and the permanent reelection drive conducted by incumbent members of Congress, the campaign that most voters pay attention to occupies the weeks from Labor Day in September to election day in November. In presidential elections the percentage of voters who make their decision after the party conventions has increased, as the number of strong party identifiers in the electorate has diminished over the past three decades. In congressional elections, the quality of House and Senate challengers varies considerably across constituencies, but when strong contenders do emerge they, too, target resources and messages at the "movable" voters whose weak partisanship makes them susceptible to concentrated, last-minute campaigning.

This potential volatility of the electorate can tempt candidates to take a cheap shot at their opponents, especially if they are behind. At the same time, the uneven coverage of races below the presidential level raises the possibility that unsavory campaign tactics will seldom attract public notice. Reporters are far more likely to report on opinion polls because their idea of a good campaign story is a horse race—who's ahead and by how much. When a contest is perceived as one-sided, in fact, they may cease coverage altogether, as the discussion in Chapter 9 pointed out. Similarly, members of the news media are more interested in the total sums of money raised and spent by candidates—more horse-race coverage. Rarely does the press focus on the source of a candidate's campaign contributions or examine the FEC reports for patterns, such as bundling (the practice of an individual or PAC collecting checks from a number of individuals or PACs and then presenting all the checks as a group, or "bundle," to a campaign or candidate), that signify undue influence by special interests.

Given the episodic public scrutiny of campaign operations, candidates may figure that the advantages of an unethical strategy may greatly exceed the drawbacks and that their behavior may not be known to the public until the election is over and the winner chosen. For every case like the New York Senate primary in which political expedience was highlighted by the press and punished by the electorate, there are many examples when it has brought the reward of victory.

Political activists, party stalwarts, and opposing candidates are in a position to monitor unethical campaign practices firsthand, but they have few incentives or resources to punish misconduct. Their influence is limited because electoral politics in the United States is extremely fragmented. Parties, for example, are broken into state and county organizations; the national headquarters cannot impose universal standards on the state affiliates and the states cannot discipline local committees. Regional differences compound the problem, for what might be considered reprehensible in Indiana could be acceptable in Louisiana. The system of direct primaries further undermines the development of an ethical code for campaigns because candidates can seek their party's nomination, whether or not the party approves of their behavior. In such a far-flung system of multiple jurisdictions and diverse political cultures, it is difficult to establish and enforce consensus on campaign ethics.

Individual candidates also perpetuate a laissez-faire approach to standards of campaign conduct. They tend to be self-starters and to assume responsibility for organizing and executing their own campaigns. Although they get help from party organizations in raising money and mobilizing grassroots support, nominees stand or fall primarily on their own efforts. Unless there is a scandal of major proportions, such as Watergate, they are rarely penalized when a fellow candidate of the same party behaves badly, and they do not bear collective responsibility for the general disrepute of their fellow politicians. Indeed, a favored ploy of all candidates is to run against the political establishment and differentiate themselves from the rest of the scoundrels at the capital. Rather than exposing unethical behavior, candidates have every reason to distance themselves from it.

Taken as a whole, the political environment in which candidates run for office permits politicians a considerable degree of ethical leeway. The laissez-faire atmosphere is reinforced by the public, which seems to relax its double standard for political figures during the brief period of the campaign. Whereas citizens are intensely interested in the private morality of elected officials, including actions that took place years before the election, they seem to expect that politicians will cut a few corners in order to get elected. Distortions of the truth and manipulation of the facts that ordinarily would provoke outrage excite far less reaction from the public in the heat of a campaign. Such voter tolerance is the primary reason candidates and their consultants have so much difficulty deciding when negative campaigning crosses the line from merely distasteful to truly noxious. In the end, relativism is the general rule: If the voters do not reject a particular tactic, then it is, ipso facto, ethical.

In sum, citizens have understandable reasons for establishing more stringent rules of behavior for elective officials than for private citizens. Their double standard is consistent with the long-standing tension in the nation's political culture, with the undeniable importance of individual character in a representative democracy, and with voters' reliance on personal behavior as a cue to public action. But citizens are hard-pressed to sustain their expectations during a campaign. At best, elections turn out to be a crude, episodic corrective to unethical behavior. Consequently, citizens are dependent—far more than they like to admit—on the integrity and sense of public purpose of politicians.

THE CODIFICATION OF ETHICS

Recent efforts to codify standards for official behavior in the legislative and executive branches of the federal government attempt to reduce the uncertainty about what constitutes ethical conduct and to ease the problems of enforcement. Making the rules more explicit regarding campaign contributions, lobbying, acceptance of honoraria, and the like reduces the leeway politicians enjoy to make their own ethical judgments. By clarifying violations, such codes also promise a greater likelihood that public officials will be made to answer for their actions. However, this legalistic approach to political ethics is only a partial solution, and it may actually make politicians less accountable for certain types of wrongdoing.

One of the greatest sources of controversy about ethics in public life concerns the political relevance of private actions. As we have seen, citizens use personal behavior as a cue to assess a politician's trustworthiness. Many of the deeds citizens condemn are not only legal but often take place before a politician has entered the public domain. It hardly seems feasible to legislate restrictions against citizens making use of such information. Therefore, opposing candidates and the news media are likely to keep bringing up these matters. Similarly, it makes no sense to legislate a set of ethical criteria that politicians must have satisfied before they decided to run for office. Common sense suggests that legal codes will not lessen the public's demand for ever greater disclosure about a candidate's personal affairs. Nor will they lessen the risk that would-be officeholders will find themselves justifying past actions. In politics, there seems to be no statute of limitations and no prohibitions against defining offenses ex post facto.

Furthermore, the fragmented nature of politics in the United States is likely to thwart any serious efforts to set strict ethical standards. The institutional mechanisms to develop a national consensus on norms and to make them binding simply do not exist. Most important, there is always the risk that a genuinely tough code—one both stringent enough to force compliance in the face of the very natural temptations inherent in election campaigns and broad enough to cover all possible transgressions— would have a chilling effect on competition. How could the public protect against ethical rules being used to hinder opponents, to drive people from the electoral arena on technicalities, and to muzzle unpopular points of view?

Apart from these practical objections to codification of political ethics, I fear that a legalistic approach will have the perverse effect of making public life less ethical. Such a tendency is already very apparent in the Congress when the House and Senate Ethics Committees investigate their colleagues for alleged misdeeds. These proceedings have become adversarial sessions, with counsel, cross-examination of witnesses, and procedural guarantees. As they have become more like trials, the principle that the accused is innocent unless proven guilty has gradually become the standard for assessing blame and punishment. Lawmakers have insisted that their detractors produce a "smoking gun" and have taken refuge in the defense that having committed no crime they should not be censured or removed from office.

In my view, this perspective debases the whole idea of public office as a trust. It establishes an entitlement to the perquisites of Congress as an institution for any incumbent who is not a proven crook. It defines fitness for office in terms of minimum criteria: In other words, anyone is suitable who has not been caught and convicted of breaking the criminal code. Hence, when the Senate Ethics Committee declined to sanction Alfonse D'Amato in 1991 because it could not prove D'Amato had participated in his brother's schemes, he trumpeted his exoneration in newspaper ads and letters to voters across the state. What the senator neglected to mention was that the committee criticized his conduct as a breach of the public trust. It found no smoking gun, but it did condemn his bad judgment.

CONCLUSION

Is there a way to make character a requirement for public office? Citizens and candidates alike will have to live with a certain degree of ambiguity about when private life spills over into public life. They will also have to accept the fact that campaigns will often skirt the bounds of probity. I have my own rules of thumb for deciding when politicians have crossed the line between human frailty and unethical conduct. I offer them here:

1. Judge incumbents more strictly than challengers because they are in a position to abuse power and because they have an obligation to promote the dignity of their office. Besides, they enjoy so many electoral advantages they should not need to resort to dirty tricks.
2. Employ higher standards for higher offices because the potential for abuse is greater.
3. Be harsh with politicians who tell falsehoods or do violence to the facts.
4. Do not judge actions from the past with standards from the present. A senator who pinched female bottoms in the elevator twenty years

ago when such harassment was commonplace is different from a senator who is still doing it.
5. Require politicians to take responsibility for what their staffs and political consultants do in their name. Individuals who hide behind their subordinates are unworthy of the public trust.

Ultimately, it is up to citizens to devise their own commonsense rules for judging politicians' conduct. Unless voters require their elected representatives to be men and women of proven character, the integrity of democratic government is compromised.

17

Strategic Perspectives on the 1992 Campaign

SAMUEL POPKIN

The worlds of campaign strategists and academic analysts of elections seldom overlap. Campaign strategists focus on the role of variables over which they have control, such as advertising and media appearances. Academic analysts, on the other hand, tend to ignore the role of campaigns and focus on such variables as the state of the economy, attitudes about the political parties, and the images of the candidates. The 1992 campaign illustrates how campaigns make connections between political parties, candidates, and economics by addressing the concerns voters have about the issues and candidates.

A slogan on the wall in the Clinton campaign's "war room"—"The economy, stupid"—became so well known that it was used in campaigns throughout the world. Ironically, neither inflation nor unemployment was high in 1992, and a standard economic model of presidential elections, based on changes in inflation and economic growth (growth for the first two quarters of 1992 was barely above 1 percent), predicted that President Bush would win comfortably with 57 percent of the vote.[1] Bush's job performance rating as of July 1992 was at only 31 percent (Campbell and Mann, 1992). That the economy mattered but some traditional economic models were so spectacularly wrong emphasizes what an unusual year 1992 was. George Bush was not defeated because knee-jerk pocketbook voters voted against him. George Bush was defeated because voters who were concerned about their long-term economic future no longer believed that the Republican Party had a program for prosperity and for governing the country, and because Bill Clinton was able to use the campaign to convince voters unhappy with the Democratic Party that he was a different kind of Democrat.

In 1992 no candidate could rely on his party's historical record to justify a claim for the right to the next four years. Internationally, the end of the Cold War meant the Republican record on defense was no longer as relevant as it had been. Domestically, Reaganomics had not meant either lower taxes, less government spending, or sustained growth. Democratic candidates, on the other hand, had to convince voters skeptical about government that they were not tax-and-spend traditional Democrats concerned about social programs but Democrats who would emphasize private-sector job creation and deficit reduction.

Unemployment and inflation were low in 1992, but potential voters had a pervasive sense of stagnation and of a slow economic decline. Americans during the Reagan and Bush presidencies had come to believe that the next generation would not prosper as they had. The long-term economic future looked uncertain compared to their own past, and they doubted whether their country would remain a world economic leader. In fact, expectations about the economic future were far lower than would have been expected on the basis of actual measures of the economy. For decades the Conference Board, a business think tank, and the University of Michigan's Institute for Social Research had been calculating indices of consumer confidence based on surveys that asked people their evaluations of local employment opportunities and economic activity and their expectations about employment opportunities, family income, and economic activity in the future. For decades both of these measures of consumer confidence had closely mirrored actual changes in employment opportunities and economic activity. When Iraq invaded Kuwait, however, consumer confidence dropped far below where it would have been based on the historical relationship with the aggregate predictors of consumer confidence. After the victorious 100-hour air war, moreover, there was only a momentary upsurge in consumer confidence before it once again dropped far below the predicted level, and it stayed there for the rest of the Bush presidency.[2]

READ MY PLAN

In 1976 many voters in the primaries had distrusted Democratic insiders because of the Democrats' support for busing and because the taint of Watergate affected everyone in Washington. In 1992 Democrats had to convince voters that they were not traditional tax-and-spend liberals from Washington who would raise taxes to start social programs of dubious potential at a time when the public was concerned about the slow but real decline in net wages. In sum, the concern with wages and jobs, the debt ($4 trillion as of 1992), and the deficit ($399.7 billion as of March 1992) accentuated all voters' concerns over whether Democrats could address the economy and not simply tackle social problems such as education and health care.

The loss of faith in Reaganomics did not revive the voters' faith in lib-

eralism; the weaknesses of the Democratic establishment were not obscured by the failures of Presidents Reagan and Bush. Throughout 1992
voters said their single greatest economic fear about a second term for
George Bush was "gridlock" and "economic decline"; their greatest fear
about a potential Democratic administration was increased taxes.[3]

Democratic primary voters angry about gridlock, broken promises,
and privileged politicians and concerned about economic decline looked
to cold economic plans, not angry rhetoric. The debate in New Hampshire and subsequent primaries was dominated by Paul Tsongas and Bill
Clinton. In New Hampshire these two candidates garnered 60 percent of
the vote, with Tsongas winning by 35 percent to Clinton's 26 percent.

What distinguished them from the others was the ability of their campaigns to focus on concrete steps for dealing with the economy, to the
point of publishing actual plans for voters to read. Few voters believed
that candidates such as Senator Tom Harkin of Iowa, Senator Robert Kerrey of Nebraska, or former Governor Edmund ("Jerry") Brown, Jr., of
California had credible approaches to the economy. Harkin, for example,
emphasized that the traditional liberalism of the past would still work;
but votes for him, combined with the write-in votes for New York Governor Mario Cuomo and consumer advocate Ralph Nader, amounted to
fewer than one-fifth of all the votes cast in New Hampshire.

Although the press often regarded these plans as gimmicks devoid of
substance, thousands of voters in New Hampshire obtained copies of the
Tsongas and Clinton economic plans, and thousands more actually went
to public libraries to read them. The Clinton plan was released, along
with a television commercial promoting the plan, during the first week of
January; in the next week Clinton moved from 16 percent and fourth
place to 33 percent and first place in the polls. In the next six weeks,
18,000 people in New Hampshire telephoned Clinton headquarters to re-
quest a copy of the plan—the equivalent of more than 10 percent of the
primary electorate (Rosenstiel, 1993).

The experience of the 1992 campaign suggests that whenever a candidate makes a clear and confident offer such as "Read my plan" or "Call
my 800 number," voters perceive it as an important cue. A candidate
who is willing to have his or her program examined, and thus be sub-
jected to the scrutiny of the electorate, is giving people a chance to see his
or her flaws. Furthermore, voters need not personally read the plan in
order to believe in its content; they can assume that its meaning will
emerge from public debate as the candidate rebuts attacks on it by the
other candidates and their surrogates. If voters reasoned that what they
had not read was credible, it was largely because they expected that the
flaws in the plan would be attacked by the other candidates.

The actual content of the plans mattered in 1992; the plans were not merely window dressing like the "secret plan" for ending the war in Vietnam that Richard Nixon said he had in 1968. Voters were sensitive enough to the content of the plans for the Clinton campaign to marginalize Tsongas by focusing on the difference between the Clinton and Tsongas plans. Blue-collar, high school–educated voters and white-collar, college-educated voters evaluated these plans differently. Blue-collar workers, who as a group had experienced a decline in wages and jobs during the course of the 1980s, were attracted to an emphasis on investment in human capital; white-collar workers were drawn to an emphasis on making more capital available to businesses (*Washington Post*, March 11, 1992). In every primary, Tsongas's support was much stronger among college graduates and professionals, and Clinton's was much stronger among blue-collar, high school–educated voters (*Washington Post*, March 11, 1992). In the critical Florida primary, Clinton defeated Tsongas among high school–educated whites by three to one, while Tsongas beat Clinton among college graduates. In other words, it was not simply the move to the South that led to Clinton's defeat of Tsongas; it was the Clinton campaign's focus on a clear distinction between the two economic plans that emphasized Tsongas's lack of attention to working families.

THE MAN FROM HOPE

As the only candidate with an economic plan that spoke to the concerns of the majority of blue-collar and minority Democrats, Clinton won the nomination despite a staggering load of negatives in the mind of the public. After the charges of marital infidelity and draft dodging and countless stories about prevaricating, less than candid replies, his public image was very much that of "Slick Willie."

Most voters did not believe that Clinton's all-but-admitted adultery and alleged evasion of the draft disqualified him from the presidency. Between 10 and 20 percent of voters thought the charges were serious, but far more important was the inference by many more from the way he handled the charges that he was insincere and overly political.[4] At the end of the primaries, 62 percent thought he said "what he thinks voters want to hear," and only 28 percent of registered voters thought he was a person who "says what he believes most of the time."[5] Phrases such as "I didn't inhale" and "maintain my political viability" were interpreted as evidence that he was an ambitious politician who would say anything and who could not be trusted personally.[6] When *Washington Post* reporters Dan Balz and David Broder conducted a focus group in Chicago, participants described Clinton with words such as "slick," "slimy," and "cunning." They also compared him to television evangelists Jimmy

Swaggart and Jim Bakker.[7] When shown television commercials of Clinton discussing his programs, potential voters in focus groups reacted derisively and discounted most of what he said as slick propaganda.[8]

Voters had inferred erroneously from the draft evasion stories that Clinton had led a life of privilege. His personal history—successful avoidance of the draft during the Vietnam War, a Rhodes scholarship, attendance at Yale Law School—suggested that he had been born to a life of social connections and privilege. This misperception raised suspicions about whether he had any genuine concern for average people or whether he was just posturing.

Less than six weeks after most voters were discounting everything Clinton did and said as "political," Clinton was rising quickly in the polls. Clinton came back because a "campaign within a campaign" launched in June after the primaries, a month-long campaign to get voters to give him a second look, did cause many voters to reassess their initial impressions of him. Partially because of Clinton's quick rise, Ross Perot dropped out of the race and attributed his decision, in part, to a revitalized Democratic Party.

The decision to use June to reintroduce Bill Clinton and to use alternate channels and venues to do so was key to overcoming the "Slick Willie" image. If Clinton won the nomination by talking about the economy, he overcame the damage he had sustained in the primaries by talking about himself and connecting the issues with which he was concerned to his own personal history. To counter the impression that many people had of him as a privileged, slick, adulterous draft dodger, albeit a smart one with a plan for the economy, the campaign provided voters with a fuller portrait of him by giving the public a sense of his past.

Clinton's comeback would not have been possible ten years earlier because it depended upon new television networks such as MTV, Fox, and CNN and on specific types of programs and formats, particularly viewer call-in shows, that had only recently risen in prominence. These programs afforded Clinton a greater chance than traditional news outlets would have to discuss issues. On the call-in shows, more of the questions were about issues and fewer concerned personal charges than in the more traditional formats (Rosenstiel, 1993).

More important, the interview programs and call-ins gave him the opportunity to give longer answers. The campaign's focus groups had shown that short sound bites of Clinton speaking were insufficient to overcome the people's preexisting beliefs about him. However, viewers who saw him talking at length, as well as those who saw him in situations where traditional politicians had seldom appeared, often noticed that there was something more to Clinton than they had expected.

After two weeks of talk-show appearances, Clinton had made major progress in breaking through the cynicism about him. On May 30, when voters were asked whether each of the candidates was "telling enough about where he stands on the issues for you to judge what he might do if he won the presidential election," 33 percent thought Bush, who had no plan, was telling enough, 32 percent thought Clinton, who did have a plan, was telling enough, and 15 percent thought Perot, who said he would soon present a plan, was telling enough (CBS–*New York Times* polls, May 27–30, 1992). Over the next three weeks, Clinton was ignored by the traditional networks, which devoted most of their coverage to Perot, who had just hired Ed Rollins, Ronald Reagan's 1984 campaign manager, and Hamilton Jordan, Jimmy Carter's campaign manager in 1976 and 1980, and who thus became the center of a media firestorm. At the same time, however, using talk shows and alternate settings, Clinton made major strides in informing voters about his plan. In mid-June 22 percent thought Perot was telling enough, and 32 percent thought Bush was telling enough, but 43 percent now thought Bill Clinton was telling enough.[9]

The second part of the plan to reintroduce Clinton was a decision to use the Democratic convention to give people more of Clinton's personal, as opposed to political, biography. On the evening of July 16 at the Democratic National Convention, the biographical film shown about Clinton, "The Man from Hope," successfully brought forward an important part of Clinton's life story: He had been born poor in the small town of Hope, Arkansas, had an alcoholic stepfather and a brother who later had drug problems, and had attended college on scholarships. This film and Clinton's subsequent acceptance speech directly challenged inferences about him that the public had drawn from the earlier stories that had erroneously led them to conclude Clinton had led a life of privilege.

After the Democratic convention, 84 percent of the public said they thought Bill Clinton had worked his way up from humble origins; 62 percent said they thought he shared the values of most Americans; and approximately half said they thought he was telling them enough about his stands on issues for them to know what he would do in office.[10] With a more complete biographical picture of Clinton, people were more willing to listen to him talk about issues and were more willing to decide whether his plans for the economy were better than those offered by the other candidates.

The new information did not actually erase old information about Clinton; after the convention, people did not forget the allegations of Clinton's draft evasion or adultery or "I didn't inhale." Throughout the campaign, more than half the public thought he was "telling people what he thought they wanted to hear, not what he believed." From March until October, a nearly constant 20 percent said they were disturbed by his draft evasion, and by a margin of more than two to one, voters said they were not confident he had the experience to deal with a difficult international crisis.[11]

This evolution in voters' perceptions of Clinton suggests that the best way to fight charges or problems involving a candidate's character during a campaign is to provide additional information about other aspects of his or her character, in order to give voters the fullest possible picture.

A NEW KIND OF DEMOCRAT

The Clinton campaign sought to convince voters that the most telling distinction between Clinton and Bush was "change versus more of the same." People felt major change was needed, and the Clinton campaign sought to remind voters that George Bush, who failed to make the changes he had promised in 1988, could only offer "more of the same." Indeed the much-cited sign on the wall of the war room in Clinton campaign headquarters had "Change versus more of the same" as the top line, followed by "It's the economy, stupid" and "Don't forget health care."

The distinction the Bush campaign sought to emphasize was "trust versus taxes." George Bush was a leader who could be trusted; Bill Clinton would only raise taxes. This meant, in effect, that Bush had to convince the public that his second term would be different from his first term, when he had broken his "no new taxes" pledge and ignored domestic concerns. In short, he had to convince people that "This time I really mean it" and "Now I really care." Given the difficulty of raising his own ratings, a good part of his campaign was devoted to lowering ratings of Clinton and the Democratic Party.

Maintaining the focus on a simple, clear distinction between "change" and "more of the same" was possible only because the Clinton campaign neutralized attacks by the Bush campaign that had attempted to turn the debate from economic plans and toward taxes or international affairs or to character flaws that would discredit Clinton's ability to bring about change. The Clinton campaign had to reassure people that Bill Clinton was not a typical "tax-and-spend" Democrat and that he had the character necessary in a president. To do this, the Clinton campaign had to negate all the peripheral attacks designed to shift the focus to trust or taxes or personal character. A simple campaign message emphasizing one clear distinction between programs required a complicated set of counterattacks and operations just to fend off all the attempts by the Bush campaign to turn the debate away from jobs and the economic future.

The Bush attack on Clinton borrowed heavily from the recent British election, in which the Conservative prime minister, John Major, had won an eleventh-hour, come-from-behind victory over the Labour Party. The Bush offensive focused on the argument that Clinton was radical, that the Democratic Party was a party of minorities and losers, and thus that any changes the Democrats made would be the wrong changes for the majority of Americans.

The Democratic convention and the selection of Senator Al Gore as vice-presidential candidate, however, had convinced the public that Bill Clinton was a "new kind of Democrat," and the Republican campaign proved unable to change that impression. The week after the Democratic convention, when the CBS–*New York Times* poll asked potential voters whether Bill Clinton and Al Gore were "different from Democratic candidates in previous years" or were "typical Democrats," 44 percent thought Clinton and Gore were a "new kind of Democrat." After the Republican convention, the number dropped to 41 percent, but in October it was up to 48 percent (CBS–*New York Times* surveys). At no time during the election did a plurality of independents and Republicans ever think of Clinton as another Mondale or Dukakis.

In September the Bush campaign resorted to implying that Clinton was a pawn of the former Soviet Union because he had visited Moscow while a Rhodes scholar at Oxford; these attempts resulted in making Bush a target of some ridicule.[12] That these attacks on Clinton were viewed as necessary at all was a testament to the ability of the Clinton campaign planners to keep the focus clearly on the distinction they sought to emphasize—"change versus more of the same"—by convincing people Bill Clinton was a "new kind of Democrat."

When Bush attacked Clinton as a draft dodger and a possible dupe of Moscow, Ronald Reagan's two-term head of the Joint Chiefs of Staff, Admiral William J. Crowe, endorsed Clinton and said that he was confident of Clinton's ability to defend the country and provide continuity in foreign policy. With the Cold War at an end, Admiral Crowe's endorsement on September 20 was enough to keep the issues of foreign policy, defense, and fitness to serve as commander in chief from becoming salient during the rest of the campaign.

Clinton had an economic plan, and a large part of the electorate knew of it and believed he had told them what he would do if elected. Campaign advertisements featured nine Nobel laureates in economics as well as hundreds of business executives from prominent corporations who also endorsed the plan. Moreover, these business executives were not "losers" but the heads of some of the most successful high-technology firms in the country, such as Apple Computers and Hewlett-Packard. The percentage of the population who thought the Clinton plan was worth trying did not decline.

Most important, Clinton's campaign advertising featured the candidate's record on welfare reform. During his tenure as governor of Arkansas, Clinton had developed a training program for mothers on welfare that had succeeded in moving 17,000 women off the welfare roles and into jobs. Against millions of unemployed nationally, 17,000 was a minuscule number, but the fact that Clinton had promoted a successful welfare reform provided an important source of reassurance that he was a new kind of Democrat. In campaign surveys, after pollsters read to respondents the Republican attacks on Clinton as a tax-and-spend Democrat and then told them about his accomplishments as governor, the welfare reform program was the most reassuring element of his record as rebuttal to Republican charges against him. Welfare reform was even more reassuring than eleven consecutive balanced budgets, an Arkansas growth rate twice the national average, or a rate of creating manufacturing jobs in Arkansas that was ten times the national average. A successful record on welfare reform and an often stated philosophy that welfare was a second chance and not a way of life made it difficult for the Bush campaign to assert that Bill Clinton was out of touch with the middle class.

Clinton's poll ratings began to rise even before the Democratic convention when he selected Senator Albert Gore, Jr., of Tennessee as his running mate. Clinton's choice of Gore was a distinct departure from the usual practice of balancing a Northerner with a Southerner, a liberal with a moderate, a younger with an older person, or a Catholic with a Protestant. Clinton and Gore were both young, moderate, Baptist, and from border states. The powerful popular reaction to the two of them as young, intelligent, and vigorous, as well as the widespread stories about people driving hours to see their bus tour appearances, suggests an important cognitive explanation for Gore's importance to the ticket. A ticket of complementary, "balanced" candidates requires a difficult process of "averaging" to arrive at its expected value: What, after all, does a Bush plus a Quayle equal? Or a Kennedy plus a Johnson? Clinton and Gore, by contrast, were so similar that such a calculation was unnecessary, and the ticket psychologically was easier to understand. The presence of Gore, who served in Vietnam, had a wife and four children, and was such a straight arrow that most of the press described him as positively square, may have lessened Clinton's problems of draft evasion and marital infidelity by concentrating voters' attention on the common features of the two.

CONCLUSION

The road to Washington is littered with the geniuses of campaigns past. When H. R. Haldeman explained to Richard Nixon in 1972 that it would be easier to raise George McGovern's negatives than to raise Nixon's positives, he was summarizing the views of Republican pollster Robert Teeter, who would give much the same advice to George Bush twenty years later (Popkin, 1991). However, the attacks that had worked so well on George McGovern in 1972 and had been so prominent against Michael Dukakis in 1988 were largely ineffective in 1992. In large measure, these attacks were not sufficient to convince voters to give George Bush four more years, because the Clinton campaign negated the attacks and kept the focus on the economic future of the country.

Campaigns do make a difference. As Vice President Quayle said of Bill Clinton in his concession speech, "If he runs the country as well as he ran his campaign, we'll be all right."[13] Bill Clinton won the Democratic primary by convincing a majority of Democrats that his plan offered them more than did Paul Tsongas's plan, and he forced the issue by challenging Tsongas to explain how his plan would move the country beyond its current economic crisis, which despite his personal credibility Tsongas could not do.[14] Clinton overcame voters' doubts about his personal character by giving them sufficient reasons to judge him instead by his political character. He then used the Democratic convention movingly to tell his extraordinary life story and to overcome the misperception that he had been born to privilege. In his choice of a running mate, he demonstrated that he was indeed a new kind of Democrat. Finally, he used his record of commitment to welfare reform to rebut charges that he was just another tax-and-spend Democrat.

NOTES

1. The model of Yale economist Ray Fair, which was based only upon economic variables, predicted that Bush would win 57 percent. Other models based upon various combinations of economic data and public opinion data proved more accurate, and the divergence between the models with and without opinion data emphasizes that assessments of the president's economic efforts, not simply the actual economy, are what matter to voters. Fair's model is described in Ray C. Fair, "The Effect of Economic Events on Votes for President: 1984 Update," *Political Behavior* 10, 2 (1988):168–179. For a summary of 1992 predictions, see Jay P. Greene, "Forewarned Before Forecast: Presidential Election Forecasting Models and the 1992 Election," *PS* 26, 1 (March 1993):17–21. For a summary of the major models, including those incorporating economic data and opinion data, see Michael S. Lewis-Beck and Tom W. Rice, *Forecasting Elections*, Washington, D.C.: Congressional Quarterly Press, 1992.

2. Similar analyses of the changed relation between consumer confidence and aggregate economic activity were presented to the New England Economic Project by Roger Brinner of Data Resources Incorporated (DRI) and Mark Zandi of Regional Financial Associates. The finding of a 1990 "gap" between confidence and aggregate economic activity is robust support for both Conference Board and Michigan measures of consumer confidence and a wide range of aggregate mea-

sures of current employment, growth, and inflation. Conversations with Mark Zandi and John Gorman of Opinion Dynamics, November 1993.

3. On four of the Clinton surveys, voters were asked to express their worries about a second Bush term and about a Clinton presidency. The two most common answers for Bush were gridlock and decline; for Clinton they were inexperience and taxes.

4. In ABC polls in New Hampshire, for example, only 11 percent of the respondents thought the information on Clinton's marriage was relevant; 80 percent thought the press was wrong to discuss the charges. Tom Rosenstiel, *Strange Bedfellows: How Television and the Presidential Candidates Changed American Politics* (New York: Hyperion, 1993), p. 70. National polls showed similar figures, whereas the number of voters thinking the draft charges were relevant was generally around 20 percent. However, only 24 percent of respondents in the April CBS–*New York Times* poll said they thought Clinton had more integrity than most people in public life.

5. CBS–*New York Times* poll, June 1992. These figures had been relatively stable since March.

6. The Clinton campaign's research, including surveys and focus groups, about the "character problem" is described in "How He Won," *Newsweek* special election issue, November–December 1992, pp. 40–41.

7. *Washington Post*, March 20, 1992. See also Rosenstiel, *Strange Bedfellows*, p. 143.

8. *Newsweek*, "How He Won," p. 41.

9. CBS–*New York Times* polls May 27–30 and June 17–20, 1992.

10. The last two questions were from CBS–*New York Times* polls for July and August 1992. The first question was from a poll conducted for the Clinton campaign by Greenberg-Lake Research.

11. CBS–*New York Times* polls for March, June, July, August, and October 1992.

12. *Newsweek*, "How He Won," pp. 83–85.

13. Quoted in the *New York Times*, November 4, 1992, p. B5.

14. Perhaps the greatest irony of the 1992 campaign was that the man regarded as the epitome of integrity for telling hard, unvarnished truths misled the public about his health. Tsongas told reporters that he had been cancer-free since his treatments in 1984 when he had, in fact, suffered a relapse; "Tsongas Says He Mishandled Issue of His Cancer," Lawrence K. Altman, *New York Times*, December 1, 1992, p. A1.

18

Do Campaigns Matter?

MARNI EZRA AND CANDICE J. NELSON

The one clear difference that emerges in an examination of the way political scientists and political practitioners look at elections is that political scientists assume, by and large, that election outcomes are determined by forces other than the actual election campaign, whereas political practitioners assume that the campaign itself determines the outcome. Perhaps one reason for these differing perspectives is that practitioners are looking at election day prospectively; academics are analyzing the same event, except they are doing so retrospectively. Political scientists look at the roles that partisanship, incumbency advantage, candidate image, and issues play in election outcomes and conclude that these four factors are, in varying degrees in different elections, responsible for the outcome of the election. Campaign practitioners, in turn, look at campaign strategies and messages, campaign media, both earned and paid, and campaign field operations as determinants of election outcomes. Yet it seems that both the political environment in which the campaign occurs and the campaign itself impact on the election outcome. It is therefore important to study elections from both the pre- and post-election day perspectives. The combination of these perspectives will help students of elections to obtain a more complete understanding of the campaign process.

ACADEMIC AND NONACADEMIC PERSPECTIVES

The early voting studies of presidential and congressional elections concluded that party identification was the primary determinant of vote choice in the United States; the authors of *The American Voter* found that "party identification had a profound impact on behavior" (Campbell et al., 1960, p. 79). In the years following the publication of *The American Voter*, many scholars examined the roles that candidate image and issues played in elections and found that under the right circumstances, both candidates and issues could influence election outcomes, though candidates were generally more important than issues.[1] The authors of *The*

American Voter argued that there are both long-term and short-term forces that influence elections; candidate image and issues are short-term forces, and partisanship is a long-term force. Absent short-term forces, partisanship is the strongest predictor of vote choice, and in races in which little or nothing is known about the candidates, vote decisions are usually made on the basis of party identification.

After the 1978 congressional elections, election scholars were able to verify what had been suspected for some time: namely, that when one candidate was an incumbent, incumbency had a profound effect on the election outcome (Mann and Wolfinger, 1980). They were able to do so because the National Election Survey (NES) added a battery of questions to its survey that had not been asked in previous years. Before 1978, respondents were asked if they could name their member of congress, and many could not. This presented scholars with a dilemma. Although respondents could not name their member of Congress, incumbents were winning their elections in overwhelming numbers. The new questions asked respondents if they could identify their member among a list of names, a scenario that more accurately depicts what is presented to the voter in a voting booth. These questions allowed academics to conduct more accurate studies on the importance of incumbency.

Incumbency advantage also began to be viewed as a voting cue that could rival (or support) party identification, depending on the party of the incumbent (Nelson, 1978). Incumbents find themselves advantaged over their challengers for many reasons, including advantages in raising money (Jacobson, 1992), higher name recognition (Abramowitz, 1975), casework provided by their office (Yiannakis, 1981; Johannes and Mc-Adams, 1981), and the ability to claim credit for projects they have brought to their district (Mayhew, 1974).

Some of the advantages of incumbency certainly drop off when the incumbent faces a high-quality challenger (Green and Krasno, 1990). Scholars argue that in highly visible electoral contests in which both candidates are well known, candidate characteristics are often the most important determinant of vote choice. In presidential elections, the most visible elections in the United States, most voters know at least something about the two major party candidates on the ballot and cast their votes accordingly. For example, Morris Fiorina argued that presidential elections are a referendum on the incumbent president or his political party (Fiorina, 1981). This line of argument would suggest that Ronald Reagan was elected president in 1980 because the American people rejected Jimmy Carter, and that Reagan was reelected in 1984 because the American people were satisfied with his handling of the presidency during his first term. In short, when Reagan asked the American people to ask themselves in 1980, "Are you better off now than you were four years ago?" a majority of Americans answered no; four years later, if the same question had been asked, the answer would have been yes.

As the preceding discussion implies, candidate image can have an issue component to it. In presidential elections, the issue component is usually the state of the economy, though an unpopular war, such as the Vietnam War in 1968, can also affect a candidate's election prospects. Beginning with the work of Edward R. Tufte in 1975, political scientists developed models to predict the outcome of presidential and congressional elections based on various calculations of the incumbent president's popularity and the state of the economy (Tufte, 1975). Tufte also agreed with the assumption that the president's party will lose seats at the midterm (and has done so since 1934). At the subpresidential level, the issue component may also be the economy, for example, in a gubernatorial race, or may be an issue of particular importance to a state or district at the congressional level.

Candidate image can play an important role at the subpresidential level as well, particularly in statewide races for governor and U.S. senator. If both candidates are well known to the voters, the characteristics of the candidates are often the determining factor in the election. In congressional elections, in which usually only the incumbent has high name recognition, the most important factor is not the image of the candidate but whether or not the candidate is an incumbent; in the late 1980s and early 1990s, over 90 percent of House members who ran for reelection were successful. Even after the House bank scandal in 1992, when many incumbents' reputations were tarnished, the reelection rate was still 88 percent.

Whereas candidate image and issues play a role in more visible elections, down-ballot races, such as state legislative races and contests for local offices, are most influenced by partisanship and incumbency. In these low-visibility races, voters do not know much about the candidates and will use the voting cues that are most obvious to them.

Political scientists study elections by comparing the relative importance of these four factors within any one election and across elections. It is assumed that what happens during an election is relatively unimportant. Raymond Wolfinger presents this argument in Chapter 14; political scientists would argue that Bill Clinton was elected president in 1992 because the Democrats were the majority party in the United States, the country was perceived to be in a recession, and George Bush was perceived to be out of touch with the problems facing the country. In a poll conducted by NBC and the *Wall Street Journal* September 12–15, 1992, when respondents were asked "who is better at dealing with the economy," only 26 percent chose George Bush. For jobs, 19 percent chose

Bush, and 25 percent said that he would be better at dealing with the deficit. The survey data confirmed for many academics that there were forces other than campaign-centered factors at work.

Nowhere in the analysis is there any mention of the Republican convention, the Clinton-Gore bus trip through the heartland of America following the Democratic convention, scandals, field organizations, or get-out-the-vote (GOTV) efforts on election day. For political scientists, the events of the campaign itself have little relationship to the outcome of the campaign.

For campaign professionals, on the other hand, the activities that take place between when a candidate decides to run for office and election day are what determine the outcome of the election. From the initial campaign planning process, through the development of a strategy, theme, and message for the campaign, fund-raising, the use of paid and earned media, the implementation of a field organization plan, and finally the GOTV effort on election day, campaign professionals assume that the campaign that most successfully executes its campaign plan will win.

To campaign professionals, the aspects of the campaign discussed throughout this book are the determinants of success. Campaigns focus on fund-raising; as David Himes argues in Chapter 5, no campaign ever lost because the campaign raised too much money, but many campaigns have lost because they did not raise enough money to implement the campaign plan. Campaigns are affected both by the absence of media coverage, as Anita Dunn points out in Chapter 9, and, if a campaign does get media coverage, by the type of coverage it gets. One would be hard pressed to find a campaign consultant to argue that paid media, be it radio or television advertisements, played no role in election outcomes. Field organizations, as Will Robinson argues in Chapter 11, can be the difference between winning and losing in a close election. William Hamilton is convincing in arguing in Chapter 13 that by the 1980s survey research had become an integral part of campaign strategy. Clearly, to campaign practitioners, campaigns do matter.

The differences in approaches to campaigns by academics and practitioners lead to differences in the interpretations of campaign outcomes. As was outlined previously, the political scientists' explanation of Bill Clinton's success in 1992 was based on the following: He was a candidate of the major political party in the United States, the economy was perceived to be in a recession, and the incumbent president was seen as out of touch with the problems and people of the United States. Campaign professionals analyzed the 1992 presidential election differently: Bill Clinton won because he had a campaign strategy and a message ("It's time for a change"), whereas George Bush had either no strategy, or at best a flawed strategy, and no message. Polling led to the development and refinement of Clinton's message; paid media, earned media, and the field organization reinforced the Clinton message.

Examining both the 1988 and 1992 presidential elections suggests that the campaign itself can affect the outcome of the election. In Chapter 3 Joel Bradshaw discusses the importance of strategy, theme, and message in a campaign. Comparing the 1988 Republican and 1992 Democratic campaigns illustrates the role that a strategy can play in a presidential campaign. Both the Republicans in 1988 and the Democrats in 1992 decided not to campaign in all fifty states. In 1988 the Bush campaign decided to campaign in only twenty-five states; in 1992 the Clinton campaign concentrated its resources in thirty-two states. By restricting the number of states the candidates campaigned in, the Bush campaign in 1988 and the Clinton campaign in 1992 were able both to marshal and to target their resources.

Analysis of the 1988 Bush and 1992 Clinton campaigns use of survey research also suggests that the measurement of public opinion during the campaign can affect the outcome of the campaign. It was a focus group conducted in New Jersey by the Bush campaign that led the campaign to concentrate on Michael Dukakis's support of a furlough program for convicted felons—the program that led to the release of Willie Horton and the subsequent negative advertisements against Governor Dukakis. Survey research was also important during the 1992 election, as Samuel Popkin points out in Chapter 17, because it enabled campaign planners to see how voters viewed Bill Clinton's background and they could then respond accordingly.

Finally, Will Robinson's discussion in Chapter 11 of the Clinton campaign's use of the field operation suggests that the Clinton field operation may have been important in the consistency with which the Clinton message was viewed during the campaign. As Robinson points out, in 1992 the Clinton campaign used the field operation not only to identify Clinton supporters and persuadable voters but also to deliver the campaign message. The field staff received, on a daily basis, the messages the candidate and the campaign were delivering, and local field operatives used that information to deliver the same message in their local jurisdictions.

It is difficult to measure, in an empirical sense, whether these campaign tactics influenced the outcome of the elections in 1988 and 1992, but it is even more difficult to dismiss the events of the campaigns themselves as completely unrelated to the outcomes. To imply that campaigns do not matter would suggest that any Democrat could have run against Bush and won, simply because Democrats were in the majority, Bush was perceived to be out of touch, and the economy was weak. Examining the presidential campaigns of 1988 and 1992 suggests that campaigns do, in fact, matter.

DIFFERING FOCUSES OF
ACADEMICS AND PRACTITIONERS

Not only do academics and practitioners differ in their views of whether campaigns themselves influence election outcomes, but they also differ in what interests them about the factors that are a part of elections in the United States. For example, both academics and practitioners are interested in the role of money in elections, but their interests in money and the way they go about looking at the role of money are very different.

Academics look at money in elections as a way for candidates to communicate with voters. Without sufficient money, candidates are unable to get their messages out to voters, and thus voters have information either about only one candidate, most often the incumbent, or, in down-ballot races, about neither candidate. For practitioners, money is a way to get candidates elected, and thus the focus is on raising enough money to implement the campaign plan.

As a result of their differing interests, academics and practitioners look at the debate over campaign finance reform differently. Academics are interested in increasing competition in elections—that is, enabling both candidates in a race to have enough money to get their messages out to the voters. Academics often discuss the need to create a "level playing field" and consequently support spending limits, public financing, or subsidies for broadcast or print communication with voters (Magleby and Nelson, 1990). Not all academics agree on these reforms. Some argue that spending limits affect both incumbents as well as challengers and would therefore affect the outcomes of elections (Green and Krasno, 1990). Academics of this view support spending limits and contend they are not a form of incumbency protection. Others disagree with such evidence and do not support spending limits because they are viewed as another shield in the armor of incumbents (Jacobson, 1990).

Practitioners, on the other hand, worry that campaign finance reform will reduce the sources of money in a campaign or increase the amount of time a candidate must spend raising money. Thus practitioners worry about proposals to restrict contributions from PACs or ban PAC contributions altogether, because, as both David Himes (Chapter 5) and Frank Sorauf (Chapter 6) point out, PAC contributions are a significant source of money for incumbents.

Another difference in the focus of academics and practitioners is in the relative interest paid to a candidate's base and persuadable voters. As Joel Bradshaw points out in Chapter 3, practitioners tend to divide voters into base voters and undecideds. Base voters are those who will support either the candidate or the candidate's opponent. Undecideds, or persuadables, are the focus of a campaign. Although some of a campaign's resources may be spent to make sure base voters turn out to vote on election day, most is used to persuade undecided voters to support a campaign's candidate. Consequently, the voters who are most interesting to a campaign are the undecideds, and polling, targeting, and field operations are primarily focused on those voters who will be the difference between success and defeat on election day.

Academics, on the other hand, are most interested in base voters. They are interested in why people choose to be Democrats or Republicans and in the stability of partisanship over time. Academics look at differences among party identifiers—on issues, ideology, evaluations of candidates, and voting behavior. Although academicians study swing voters (and there is a fair amount of research on ticket splitting), the main interest of academics is party identifiers. There has also been some scholarship on independent voters. To the surprise of many, Keith et al. (1992) found that two-thirds of independent voters are actually partisans and display the qualities that were thought to be reserved only for those who immediately identified themselves as belonging to one party or another. Whereas academics study independents to determine whether they resemble partisans, practitioners view independents as the key to winning on election day and attempt to figure out ways to win over the independent vote.

A third area in which academic and practitioner interests differ is in the analysis of elections. Academicians are interested in the various external influences that can influence election outcomes: partisanship, incumbency advantage, candidate image, issues, registration laws, national forces, and past voting behavior, to name a few. Practitioners, in contrast, are interested in manipulating the internal factors of a campaign—paid and earned media, targeting, and field operations, for example—to achieve success on election day. Academics focus on the objective environment in which a campaign occurs; practitioners focus on the campaign itself.

CONCLUSION

The essays in this book have illustrated the differing ways in which academic students of elections and political practitioners approach eight different aspects of campaigns. Although their interests and approaches to elections differ, both academics and practitioners are, in the broad sense, students of elections. Practitioners seek to influence election outcomes and thus are continually trying new approaches to achieve success for their candidates on election day. Academics seek to understand election outcomes and thus continually try new models to explain those outcomes. Practitioners must deal with the day-to-day problems that face a campaign as they are happening; academics have the luxury of examining events after they have occurred. The different atmospheres in which these two groups work and the different ways in which they view elections—one prospective, the other retrospective—affect whether they believe that campaigns matter. Although they differ in their approaches, both academics and practitioners contribute to a more general understanding of elections and their importance in the political system.

NOTES

1. See, for example, Larry Bartels, "Candidate Choice and the Dynamics of the Presidential Nominating Process," *American Journal of Politics* 31 (1987):1–30; Edward Carmines and James Stimson, "The Two Faces of Issue Voting," *American Political Science Review* 74 (March 1980):78–91; Benjamin Page and Richard Brody, "Policy Voting and the Electoral Process: The Vietnam War Issue," *American Political Science Review* 66 (1972):975–995; Larry Bartels, "Issue Voting Under Uncertainty," *American Journal of Political Science* 30 (1986):709–729.

References

Abramowitz, Alan. (1975). "Name Familiarity, Reputation and the Incumbency Effect in a Congressional Election." *Western Political Quarterly* 28:668–684.

Alexander, Herbert E., and Monica Bauer. (1991). *Financing the 1988 Election.* Boulder, Colo.: Westview Press.

Allen, Cathy. (1990). *Political Campaigning: A New Decade.* Washington, D.C.: National Women's Political Caucus.

Altman, Lawrence K. (1992). "Tsongas Says He Mishandled Issue of His Cancer." *New York Times,* December 1, p. A1.

Ansolabehere, Stephen, Roy Behr, and Shanto Iyengar. (1992). *The Media Game: American Politics in the Television Age.* New York: Macmillan.

Ansolabehere, Stephen, and Shanto Iyengar. (1993a). "Riding the Wave and Claiming Ownership over Issues: The Joint Effects of Advertising and News in Campaigns." Unpublished paper, University of California, Los Angeles.

———. (1993b). "Competing for Votes: Advertising Strategy in Political Campaigns." Unpublished paper, University of California, Los Angeles.

Arterton, Christopher. (1992). "The Persuasive Art in Politics: The Role of Paid Advertising in Presidential Campaigns." In Mathew D. McCubbins, ed., *Under the Watchful Eye: Managing Presidential Campaigns in the Television Era.* Washington, D.C.: Congressional Quarterly Press, pp. 83–126.

Asher, Herbert. (1983). "Voting Behavior Research in the 1980s." In Ada W. Finifter, ed., *Political Science: The State of the Discipline.* Washington, D.C.: American Political Science Association, pp. 339–388.

———. (1992). *Presidential Elections and American Politics.* 5th ed. Pacific Grove, Calif.: Brooks/Cole.

Auden, W. H., and Lewis Kronenberger. (1981). *The Viking Book of Aphorisms: A Personal Selection.* New York: The Viking Press.

Axelrod, Robert. (1972). "Where the Votes Come From: An Analysis of Presidential Election Coalitions, 1952–1968." *American Political Science Review* 66:11–20.

Baer, Denise L. (1993). "Political Parties: The Missing Variable in Women and Politics Research." *Political Research Quarterly* 46:547–576.

Baer, Denise L., and David A. Bositis. (1988). *Elite Cadres and Party Coalitions: Representing the Public in Party Politics.* New York: Greenwood Press.

Baer, Denise L., David A. Bositis, and John S. Jackson III. (1991). "The 1988 Party Elite Study." *Vox Pop* 10:3–5.

Baer, Denise L., and Julie Dolan. (1994). "Intimate Connections." *American Review of Politics.* Special issue edited by Sara Morehouse and Malcolm Jewell.

Bartels, Larry. (1986). "Issue Voting Under Uncertainty." *American Journal of Political Science* 30:709–729.

———. (1987). "Candidate Choice and the Dynamics of the Presidential Nominating Process." *American Journal of Politics* 31:1–30.

Beck, Paul Allen, and Frank J. Sorauf. (1992). *Party Politics in America.* New York: HarperCollins.

Berelson, Bernard, Paul Lazarsfeld, and William McPhee. (1954). *Voting.* Chicago: University of Chicago Press.

Berry, Jeffrey M. (1993). "Citizen Groups and the Changing Nature of Interest Group Politics in America." *Annals of the American Academy of Political and Social Science* 528:30–41.

Black, Christine M., and Thomas Oliphant. (1989). *All By Myself: The Unmaking of a Presidential Campaign.* Chester, Conn.: Globe Pequot Press.

Blumenthal, Sidney. (1982). *The Permanent Campaign.* New York: Simon and Schuster.

———. (1990). *Pledging Allegiance: The Last Campaign of the Cold War.* New York: HarperCollins.

Bode, Kenneth. (1992). "Pull the Plug, Empower the Voters." *The Quill* 80:10–14.

Brenner, Marie. (1992). "Politics: Perot's Final Days." *Vanity Fair* 55:74–80.

Broder, David. (1992). "Hit the Streets." *The Quill* 80:8–9.

Burnham, Walter Dean. (1985). "The 1984 Election and the Future of American Politics." In Ellis Sandoz and Cecil Crabb, eds., *Election '84.* New York: Mentor, pp. 204–260.

Campbell, Angus, Philip Converse, Donald Stokes, and Warren Miller. (1960). *The American Voter.* New York: Wiley.

———. (1964). *The American Voter: An Abridgement.* New York: Wiley.

———. (1966). *Elections and the Political Order.* New York: Wiley.

Campbell, James E., and Thomas Mann. (1992). "Forecasting the 1992 Elections: A User's Guide to the Models." *Brookings Review* 10:22–27.

Carmines, Edward G., and James A. Stimson. (1989). *Issue Evolution: Race and the Transformation of American Politics.* Princeton: Princeton University Press.

Center for National Policy. (1991). *The Real Story of the U.S. Economy, 1950–1990.* Washington, D.C.: Center for National Policy, pp. 61–78.

Converse, Philip E., et al. (1969). "Continuity and Change in American Politics: Parties and Issues in the 1968 Election." *American Political Science Review* 63 (December):1083–1105.

Cook, Timothy E. (1989). *Making Laws and Making News: Media Strategies in the United States House of Representatives.* Washington, D.C.: Brookings Institution.

Cotter, Cornelius. (1984). *Party Organizations and American Politics.* New York: Praeger.

Cramer, Richard Ben. (1992). *What It Takes: The Way to the White House.* New York: Random House.

Crawford-Mason, Claire, and Lloyd Dobyns. (1991). *Quality or Else: The Revolution in World Business.* Boston: Houghton Mifflin.

Crotty, William. (1991). *Political Participation and American Democracy.* New York: Greenwood Press.

Downs, Anthony. (1960). *An Economic Theory of Democracy.* New York: Harper and Row.

Duverger, Maurice. (1954). *Political Parties.* New York: John Wiley and Sons.

Edsall, Thomas B., and E. J. Dionne, Jr. (1992). "Younger, Lower-Income Voters Spurn GOP." *Washington Post,* November 4, p. 1.

Ehrenhalt, Alan. (1991). *The United States of Ambition: Politics, Power, and the Pursuit of Office.* New York: Times Books.

Fair, Ray C. (1988). "The Effect of Economic Events on Votes for President: 1984 Update." *Political Behavior* 10 (2):168–179.

Fiorina, Morris. (1981). *Retrospective Voting in American National Elections.* New Haven: Yale University Press.

Frendreis, John P., James L. Gobson, and Laura L. Vertz. (1990). "The Electoral Relevance of Local Party Organizations." *American Political Science Review* 84:225–235.

Germond, Jack, and Jules Witcover. (1985). *Wake Us When It's Over: Presidential Politics of 1984.* New York: Macmillan.

Ginsberg, Benjamin. (1989). "How Polling Transforms Public Opinion." In Michael Margolis and Gary A. Mauser, eds., *Manipulating Public Opinion: Essays on Public Opinion as a Dependent Variable.* Pacific Grove, Calif.: Brooks/ Cole Publishing, pp. 271–293.

Goldenberg, Edie, and Michael W. Traugott. (1984). *Campaigning for Congress.* Washington, D.C.: Congressional Quarterly Press.

Green, Donald Philip, and Jonathan Krasno. (1990). "Rebuttal to Jacobson's 'New Evidence for Old Arguments.'" *American Journal of Political Science* 34:363–372.

Greene, Jay P. (1993). "Forewarned Before Forecast: Presidential Election Forecasting Models and the 1992 Election." *PS* 26 (March):17–21.

Grenzke, Janet M. (1989). "Shopping in the Congressional Supermarket: The Currency is Complex." *American Journal of Political Science* (February):1–24.

Guber, Susan. (1988). *How to Win Your First Election: The Candidate's Handbook.* Miami: Pickering Press.

Herrnson, Paul S. (1988). *Party Campaigning in the 1980s.* Cambridge: Harvard University Press.

———. (1992). "National Party Organizations and the Postreform Congress." In Roger H. Davidson, ed., *The Postreform Congress.* New York: St. Martin's Press.

———. (1994). *Congressional Elections: Campaigning at Home and in Washington.* Washington, D.C.: Congressional Quarterly Press.

Hershey, Marjorie Randon. (1984). *Running for Office: The Political Education of Campaigners.* Chatham, N.J.: Chatham House.

Hess, Stephen. (1978). *The Presidential Campaign.* Washington, D.C.: Brookings Institution.

Honomichl, Jack J. (1980). "Marketing of a Candidate." *Advertising Age,* December 15, pp. 3, 65–66.

Huckfeldt, Robert, and John Sprague. (1992). "Political Parties and Electoral Mobilization: Political Structure, Social Structure, and the Party Canvass." *American Political Science Review* 86:70–86.

Institute for Strategic Management. (1984). "Campaign Groundwork: Strategy, Planning and Management." Washington, D.C.

Iyengar, Shanto. (1991). *Is Anyone Responsible? How Television Frames National Issues.* Chicago: University of Chicago Press.

———. (1993). "Agenda-Setting and Beyond: Television News and the Strength of Political Issues." In William Riker, ed., *Agenda Formation*. Ann Arbor: University of Michigan Press.

Iyengar, Shanto, and Donald Kinder. (1987). *News That Matters*. Chicago: University of Chicago Press.

Iyengar, Shanto, and Adam Simon. (1993). "News Coverage of the Gulf Crisis and Public Opinion: A Survey of Effects." *Communication Research* 20:365–383.

Jacobson, Gary. (1990). "The Effects of Campaign Spending in House Elections: New Evidence for Old Arguments." *American Journal of Political Science* 34:334–362.

———. (1992). *The Politics of Congressional Elections*. San Diego: HarperCollins.

Jacobson, Gary, and Samuel Kernell. (1981, 1983). *Strategy and Choice in Congressional Elections*. New Haven: Yale University Press.

Jensen, Richard. (1969). "American Election Analysis." In Seymour Martin Lipset, ed., *Politics and the Social Sciences*. New York: Oxford, pp. 226–243.

———. (1980). "Armies, Admen and Crusaders." *Public Opinion* 3 (5): pp. 44–53.

Johannes, John R., and John C. McAdams. (1981). "The Congressional Incumbency Effect: Is it Casework, Policy Compatibility or Something Else?" *American Journal of Political Science* 25:512–542.

Kaid, Lind L., et al. (1993). "Television News and Presidential Campaigns: The Legitimization of Televised Political Advertising." *Social Science Quarterly* 74:274–285.

Keith, Bruce E., David B. Magleby, Candice J. Nelson, Elizabeth Orr, Mark C. Westlye, and Raymond Wolfinger. (1992). *The Myth of the Independent Voter*. Berkeley: University of California Press.

Kessel, John H. (1988). *Presidential Campaign Politics*. Chicago: Dorsey.

Krassa, Michael A. (1988). "Context and the Canvass: The Mechanisms of Interactions." *Political Behavior* 10:233–246.

Ladd, Everett Carll, and John Benson. (1992). "The Growth of News Polls in American Politics." In Thomas E. Mann and Gary R. Orren, eds., *Media Polls in American Politics*. Washington, D.C.: Brookings Institution, pp. 19–31.

Lake, Celinda, and Nikki Heidepriem. (1988). "Whatever Happened to the Gender Gap?" *Campaigns and Elections* 2:37–40.

Lazarsfeld, Paul, Bernard Berelson, and Hazel Gaudet. (1944). *The People's Choice*. New York: Columbia University Press.

Lewis-Beck, Michael, and Tom W. Rice. (1992). *Forecasting Elections*. Washington, D.C.: Congressional Quarterly Press.

Loomis, Burdett. (1988). *The New American Politician: Ambition, Entrepreneurship, and the Changing Face of Political Life*. New York: Basic Books.

Luntz, Frank. (1991). "Preparing Your Campaign Playbook." *Campaigns and Elections* (July) 12:40–46.

MacDougall, Malcolm D. (1977). *We Almost Made It*. New York: Crown Publishers.

Maddox, William, and Stuart Lilie. (1984). *Beyond Liberal and Conservative: Reassessing the Political Spectrum*. Washington, D.C.: Cato Institute.

Magleby, David, and Candice J. Nelson. (1990). *The Money Chase*. Washington, D.C.: Brookings Insitution.

Maisel, L. Sandy. (1986). *From Obscurity to Oblivion: Running in the Congressional Primary*. Knoxville: University of Tennessee Press.

Mann, Thomas E., and Raymond Wolfinger. (1980). "Candidates and Parties in Congressional Elections." *American Political Science Review* 74:617–632.

Markle Foundation. (1993). "Draft Report on the 1992 Election." Mimeographed.

Markus, Hazel, and Robert B. Zajonc. (1984). "The Cognitive Perspective in Social Psychology." In G. Lindsey and E. Aronson, eds., *Handbook of Social Psychology*. 2d ed. New York: Random House.

Mauser, Gary A. (1989). "Marketing and Political Campaigning: Strategies and Limits." In Michael Margolis and Gary A. Mauser, eds., *Manipulating Public Opinion: Essays on Public Opinion as a Dependent Variable*. Pacific Grove, Calif.: Brooks/Cole Publishing, pp. 19–46.

Mayhew, David. (1974). *Congress: The Electoral Connection*. New Haven: Yale University Press.

McCabe, Ed. (1988). "The Campaign You Never Saw." *New York* 21:33–48.

McCubbins, Mathew D. (1992). "Party Decline and Presidential Campaigns in the Television Age." In Mathew D. McCubbins, ed., *Under the Watchful Eye: Managing Presidential Campaigns in the Television Era*. Washington, D.C.: Congressional Quarterly Press.

Miller, Warren E. (1991). "Party Identification, Realignment, and Party Voting: Back to the Basics." *American Political Science Review* 85 (June):557–568.

Mueller, Carol M. (1988). "The Empowerment of Women: Polling and the Women's Voting Bloc." In Carol M. Mueller, ed., *The Politics of the Gender Gap*. Beverly Hills: Sage, pp. 16–36.

Napolitan, Joe. (1972). *The Election Game and How to Win It*. Garden City, N.Y.: Doubleday.

Natchez, Peter B. (1985). *Images of Voting/Visions of Democracy*. New York: Basic Books.

Nelson, Candice. (1978). "The Effects of Incumbency on Voting in Congressional Elections." *Political Science Quarterly* 93:665–678.

Neuman, Russell W. (1986). *The Paradox of Mass Politics*. Cambridge: Harvard University Press.

Newsweek. (1992). Special election issue, November–December.

Nimmo, Dan. (1970). *The Political Persuaders*. Englewood Cliffs, N.J.: Prentice-Hall.

Nimmo, Dan, and Robert L. Savage. (1976). *Candidates and Their Images: Concepts, Methods, and Findings*. Pacific Palisades, Calif.: Goodyear Publishing.

O'Brien, Lawrence F. (1975). *No Final Victories: A Life in Politics from John F. Kennedy to Watergate*. New York: Ballantine Books.

O'Neill, Tip. (1987). *Man of the House: The Life and Political Memoirs of Speaker Tip O'Neill*. New York: Random House.

Ornstein, Norman J., Thomas E. Mann, and Michael J. Malbin. (1994). *Vital Statistics on Congress: 1993–1994*. Washington, D.C.: Congressional Quarterly Press.

Otten, Alan. (1992). "TV News Drops Kid-Gloved Coverage of Election, Trading Staged Sound-Bites for Hard Analysis." *Wall Street Journal*, October 12, p. A12.

Page, Benjamin, and Richard Brody. (1972). "Policy Voting and the Electoral Process: The Vietnam War Issue." *American Political Science Review* 66:975–995.

———. (1976). "A Theory of Political Ambiguity." *American Political Science Review* 70:742–752.

Peterson, Bill. (1985). "Reagan Did Understand Women." *Washington Post*, March 3.

Petrocik, John R. (1991). "Divided Government: Is It All in the Campaigns?" In Gary W. Cox and Samuel Kernell, eds., *The Politics of Divided Government*. Boulder, Colo.: Westview Press.

––––––. (1992). "The Theory of Issue Ownership." Unpublished manuscript, University of California, Los Angeles.

––––––. *Issue Ownership in Elections*. Manuscript in progress.

Popcorn, Faith. (1992). *Popcorn Report: Faith Popcorn on the Future of Your Company, Your World, Your Life*. New York: Harper Business.

Popkin, Samuel. (1991). *The Reasoning Voter: Communication and Persuasion in Presidential Campaigns*. Chicago: University of Chicago Press.

––––––. (1992). "Campaigns That Matter." In Mathew D. McCubbins, ed., *Under the Watchful Eye: Managing Presidential Campaigns in the Television Era*. Washington, D.C.: Congressional Quarterly Press, pp. 153–170.

Pratto, Felicia, and Oliver P. John. (1991). "Automatic Vigilance: The Attention-Grabbing Power of Negative Social Information." *Journal of Personality and Social Psychology* 61:382–391.

Riker, William. (1986). *The Art of Political Manipulation*. New Haven: Yale University Press.

Rogers, E. M., and J. W. Dearing. (1988). "Agenda-Setting Research: Where Has It Been and Where Is It Going?" In J. A. Anderson, ed., *Communication Yearbook*, vol. 11. Beverly Hills: Sage Publications.

Rohde, David. (1991). *Parties and Leaders in the Postreform House*. Chicago: University of Chicago Press.

Rosen, Jay, and Paul Taylor. (1992). *The New News v. the Old News: The Press and Politics in the 1990s*. New York: Twentieth Century Fund.

Rosenstiel, Tom. (1993). *Strange Bedfellows: How Television and the Presidential Candidates Changed American Politics*. New York: Hyperion Books.

Rosenstone, Stephen, Roy L. Behr, and Edward H. Lazarus. (1984). *Third Parties in America: Citizen Response to Major Party Failure*. Princeton: Princeton University Press.

Rosenstone, Steven J., and John Mark Hansen. (1993). *Mobilization, Participation, and Democracy in America*. New York: Macmillan.

Runkel, David, ed. (1989). *Campaigning for President: The Managers Look at 1988*. Boston: Auburn House.

Sabato, Larry J. (1981). *The Rise of Political Consultants*. New York: Basic Books.

Safire, William. (1978). *Political Dictionary*. New York: Random House.

Schattschneider, E. E. (1942). *Party Government*. New York: Farrar and Reinhart.

––––––. (1960). *The Semi-Sovereign People*. Hinsdale, Ill.: Dryden Press.

Schlesinger, James A. (1966). *Ambition and Politics*. Chicago: Rand McNally.

Semetko, Holli, Jay G. Blumer, Michael Gurevitch, and David H. Weaver. (1991). *The Formation of Campaign Agendas: A Comparative Analysis of Party and Media Roles in Recent American and British Elections*. Hillsdale, N.J.: Lawrence Erlbaum and Associates.

Smith, Hedrick. (1988). *The Power Game*. New York: Random House.

Sorauf, Frank J. (1980). "Political Parties and Political Action Committees: Two Life Cycles." *Arizona Law Review* 22:445–464.

Squire, Peverill. (1991). "Preemptive Fundraising and Challenger Profile in Senate Elections." *Journal of Politics* 53:1150–1164.

Stokes, Bruce. (1988). "The Right Readies Soldiers for Bush." *National Journal Convention Daily,* August 16, p. 6.

Thurber, James A. (1991). "Dynamics of Policy Subsystems in American Politics." In Allan J. Cigler and Burdett A. Loomis, eds., *Interest Group Politics.* 3d ed. Washington, D.C.: Congressional Quarterly Press.

Tufte, Edward. (1975). "Determinants of the Outcomes of Midterm Congressional Elections." *American Political Science Review* 69:812–826.

Vallone, R., L. Ross, and M. Lepper. (1987). "The Hostile Media Phenomenon: Biased Perception and Perceptions of Media Bias in Coverage of the Beirut Massacre." *Journal of Personality and Social Psychology* 49:577–585.

White, Theodore. (1973). *The Making of the President, 1972.* New York: Atheneum.

Williams, Marjorie. (1992). "His Master's Voice." *Vanity Fair* 55:214–218.

Winter Park Group. (1986). "Proposed Gary Hart 1988 Business Plan." Unpublished manuscript, Winter Park, Colo.: Winter Park Group.

Wirthlin, Richard, Vincent Breglio, and Richard Beal. (1981). "Campaign Chronicle." *Public Opinion* (February/March) 4:43–49.

Witt, Evans. (1985). "What the Republicans Have Learned About Women." *Public Opinion* 8 (October/November) 13:49–52.

Wolinsky, Leo, et al. (1991). "Refereeing the TV campaign." *Washington Journalism Review* (January/February):22–28.

Womack, James P., Daniel P. Jones, and Daniel Roos. (1988). *The Candidate's Handbook.* Miami: Pickering Press.

Wright, John R. (1985): "PACs, Contributions, and Roll Calls: An Organizational Perspective." *American Political Science Review* 79(2):400–414.

Yiannakis, Diana Evans. (1981). "The Grateful Electorate: Casework and Congressional Elections." *American Journal of Political Science* 25:568–580.

About the Book and Contributors

For the first time, leading political scientists and experienced campaign professionals (many instrumental in the 1992 and 1994 elections) have come together to consider the nuts-and-bolts of American campaigns and elections in conjunction with academic theories and research. Offering a careful mix of Democratic and Republican, academic and practitioner, male and female campaign perspectives, this volume scrutinizes national- and local-level campaigns with the 1996 elections in mind. It explores issues of money, media (including MTV and infomercials), volunteerism, survey research, and focus groups to show not only how to win elections, but why it has become imperative to do so in an ethical way. Perfect for a variety of courses in American government, *Campaigns and Elections American Style* paints a clear, detailed portrait of the professionalization and transformation of American election campaigns over the last 30 years.

STEPHEN ANSOLABEHERE is associate professor of political science at Massachusetts Institute of Technology. He is a coauthor of *The Media Game: American Politics in the Media Age* with Shanto Iyengar and Roy Behr. He has specialized in campaign finance, congressional elections, and research methodology. He received his Ph.D. from Harvard.

DENISE BAER is visiting associate professor at American University. In 1992 and 1993 she was an American Political Science Association Congressional Fellow with the U.S. House of Representatives Democratic Caucus and Representative David Price. Her research focuses on factions, interest groups, social movements, and political parties. She is the author of the forthcoming *Party Organization and Interest Advocacy in the Post-Reform Era* and has coauthored *Politics and Linkage in a Democratic Society* and *Elite Cadres and Party Coalitions,* both books with David Bositis.

JOEL BRADSHAW is president of Campaign Design Group, a Democratic political consulting firm that specializes in designing and directing campaigns for local, state, and federal office. He served as senior consultant to Senator Gary Hart's 1984 presidential campaign and also directs a campaign management training program for the American Medical Association's political action committee.

JAY BRYANT has been a private communications consultant since 1979 and has created political campaign advertising programs in more than forty winning senatorial and congressional elections. From 1976 to 1979 he was director of communications for the National Republican Congressional Committee and has extensive experience on Capitol Hill. He was producer of the television program *At Issue,* which appeared nationally.

ANITA DUNN is senior vice president at Squire Knapp Ochs Communications, a political media consulting firm. She previously served as senior counselor to Senator Bill Bradley. Prior to joining Senator Bradley, she was director of communications for the Democratic Senatorial Campaign Committee during the 1988 and 1990 election cycles.

MARNI EZRA is a doctoral student at American University. She previously worked at Peter Hart Research, a Democratic political polling firm, and at the Center for Responsive Politics, a public interest group that specializes in campaign finance issues. Her fields of interest are campaign finance, interest groups, and congressional elections.

LINDA L. FOWLER is professor of political science at the Maxwell School at Syracuse University. She is coauthor, with Robert D. McClure, of *Political Ambition: Who Decides to Run for Congress* and *Candidates, Congress, and the American Democracy.* Her present research examines the role of attentive constituencies in shaping congressional policymaking.

WILMA GOLDSTEIN is a political consultant and has extensive campaign and research experience. She has served as director of the National Women's Business Council, a federal government commission, and has been director of survey research for the National Republican Congressional Committee. For the past decade she has combined work for Republican political candidates and committees with teaching and consulting for various women's political organizations.

WILLIAM R. HAMILTON is a pioneer in private public opinion research. Established in 1964, his firm Hamilton and Staff has conducted over 7,000 research studies for political candidates and public affairs clients, both in the United States and internationally. He is immediate past president of the American Association of Political Consultants and an adjunct professor in the graduate program in political campaigning at the University of Florida.

PAUL S. HERRNSON is associate professor of government and politics at the University of Maryland. He is the author of *Party Campaigning in the 1980s,* and as well as many articles on political parties, campaign finance, and congressional elections. He has also served as a consultant for the Democratic Caucus of the U.S. House of Representatives and as an American Political Science Association Congressional Fellow.

DAVID HIMES is senior vice president of AB&C group, a direct-mail marketing firm. Previously he was deputy director of finance for the National Republican Congressional Committee and was responsible for raising $15–$20 million each year for the committee. Before that post, he worked as director of marketing for KCI Communications, Inc., publisher of several financial and investment newsletters.

SHANTO IYENGAR is professor of communications studies and political science at the University of California at Los Angeles. He is a coauthor, with Stephen Ansolabehere and Roy Behr, of *The Media Game: American Politics in the Media Age*. He received his Ph.D. from the University of Iowa, and his fields of study are political psychology and sociology, election behavior, and public opinion.

CANDICE J. NELSON is assistant professor of government at American University and director of the university's Campaign Management Institute. Previously she was a visiting fellow at the Brookings Institution, where she coauthored, with David B. Magleby, *The Money Chase*. A former American Political Science Association Congressional Fellow, she coauthored *The Myth of the Independent Voter* and has written numerous articles on congressional elections, political action committees, and campaign finance.

JOHN R. PETROCIK is professor of political science at the University of California at Los Angeles, where he specializes in mass attitudes and behavior, political parties, elections and campaigns, and survey research and analysis. He has authored or coauthored several books and research articles on these topics, including *The Changing American Voter*, and has worked on behalf of Republican candidates for municipal, state, and national offices.

SAMUEL POPKIN is professor of political science at the University of California at San Diego. He served as a consultant to the Clinton campaign, working on polling and strategy, and has been an active participant and academic analyst for many presidential elections. He has authored or coauthored several books, including *The Reasoning Voter: Communication and Persuasion in Presidential Campaigns; Candidates, Issues, and Strategies: The Computer Simulation of Presidential Elections;* and *Chief of Staff: Twenty-Five Years of Managing the Presidency*.

WILL ROBINSON is a partner at MacWilliams Cosgrove Snider Smith and Robinson, a political media consulting firm. He previously served as campaign director of the Democratic National Committee (DNC), as political director of the National Committee for an Effective Congress (NCEC), and as deputy political director of the Dukakis campaign. He is on the board of advisers for the Center for Presidential Study at the LBJ Library in Austin, Texas, and is consultant to the National Democratic Institute for International Affairs.

FRANK J. SORAUF is a Regents' Professor at the University of Minnesota. He has published books and articles on political parties and judicial politics, but since 1980 his research has centered almost exclusively on campaign finance. He has published two books on the topic, *Money in American Elections* and *Inside Campaign Finance.*

WILLIAM R. SWEENEY is director of government relations for Electronic Data Systems (EDS). He previously served as research director (1974–1977) and executive director (1977–1981) of the Democratic Congressional Campaign Committee, as deputy chairman of the Democratic National Committee (1981–1985), and as senior adviser to the presidential campaign of Senator Albert Gore, Jr. (1988). He is currently a member of the board of directors of the International Foundation for Electoral Systems.

JAMES A. THURBER is professor of government and director of the Center for Congressional and Presidential Studies at American University. He has written and edited books, monographs, and articles on Congress, congressional-presidential relations, congressional budgeting, interest groups and lobbying, including *Divided Democracy* and *Setting Course: A Congressional Management Guide.* His previous posts include legislative assistant for U.S. Senator Hubert H. Humphrey, senior staff analyst for Representative David Obey, and consultant to the Joint Committee on the Organization of Congress.

RAYMOND E. WOLFINGER, professor of political science at the University of California at Berkeley, is a former chairman of the Board of Overseers of the National Election Studies. He is a coauthor of *The Myth of the Independent Voter* with Bruce E. Keith, David B. Magleby, Candice J. Nelson, Elizabeth Orr, and Mark C. Westlye.

Index

Abortion issue, 52
Abrams, Robert, 205–206
Absentee ballots, 145
Academics. *See* Political scientists
Advertising, campaign
  competitiveness of, 108–110
  experimental tests of, 102–103
  function of, 7–8
  mass media and, 60–61, 86–87, 103–107
  newsworthiness of, 105–107
  political communications and, 89–99, 109, 206
  polls and, 10
  product advertising vs., 87–89
  stereotypes and, 107–108
  See also Marketing
Advisors, pollsters as, 173–174
Ad-watch reports, 106–107
Agenda setting, campaign, 57–61
Ailes, Roger, 107, 109, 119–120, 125
Ambition theory, 61(n2)
American Voter, The (Campbell), 48, 224–225
Ansolabehere, Steven, 7, 101, 241
Apology defense, 98
Arterton, Christopher, 58–59
Atlanta Constitution, 122
Attack strategies
  defense strategies and, 97–99, 109
  political communications and, 95–97
Attitude research, 182–183
Attorneys, campaign, 26
Atwater, Lee, 175

Audiences, campaign, 20–22

Baer, Denise, 6, 47, 241
Baker, James, 19
Bakker, Jim, 217
Ballot review, 23
Balz, Dan, 216
Base voters, 230
Bean-Jones, Linda, 64
Benchmark poll, 172–173
Berman, Michael, 17
Billboards, 90, 140
Bishop, G. Norman, 100(nn 1, 2)
Black vote, 54
Block captains, 141–142
Blue-collar workers, 216
Blumenthal, Sidney, 50
Boxer, Barbara, 44, 108, 119
Bradley, Bill, 186
Bradshaw, Joel, 5–6, 30, 228, 229, 241
Breglio, Vincent J., 100(n2)
Brinner, Robert, 222(n2)
Broadcast messages, 51–52, 61
Broder, David, 61, 196, 216
Brooks, Jack, xvi
Brown, Edmund ("Jerry"), Jr., 215
Bryant, Jay, 7, 84, 109, 242
Buckley v. Valeo, 64
Budget. *See* Finance, campaign
Budget deficit issue, 189
Bundling, 208
Bush, George
  economic failures of, 215, 226–227
  political communications and, 92–95, 98

presidential campaign of 1992 and, xv, 4, 11, 38, 45, 156, 186–187, 213, 219–220, 222, 227–228

Cable television. *See* Television
Caddell, Patrick, 161, 165, 167
Calendar, campaign, 25
Campaign Design Group, 5
Campaign finance committee, 70
Campaign Management Institute, 5, 8
Campaign organizations, 25, 26–27, 29(n2), 61(n2)
Campaign plans. *See* Planning, campaign
Campaign professionals
  campaign finances and, 78, 229
  functions of, 3, 5
  political scientists vs., 1–2, 224, 227, 229–231
Campaigns, election
  academic vs. nonacademic perspectives on, 224–231
  advertising and, 7, 84–100, 101–111
  defined, 2–3, 14
  ethics and, 10–11, 192–199, 200–212
  field operations and, 8–9, 138–151, 152–160
  finance and, 6–7, 62–77, 78–82
  mass media and, 7–8, 84–100, 101–111, 112–125, 126–137
  non-media factors affecting, 128–131
  phases of, 171–178
  planning for, 4–6, 14–28
  political polls and, 9–10, 161–179
  strategies for, 4–6, 30–46, 47–61
  survey research in, 9–10, 181–190
Campaign strategy. *See* Strategies, campaign
Candidates
  campaign planning and, 19–20
  campaigns centered around, 55–56
  ethical issues and, 198–199, 200–212
  family of, 20, 63–64
  financial contributions from, 63–64, 68–69
  fund-raising by, xix, 62, 69–70

image and, 40–41, 61(n1), 91–93, 182–183, 226
issue agendas of, 134–135, 226
as leaders, 19, 28
media and, 134–137
political theme and, 42–45
positioning of, 38–42, 54–55, 61(n1)
strategic, 59–60
voter contact by, 141, 155–156
warnings about, 28(n1)
zero-sum games and, 3, 200
See also Politicians
Cantril, Hadley, 162
Canvassing, 140–141, 158
Carter, Jimmy, xv, 165, 186, 225
Carville, James, 117, 161
Challengers
  campaign funding for, 80–82, 83(n3)
  incumbents vs., 39, 80, 131, 225
  media bias and, 113–119, 123, 133
  See also Incumbents
Chandler, Rod, 39
Character, ethics and, 195, 211
Civilization, origin of, 84–85
Clinton, Bill
  as Arkansas governor, 221
  character questions about, 93, 195, 216–219, 223(n6)
Clinton presidential campaign
  economic issues and, 215–216, 226–227
  ethical questions during, 195
  field operations in, xix, 143–144, 156
  incumbency issue and, 38
  message of, 28, 213, 227
  Ross Perot and, xv, 187–190
  political communications and, 92–94, 96, 98
  political scientists' view of, 226–227
  polls and, 161, 167–168, 175, 220, 221, 223(nn 3, 4)
  strategies of, 4, 11–12, 214–222, 227
  survey research in, 182
  tactics used in, xix, 51–52
  talk-show appearances and, 217–218
  theme of, 45, 51, 61
  See also Presidential campaigns

Cloverdale, Paul, 121
Code of ethics, political, 198–199, 210–211
Coleman, Marshall, 52
Commercial lists, 74
Commercials, political, 86–87
Communications. *See* Political communications
Competition, electoral
  campaign of 1992 and, 78–81
  campaign advertising and, 108–110
  media bias and, 113–116
Competitive-advertising hypothesis, 101
Compiled lists, 74
Computer-assisted telephone interviewing (CATI), 179(n1)
Conference Board, 214
Conflict, political, theory of, 53–54
Congressional campaigns
  federal election law and, 121–123
  life cycle of, 14, 208
  media coverage of, 112–125
  non-media factors affecting, 127–131
  political polls and, 170–171
  See also Presidential campaigns; State and local campaigns
Congressional Campaign Study (1984), 160(n1)
Congressional Quarterly, 80, 118
Congressional Record, 118
Connally, John, 71
Contributions, financial
  from candidates, 63–64, 68–69
  for incumbents, 67, 79–81, 113
  from individuals, 64–65, 68
  from political committees, 65–67, 229
  public suspicion about, 24
  tactics for soliciting, 69–76
  See also Fund-raising
Cook, Timothy E., 118
Counterattack defense, 98–99
Crane, Bill, 122
Crossley, Arch, 162
Crowe, William J., 220
Cuomo, Mario, 215

D'Amato, Alfonse, 205–206, 211
Dawkins, Pete, 119
Defense strategies, 97–99, 100(n2), 109
Democratic Congressional Campaign Committee (DCCC), 170
Democratic National Committee (DNC), 67
Democratic National Convention (1992), 218
Democratic Party, xv, 58, 188, 213, 214, 219
Democratic Senatorial Campaign Committee (DSCC), 114, 121
Demographics, political polls and, 176, 179(n6)
Denial defense, 97–98
DeVries, Walter, 163, 164
Dinners, fund-raising, 70–71
Direct mail
  fund-raising through, 68, 73–74
  GOTV pieces by, 145–146
  political communications through, 95, 97
  voter contact through, 142–143
Door-to-door canvassing
  GOTV programs and, 147, 149
  voter contact through, 140–141
Dukakis, Michael, 95, 99, 155, 228
Duke, David, 54
Dunn, Anita, 7, 112, 126–127, 227, 242
du Pont, Pete, 64

Early campaign phase, 172–173
Econometric model, 48–49
Economy
  campaign strategy and, 4, 11, 23
  as issue in 1992 campaign, 214–216, 220–221, 226–227
Edwards, Edwin, 54
Election campaigns. *See* Campaigns, election
Election-day volunteers, 148–149
Election outcomes
  academic study of, 224, 226–231
  field operations and, 157–158
  geography and, 128–129, 137(n1)
  incumbency and, 225–226

issues and, 130, 137(n2), 226
partisanship and, 128–130, 137(n1), 224–225
survey research and, 182–183
Endgame campaign phase, 176–178
Endorsers, campaign, 22
Engel, Rob, 179(n4)
Environment. *See* Political environment
Ethics
campaign practices and, 10–11, 207–212
codification of, 198–199, 210–211
defining, 192–193, 196–198
elections of 1992 and, 194–195
legal issues vs., 192–193, 210–211
media scrutiny of, 78, 195–196, 205
political scandals and, 10, 193–195
political scientists and, 200–201
in political vs. private life, 201–207, 210
representative government and, 202–204
Evaluators, pollsters as, 174–175
Exit polls, 182, 189
Expert Testimony (Stockley), 192
Explanation defense, 98
Ezra, Marni, 12, 224, 242

Fair, Ray, 222(n1)
Family of candidate
fund-raising from, 63–64
public perception and, 20
Federal campaigns. *See* Congressional campaigns
Federal Election Campaign Act (FECA), 64, 207
Federal Election Commission (FEC), xviii, xix, 79–80, 83(n2), 112, 121–122, 179(n2), 207
Federal election law, 121–123, 179(n2)
Feinstein, Dianne, 108
Ferraro, Geraldine, 205–207
Field operations
election outcomes and, 157–158
GOTV programs and, 144–151, 156–157

in high-performance precincts, 145
in low-performance precincts, 144–145, 146–149
message communication and, 143–144, 155–156, 228
purposes of, 8–9, 138–139, 152–153
volunteers and, 158–160
voter contact through, 8, 139–143
voter identification and targeting in, 153–155
voter registration drives and, 156–157
Finance, campaign
campaign of 1992 and, 79–81, 83(nn 2, 5)
contribution solicitation tactics and, 69–76
federal election law and, 121–123
fund-raising strategies and, 63, 67–69
political scientists' view of, 78, 229
presidential campaigns and, 112
purpose of, 6–7
reforming, 81–82, 229
sources of, 63–67
strategic planning and, 24–26
See also Fund-raising
Finders' fees, 197
Fiorina, Morris, 225
Fiscal responsibility, 203
Five-functions analysis, 7, 89–99, 100(n1)
Flip-flops, 197
Florida primary (1992), 216
Florio, James, 10, 54, 185, 190(n3)
Flowers, Gennifer, 96, 98
Flying squads, 149–150
Focus groups
function of, 9, 41
political polls and, 166–167, 175, 179(n3)
Foley, Thomas, xvi
Follow-up requests, 76
Ford, Gerald, 52, 165
Foreign policy, 213–214, 220
Four-defense analysis, 97–99, 100(n2)
Fowler, Linda L., 11, 200, 242

Fowler, Wyche, 121
Fundamental analysis, 186
Fund-raising
  campaign of 1992 and, 78–81
  campaign planning and, 24, 63
  five truths of, 62
  regulation of, 197, 229
  for seed-money, 68–69
  solicitation tactics for, 69–76
  sources of, 63–67
  strategies for, 63, 67–68
  See also Contributions, financial;
    Finance, campaign

Gallup, George, 162
Gender issues
  campaign strategies and, 44–45, 52,
    55
  political advertising and, 104–105,
    108
General gifts committee, 70
Geodemographics, 176, 179(n6)
Geography
  campaign strategies and, 32–37
  election outcomes and, 128–129,
    137(n1)
Get-out-the-vote programs. *See* GOTV
  programs
Gingrich, Newt, xvi, 86
Glenn, John, 22
Glickman, Dan, xvi
Goldstein, Wilma, 11, 192, 242
Goldwater, Barry, 185
Gore, Al, 187, 220, 221
GOTV programs
  field operations and, 8, 144–151,
    156–157
  in high-performance precincts, 149–
    151
  in low-performance precincts, 146–
    149
  See also Field operations
Grassroots politics
  example of, 143–144
  function of, 8–9
  See also Field operations
Greenberg, Stanley, 161, 175

Grunwald, Mandy, 161
Gubernatorial campaigns, 170

Haldeman, H. R., 221
Hamilton, William R., 9, 161, 178, 227,
  242
Harkin, Tom, 120, 215
Harris, Louis, 162–163, 164
Hart, Gary, 15, 194
Hatfield, Mark, 121
Heffernan, Ed, 114–116
Heinz, John, 64
Herrnson, Paul S., 8–9, 152, 242
High-impact voter contact, 139, 140–
  143
High-performance precincts
  field operations in, 145
  GOTV activities in, 149–151
Hill, Anita, 96, 97, 194
Himes, David, 6, 62, 227, 229, 243
Historical analysis, campaign
  strategies and, 32–37
Holtzman, Elizabeth, 205–207
Horton, Willie, 99, 201, 228
Host committee, 71–72
Hotline, 24
House Ethics Committee, 211
House lists, 74
House of Representatives, U.S.
  elections of 1992 and, 79–80, 82,
    83(n3)
  scandals in, 195
  See also Congressional campaigns
Hypodermic model of propaganda,
  47–48

Ideology, political, 39–40
Image, candidate
  attitude research on, 182–183
  election outcomes and, 226
  party identification and, 55–56,
    61(n1)
  political communications and, 91–93
  positioning strategy and, 19–20, 40–
    41
  voting behavior and, 91–93
Image statement, 91

Incumbents
  campaign of 1992 and, 79–82
  challengers vs., 39, 80, 131, 225
  election outcomes for, 225–226
  ethical standards for, 211
  financial contributions and, 67, 79–
    81, 113, 229
  media bias toward, 113–118, 124–
    125, 133
  political ambitions of, 130–131
  positioning strategy and, 38–39, 130–
    131
  See also Challengers
Independents, political, 184–185, 230
Inside Politics (CNN), 106
Institute for Social Research, 214
Interest groups, 158–159
Issue bundles, 60–61
Issue framing, 55
Issue-ownership hypothesis, 101, 107–
  108
Issues, campaign
  development and exploitation of,
    93–95
  election outcomes and, 130, 137(n2),
    226
  media coverage of, 133–135
  partisanship and, 134–135
  strategic planning and, 27–28
  See also specific issues
Iyengar, Shanto, 7, 101, 243

Jefferson, Thomas, 202
Job descriptions, campaign, 26–27
Jordan, Hamilton, 218
Journalists
  campaign coverage by, 135–136
  political role of, 124
  tabloid journalism and, 194
  See also Media

Kennedy, John F., 163
Kennedy, Robert, 164
Kerrey, Robert, 215
Key, V. O., 56
Kickbacks, 197
King, Tom, 173

Kraft, John, 162, 163
Kurtz, Howard, 124

Laissez-faire ethics, 209
Lawyers, campaign, 26
Leaders
  candidates as, 19, 28
  political skills of, 59–60
Leafleting, 140
Legal issues
  ethical issues vs., 192–193, 210–211
  field operations and, 145
Levine, Mel, 44
Literature distribution, 139–140
Local campaigns. *See* State and local
  campaigns
Lonsdale, Harry, 120–121
Los Angeles Times, 132
Lotus diagram, 17–18
Low-impact voter contact, 139–140
Low-performance precincts
  field operations in, 144–145, 146–149
  GOTV activities in, 146–149

McCarthy, Leo, 44
McGovern, George, 185, 221
McInturff, Bill, 176
Mack, Connie, 40
Magnet issues, 58, 61
Mailing lists, 74–75
Major gifts committee, 70
Major, John, 219
Manatt, Charles T., 15
"The Man From Hope," 218
Marketing
  strategic positioning and, 54–55, 61
  telephone, 75–76
  See also Advertising, campaign
Market Opinion Research (MOR), 163
Mass media. *See* Media
Mauser, Gary, 51, 54
Mayoral campaigns, 171
Media
  campaign advertising and, 60–61,
    86–87, 103–107
  campaign strategies and, 49–50
  challengers and, 118–119, 133

competitive-advertising hypothesis and, 108–110
election coverage by, 7–8, 60–61, 112–125, 126–132
ethical scrutiny by, 78, 195–196, 205
federal election law and, 121–123
incumbency bias and, 113–118, 124–125, 133
issue coverage by, xvii, 133–135
issue-ownership hypothesis and, 107–108
journalists and, 124, 135–136, 194
"Neil Armstrong syndrome" and, 116–118
political communications and, 89–99, 119–121
political power and, 86–87
polls and, 10, 162, 167
recirculation hypothesis and, 105–107
riding-the-wave hypothesis and, 103–105
as secondary audience, 22
See also Press coverage; Television
Media pollsters, 162
Mercantilist campaign, 49
Message, campaign
attitude research and, 182
campaign theme and, 42–45, 50–52
field operations and, 143–144, 155–156, 228
strategic planning and, 27–28, 34
See also Political communications
Midcampaign phase, 173–176
Militarist campaign, 49
Mondale, Walter, 38–39, 45, 186, 194
Money. *See* Finance, campaign
Monitors, pollsters as, 174
Morella, Connie, 114–116
MTV, xviii
Murray, Patty, 39

Nader, Ralph, 215
Name identification
political communications and, 89–91
voter contact and, 140, 144
Napolitan, Joe, 164

Narrowcast messages, 51, 60–61
National Election Survey (NES), 184, 190, 225
National Enquirer, 98
National Republican Senatorial Committee (NRSC), 121–122
National Women's Political Caucus, 59–60
"Neil Armstrong syndrome," 116–118
Nelson, Candace J., 12, 224, 243
New-collar voter, 153
New Hampshire primary (1992), 215
Newman, Paul M., 100(n2)
News coverage. *See* Media; Press coverage
Newspapers, 91, 95, 131–134
Newsweek, 92, 161
New York Senate Race of 1992, 205–207
Nimmo, Dan, 49–50, 61(n1)
900 numbers, fund-raising through, 76
1992 election campaign
advertising tests during, 102–103
competitiveness of, 78–81
economic issues and, 215–216, 226–227
unusualness of, 213–214
See also Clinton presidential campaign
Nixon, Richard, 11, 216, 221
Nonacademic survey research, 183–186

O'Neill, Thomas P., Jr., xvi, 15
Opinion leaders, 22
Opinion surveys. *See* Polls; Survey research
Opposition research, 172, 179(n5)
Organizations, campaign, 25, 26–27, 29(n2), 61(n2)
Outcomes. *See* Election outcomes
Outside lists, 74

PACs. *See* Political action committees
Page, Gideon, 192
Parties, political. *See* Political parties

Partisanship
  academic study of, 224–226, 230
  campaign strategy and, 57–59
  candidate issues and, 134–135
  election outcomes and, 128–130,
    137(n1), 224–226
  survey research and, 183–186,
    190(n2)
  tracking polls and, 177
  See also Political parties
People resources, 25
Percent-of-effort (PEI), 35, 36
Perot, Ross, xv, 11, 79, 96, 186–190, 201,
    217, 218
Personality, candidate, 19–20
  See also Image, candidate
Personal lives, of politicians, 201–207,
    210
Personal solicitation tactics, 69–73
Persuadable voters, 34, 176–177, 229–
    230
Petrocik, John R., 7–8, 126, 243
"Pet rock" coverage, 118–119
Phases, of election campaigns, 171–178
Phillips, Howard, 50
Phone banks
  GOTV campaigns and, 146–147, 149
  political surveys through, 166–167
  voter contact through, 143
Planning, campaign
  attitude and, 14–15
  audiences and, 20–22
  candidates and, 19–20
  finance and, 24–26
  importance of, 5–6, 28
  lotus diagram and, 17–18
  message and, 27–28
  organizational structure and, 26–27,
    29(n2)
  political environments and, 22–24
  principles of, 15–17
  resource equations and, 15
  rigid plans and, 13(n4)
  written documents for, 17–18
  See also Strategies, campaign
Plunkett, George Washington, 11
Point of purchase, political, 89

Political action committees (PACs)
  fund-raising from, 65–66, 229
  incumbent funding by, 80–81, 113,
    229
  poll commissioning by, 166, 179(n2)
Political campaigns. *See* Campaigns,
    election
Political communications
  attack strategies and, 95–97, 109
  campaign themes and, 42–45
  candidate image and, 91–93
  defense strategies and, 97–99, 109
  field operations and, 143–144, 155–
    156
  five functions of, 7, 89–99, 100(n1)
  issues and, 93–95
  media coverage of, 89–99, 119–121
  name identification and, 89–91
  paid advertisements and, 87–89,
    101–111
  political power and, 85–87
  television and, 86–87, 101–111
  See also Message, campaign
Political environment
  academic study of, 224–226, 230
  campaign planning and, 22–24
  election outcome and, 130, 133
Political parties
  academic study of, 224–226, 230
  campaign organizations and, 61(n2)
  campaign strategies and, 5, 33–34,
    57–59
  campaign volunteers and, 158–159
  candidate-centered campaigns and,
    55–56
  election outcomes and, 128–130,
    137(n2), 183, 224–225, 227
  ideological positioning and, 39–40
  as secondary audience, 22
  voting behavior and, 48–49
  See also Partisanship
Political party committees, 66–67
Political Persuaders, The (Nimmo), 49
Political power
  origins of, 84–85
  political communications and, 85–87

Political scientists
  campaign analysis by, 3, 58
  campaign ethics and, 200–201
  campaign finance and, 78, 229
  campaign professionals vs., 1–2, 224,
    227, 229–231
  campaign strategy and, 47–49
  election outcomes and, 224, 226–231
  field work studies by, 158
  survey research and, 183–186
"Political spin," 2, 13(n3)
Politicians
  code of ethics for, 198–199, 210–212
  political ambitions of, 130–131
  political vs. private lives of, 201–207,
    210
  See also Candidates
Polls
  benchmark, 172–173
  campaign advertising and, 10
  campaign phases and, 171–178
  campaign strategies and, 36, 161,
    164, 168–169, 174–179
  exit, 182, 189
  function of, 9–10
  future trends in, 173, 175–176, 178
  in general elections, 170–171
  in presidential elections, 169–170,
    218, 220, 222(n1), 223(nn 3, 4), 226–
    227
  rolling-average technique for, 177–
    178
  short history of, 162–169
  telephone use for, 165–167, 179(n1)
  tracking, 9, 165, 177–178
  trend, 174
  See also Survey research
Pollsters, 173–174
Poll watching, 148, 149
Poll workers, 147–148, 149
Popkin, Samuel, 2, 11–12, 54, 57, 182,
    213, 228, 243
Positioning, strategic
  marketing principles and, 54–55,
    61(n1)
  three types of, 38–41
  See also Strategies, campaign

Precinct captains, 141–142, 154
Precinct house, 146
Prepolling process, 172
Presidential campaigns
  media coverage of, 112–113
  polling in, 169–170, 218, 220,
    222(n1), 223(nn 3, 4), 226–227
  talk-show appearances and, 217–218
  See also Clinton presidential
    campaign; Congressional
    campaigns
Press coverage
  of congressional campaigns, 112–125
  limitations on, 131–134
  political advertising and, 101–111
  reforming, 126–127
  See also Media
Primary audience, 20
Primary campaigns, 169, 180(n7)
Private conduct, politics and, 201–207,
    210
Product advertising, campaign
  advertising vs., 87–89
Professionals. *See* Campaign
  professionals
Propaganda, 47–48
Prospecting, telephone, 76
Prospect list, 75
Public opinion polls, 9–10, 162, 167
  See also Polls
Public politics, 124
Public relations, 86–87
Public television. *See* Television

Quayle, Dan, 222
Quayle, Oliver, 162, 163

Radio advertising, 91, 95, 97, 150
Rather, Dan, 92
Rational-choice model, 48–49
Reactivation requests, 76
Reagan, Ronald
  economic failures of, 214–215
  presidential campaigns of, 45, 55,
    186, 200, 225–226
  television medium and, 86

Receptions, fund-raising through, 70–73

Recirculation hypothesis, 101, 105–107

Reese, Matt, 179(n6)

References, 233–239

Regional disparity, 16–17

Regulatory responsibility, 203

Renewal requests, 76

Reporters. *See* Journalists

Representative government, 202–204

Republican National Committee (RNC), 67

Republican Party, xv, 58, 188

Resource equations, 15

Resources, campaign, 24–26, 32

Response as attack, 99

Reverse phone bank, 150

Rice, Donna, 194

Ride program, 148, 149–150

Riding-the-wave hypothesis, 101, 103–105

Rigid plans, 13(n4)

Robinson, Will, 8, 138, 152, 227, 228, 243

Rohde, David, 56

Roll, Charles, 162, 163

Rolling-average tracking, 177–178

Rollins, Ed, 10–11, 13(n3), 54, 218

Romney, George, 163, 164

Roosevelt, Franklin, 204

Roosevelt, Theodore, 187

Roper, Elmo, 162

Rosenberg, Simon, 143

Rosen, Jay, 124

Rostenkowski, Dan, xvi

Rund, Charles F., 100(n2), 161

Runyon, Damon, 99

Safire, William, 3

Scandals, political, 10, 193–195

Schattschneider, E. E., 53

Scholars. *See* Political scientists

Schroth, Rob, 173

Secondary audiences, 21–22

Second gift requests, 76

Seed-money, fund-raising for, 68–69

Senate Ethics Committee, 211

Senate, U.S.
  campaigns for, 83(n6), 170
  elections of 1992 and, 80–81, 205–207
  See also Congressional campaigns

Sex scandals, 96

Shapp, Milton, 164

Sharpton, Al, 205–207

Situational problems, 17

"Slick Willie," 216–217

Smith, Hedrick, 183–184

Smith, Neal, xvi

Social environment, 23–24

Soft votes, 176–177

Sorauf, Frank, 6–7, 78, 229, 244

Sound truck, 150

Special events, 70

Specialized polls, 176

Squier, Bob, 176

State and local campaigns
  media bias and, 113–118
  non-media factors affecting, 128–131
  political polls and, 171
  See also Congressional campaigns

Stephanopolous, George, 112

Stereotypes, political, 107–108

Stockley, Grif, 192

Strategic candidates, 59–60

Strategies, campaign
  agenda setting and, 57–61
  candidate and, 40–41, 55–56
  changing, 41–42
  conflict theory and, 53–54
  definition of, 31, 51
  four dimensions of, 5–6, 31–32
  historical voting behavior and, 32–37
  ideological positioning and, 39–40
  incumbency and, 38–39, 130–131
  issue bundles and, 60–61
  media and, 49–50
  opinion surveys and, 10
  partisanship and, 57–59
  political science and, 47–49
  polls and, 161, 164, 168–169, 174–179, 183
  positioning and, 38–41, 54–55
  purpose of, 4–6, 50–52, 54–55, 228
  theme and, 42–45, 50–52

voter definition and targeting and, 31–32, 53–54, 153–155
See also Planning, campaign; Tactics, campaign
Structure, organizational, 26–27, 29(n2)
Survey research
academic vs. nonacademic, 183–186
in election campaigns, 9–10, 182–183, 228
function of, 9–10
growth in nonacademic, 181–182
political partisanship and, 183–186, 190(n2)
postelection, 180(n8), 182, 189
telephone, 165–167
third-party candidates and, 187–190, 191(n4)
See also Polls
Swaggart, Jimmy, 216–217
Sweeney, William R., 5–6, 14, 244
Swing voters, 230

Tabloid journalism, 194
Tactics, campaign
ethics of, 207–210
media scrutiny of, 195–196
purpose of, 4–6, 50–52
See also Strategies, campaign
Talk shows, xviii, 217–218
Targeting, voter
attitude research and, 182
as campaign strategy, 31–32, 53–54
field operations and, 153–155
in fund-raising, 70
Tarrance, Lance, 178
Taylor, Paul, 124
Teeter, Robert, 165, 222
Telemarketing, 75–76
Telephone surveys
development of, 165–167, 179(n1), 181–182
future trends in, 176
See also Polls; Survey research
Television
ad-watch reports on, 106–107
campaign advertising and, 87–89, 91, 93, 102–110

campaign strategy and, 49–50
Clinton's talk-show appearances on, 217–218
issue messages and, 95, 107–108
as political attack medium, 97, 109
political communications and, 86–87, 101–111
political coverage on, 103–107, 196
polls and, 175–176
See also Media; Press coverage
Theme, campaign. *See* Message, campaign
Third-party candidates, 187–190, 191(n4)
Thomas, Clarence, 96, 97–98, 194
Thurber, James A., 1, 244
Today Show, 119
Tracking polls, 9, 165, 177–178
Trend polls, 174
Truman, Harry, xv
Trust
ethics and, 211
representative government and, 202–204
Truth-box reports, 61, 106–107
Tsongas, Paul, 40, 215, 216, 222, 223(n14)
Tufte, Edward R., 226
Turnout control center, 150–151

Undecided voters, 34, 176–177, 229–230
Unemployment issue, 104–105
Unethical behavior. *See* Ethics
Universal lists, 74
Unruh, Jesse, 6, 182–183

VIP receptions, 70–71, 72
Visibility activities, 140
Volunteers, campaign
on election-day, 148–149
GOTV programs and, 144–151
need for, 60, 158–160
voter contact by, 139–143
Voter contact
candidates and, 141, 155–156
field operations and, 8, 139–143

high-impact, 139, 140–143
low-impact, 139–140
programs for, 144–151, 156–157
Voter identification programs, 139,
    153–155
Voter lists, 74
Voter registration drives, 156–157
Voter Research and Surveys (VRS), 189
Voters
    defining and targeting, 31–32, 53–54,
        153–155
    as primary audience, 20
    turnout of, 53–54, 150–151, 158
Voting behavior
    campaign attacks and, 95–97
    candidate image and, 91–93
    historical analysis of, 32–37, 153–154
    issue messages and, 93–95
    name identification and, 89–91
    non-media factors affecting, 128–131
    political conflict and, 53–54
    scientific studies of, 48–49
    third-party candidates and, 188–190,
        191(n4)

WAG (wild-assed guess), 17

Wallace, George C., 191(n4)
Wall Street Journal, 226
Warmaking responsibility, 203
Washington, George, 194
Washington Post, 11, 113, 114, 124, 195,
    216
Watergate, 193–194, 195, 197, 209, 214
Wedge issues, 58, 61
Welfare reform, 221
White-collar workers, 216
Whitman, Christine Todd, 54, 190(n3)
Whouley, Michael, 143
Wilder, Doug, 52
Wirthlin, Richard, 55, 161, 163, 164
Wolfinger, Raymond E., 10, 181, 226,
    244
Women's issues. *See* Gender issues
Woodruff, Judy, 125
Written campaign plan, 16, 28
Wyden, Ron, 120

Yeakel, Lynn, 119
Yuppies, 153

Zandi, Mark, 222(n2)
Zero-sum games, 3, 200